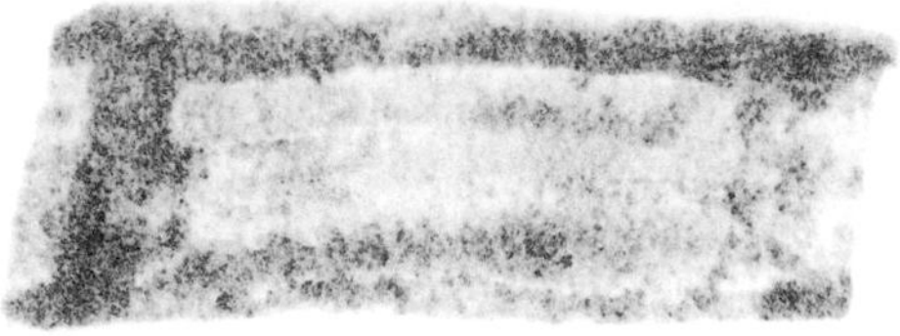

THE VIOLENCE OF CARE

The Violence of Care

Rape Victims, Forensic Nurses, and Sexual Assault Intervention

Sameena Mulla

NEW YORK UNIVERSITY PRESS
New York and London

NEW YORK UNIVERSITY PRESS
New York and London
www.nyupress.org

Library of Congress Cataloging-in-Publication Data

Mulla, Sameena.
The violence of care : rape victims, forensic nurses, and sexual assault intervention / Sameena Mulla.
pages cm
Includes bibliographical references and index.
ISBN 978-1-4798-0031-5 (hardback) — ISBN 978-1-4798-6721-9 (paper)
1. Rape victims—Medical examinations—United States. 2. Rape victims—Services for—United States—Psychological aspects. 3. Forensic nursing—United States. I. Title.
RA1141.M85 2014
362.883—dc23

2014002839

New York University Press books are printed on acid-free paper, and their binding materials are chosen for strength and durability. We strive to use environmentally responsible suppliers and materials to the greatest extent possible in publishing our books.

Manufactured in the United States of America
10 9 8 7 6 5 4 3 2 1

Also available as an ebook

CONTENTS

ACKNOWLEDGMENTS

A book comes about only when the right coalition of supportive, encouraging, and challenging people provide a would-be author with a foundation from which to write. While I have been lucky enough to be surrounded by such people all along the way, I must still lay claim to the remaining faults of the book. Let me start by thanking those people I will not name: without the women and men undergoing and conducting sexual assault forensic intervention, there would be no book. My greatest debt is to them. Their honesty, integrity, and passion were demonstrated in the thousand and one kindnesses they offered me on a daily basis.

Adequate and meaningful time to conduct research is not conjured out of thin air. I was able to conduct research only because of the openhanded generosity of the Social Science Research Council's Sexuality Research Fellowship Program, and the Law and Social Science Program of the National Science Foundation. The Women, Gender and Sexuality Program, and the Center for Africana Studies at the Johns Hopkins University, as well as a Regular Research Grant at Marquette University also supported the project along the way.

My thanks also to my teachers, Veena Das, Deborah Poole, Jane Guyer, Harry Marks, and Jennifer Culbert, who argued with each other and with me as to what book I should ultimately write. I have also benefited from the generous and insightful teaching of Naveeda Khan, Rayna Rapp, and Malathi de Alwis. Xiao-Bo Yuan was my first (and best) research assistant on this project, and I thank her for her talented handling of the interview materials. Don Selby and Valeria Procupez formed my first writing group, and they have continued to read and comment on my work over the years. Amrita Ibrahim, Sidharthan Maunaguru, Rasna Dhillon, Young-gyung Paik, Sylvain Perdigon, Aaron Goodfellow, Richard Baxstrom, Todd Meyers, and Hussein

Agrama were wonderful to learn from and with. The Department of Anthropology and Sociology at Williams College gave me a year to write as a Bolin Fellow, along with stunning vistas to keep me energized, and generous and friendly colleagues who helped me think about how to both start and finish a project as complicated as this one. In Williamstown, Cyndi Howson and Alexa Schriempf made up my second writing group, and were vital companions.

These days I am grateful for the bonhomie of my colleagues in the Department of Social and Cultural Sciences at Marquette University. My special thanks to Heather Hlavka. Additional thanks to Alison Efford, Nakia Gordon, Andrew Kahrl, and Julia Azari, who I value not only as fellow faculty but as wonderful friends. Rose Corrigan, Lesley McMillan, Gethin Rees, and Deborah White all share my interests in travel, fine dining, and research on sexual assault, and I have appreciated our CAIRRN Workshops these past few years. My brother Rashad Mulla is another source of support, as are my many siblings-in-law, Kedy Edme, Sayila Edme, Martine Edme Edouard, Jude Edouard, Ayina Verella, and Janremi Verella. Thanks also to my parents, the Mullas, and to my husband's parents, the Edmes. Veronica Cox, Alison Klein, and Lindsay Moore Monte are owed a debt of thanks for their patient friendship that stretches now into the decades.

Many thanks to NYU Press, and to my editor, Jennifer Hammer, for her able shepherding of this book through to publication, and thanks also to her assistant, Constance Grady. My gratitude also extends to the anonymous reviewers. They provided detailed comments and very nuanced readings of the text. Their insights made the manuscript into a stronger book, and I wish I had been able to implement all of their suggestions.

I will not be able to adequately express the extent of my warmth and good feeling for how grounded my partner, Tipan Verella, keeps me. With him reliably at my back, I was free to meander where this project took me, and look deeply into things that unsettled me, even if productively, for many years. It is with him that I can now happily apply myself to the task of parenting our son, Ibrahim, who stirs up our household with his energetic antics every day and instructs his parents on the art of play with zest and wisdom.

Introduction

Sexual Violence in the City

I'm in a hurry, and luckily, I see a taxicab parked at the curb less than a block away. A few steps closer and I recognize the driver. When I signal to him, he waves in acknowledgment and pulls the car forward so I don't have to take the last few steps in the summer heat. "Where you headed . . . hospital?" And when I say yes, and direct him downtown, he sighs, "It's never good news when you are headed to the hospital."

It was the summer of 2002 in Baltimore, and I was a rape crisis advocate volunteering for a local rape crisis center. I completed my training for this in February 2002, and at that time I bought my first cell phone. I was on call four or five times a week, taking as many eight-hour shifts as I could. The calls would come at all hours, and sometimes, even if I was not on the schedule, I, or another of the advocates, might be called if there wasn't enough coverage or there were multiple cases and additional rape crisis advocates were needed.

Though cell phone–equipped and therefore reachable, I was without a car. All of the other advocates drove. "No problem," I would say. I lived near a large hotel so there were usually taxis out front. The hospitals where we worked were no more than a 20-minute drive away, and once the volunteer coordinator called us, we had 45 minutes to reach the emergency room. It had been a busy summer; I was getting a call at least every other shift. The lore at the rape crisis center was that the overnight shift had the most activity, but I didn't sign up for that shift because cabs are harder to come by in the middle of the night, and I was not keen to explore the city in the darkness. Still, there didn't seem to be a particular witching hour: 6 a.m., 12 noon, 5 p.m., or 9 p.m.—the calls came. I would grab my bag and rush to one of four hospitals, wondering what I would encounter there.

In the hospital, I looked for the "ASA," or "alleged sexual assault victim," as the police, hospital personnel, and forensic nurse examiners referred to her (and, less frequently, him). I met my first forensic nurse examiner during my training as an advocate, and was immediately curious about the profession. The role of the forensic nurse examiner, a specially trained registered nurse, is to both care for and collect evidence from victims of violence. If I was unable to locate the forensic nurse examiner to buzz me into the back, I knew the codes to the emergency room doors and frequently just let myself in. I then checked the giant white board, which would tell me where the victim was—the letters "ASA" scribbled next to her name. The rape crisis center had cautioned us to reject this moniker; as rape crisis advocates, we did not have to qualify our clients as "allegedly" victimized. We, unlike the law enforcement personnel who saw them during the course of rape crisis intervention, were free to believe them and to aid their recovery to the best of our abilities. I and the other rape crisis advocates frequently wondered why nurses continued to adopt this moniker since their other patients weren't treated as if they "allegedly" had stomach pains or any other health complaints.

When meeting a patient, I introduced myself, offered information about the rape crisis center, and then stayed for as long as the patient wanted me to stay. At times, this was only a few minutes, but as often as not patients asked me to accompany them during the forensic examination. There, I held their hands, offered what comfort I could, and did my best to promote the interests of the victim by helping her to communicate her needs and desires to the forensic nurse examiner. As the months passed, I prided myself for the ease with which the forensic nurse examiners now regarded me, though initially they had been wary. For better or for worse, I had become part of the team.

By 2004, I had a driver's license and a much beloved blue 1988 Volvo 240DL station wagon. I drove myself to the hospitals, but I missed bantering with the taxi drivers and the resulting calm of friendly chitchat. In the summers, I missed the air conditioning; the Volvo's cooling system had long ago given up and was not worth fixing. I hated hospital parking lots and the extra step of validating my parking ticket before

I left. And on my way home, again, I missed chatting with taxi drivers and the way their talk helped me shake off the thrumming emergency room air. I learned to quickly return to what I was doing before the phone rang. I learned to program my cell phone so that it rang differently when it was the rape crisis center calling. I also learned that no matter how whimsical or gentle my ring tone selection, I always felt a slight jolt when the calls came.

By 2005, I was feeling odd about my city. Emergency room geography lessons began filtering my view. Steps from my home, there was the pay phone where just last week two men abducted a young man at knifepoint, drove him to a forest just north of the city, and assaulted and abandoned him there. In a well-frequented stretch of bars and clubs near the waterfront, there was a popular dance club where there had been at least two suspected cases of Rohipnol drugging. I went there once—it was a lot of fun but I avoided it in the future. A woman was kidnapped during lunch hour from the parking lot of a mall that was a favorite downtown tourist destination. Her hands were still bound by sheets when she was brought to the hospital three days later. The mall housed one of my favorite retail stores but I stopped shopping there because the manager raped one of the employees, and if the employee still worked there, I wanted to give her space. The woman who ran up to my car window to sell me my morning paper arrived in the emergency room one day. We laughed and joked at the hospital, but when she saw me drive up a week later, she looked away and I didn't stop to buy the paper. A taxicab dispatcher reported an assault by one of the drivers. When I began warily eyeing any and all taxicab drivers to see if their descriptions matched the dispatcher's assailant, I stopped missing the comfort of those brightly colored taxicabs.

Baltimore—lovingly called "Small-timore" by some joking residents—is a modestly sized city.[1] It was simply a matter of time before some of the dots connected and my work at the hospital began to seep into my daily life. My occasional unease was comparable to the occasional bouts of hypochondria experienced by medical students as they were taught new pathologies and symptoms. Awareness of the violence around me made me no more or less prone to its spell. When I wrapped up the fieldwork on which this book is based, I reflected on my experiences, concluding that while many familiar places and personalities had figured in my investigation of sexual violence, the most striking and frequent characteristic of the violence I had witnessed was that it was almost always between intimates. The myth of the threatening stranger rapist had proved to be just that, a myth, and victims more often than not named a friend, family member, co-worker, or neighbor as attacker.

In these opening pages, some of the basic elements of a "typical" sexual assault intervention come through. Each case is a surprise for the professionals who respond to it, interrupting some other activity. As a rape crisis advocate, I experienced the unpredictability of sexual assault intervention first hand, taking calls as needed, never knowing when I would be making a trip to the emergency room. Forensic nurses, police detectives, and rape crisis advocates could be called upon at any time and under any set of circumstances. None of us knew when we might be called or what violent events had set the intervention in motion. For rape crisis advocates and forensic nurses alike, the shift work was not a full-time pursuit but rather a secondary addition to one's day-to-day routine. Like the forensic nurses and police detectives, my role as a rape crisis advocate was highly dependent on a delicate network of technology and my participation was contingent on key tools such as cell phones and automobiles. Indeed, a malfunctioning pager once crippled the entire patient advocacy operation over the course of several months. The technologies upon which forensic practitioners rely varied in their sophistication, but none of the stakeholders in the sexual assault intervention were able to carry out their charges without one technology or another.

This book examines the rapidly changing world of sexual assault forensic intervention, particularly as it is mediated by the relationship between law and medicine in formal emergency room–based programs. It traces the complex of care that emerges from the interpenetration of legal and therapeutic practices. Ultimately, it argues that blending the work of care and forensic investigation into a single intervention shapes how victims of violence understand their own suffering, recovery, and access to justice—in short, what it means to be a "victim." Because of the institutional protocols governing forensic intervention, even the most well-intentioned forensic nurses tend to focus on collecting evidence, often at the expense of caring for their patients. Institutional forces frequently cast the psychological or even physical trauma of victims as a secondary priority in the emergency that requires forensic nurses to race the clock to preserve rapidly deteriorating biological evidence. The reality is that most of the evidence they do collect never reaches the courtroom, while many studies have found that at present, when cases do reach the courtroom, forensic evidence does little to increase the likelihood of a guilty verdict. The impact of the forensic intervention, then, is largely on the victims themselves, and on how they come to understand what has happened to them. These interventions weigh heavily on victims of violence, as they serve as the medium through which experiences of victimization and recovery are cultivated. Many studies have documented the tendency of formal interventions to introduce more suffering into victims' lives even as they attempt to care for the victim, a phenomenon referred to as re-victimization or "the second rape" (Campbell 2001b; Madigan and Gamble 1991). At both the federal and local levels, rape crisis management is one way in which the state responds to the immediate aftermath of violence (Corrigan 2013b). In Baltimore, Maryland, a forensic nurse examiner typically has the dual responsibilities of treatment and evidence collection, a fairly typical model of sexual assault intervention in the United States. Institutional imaginaries of sexual violence are configured as "medico-legal"; the term highlights the simultaneously distinct and conjoined therapeutic and juridical aims of intervention. Forensic training manuals, textbooks, and policy documents routinely frame sexual assault interventions as such (Crowley 1999; Office on Violence Against Women 2004; Olshaker et al. 2006). The intervention casts the sufferer of rape as both a victim within the legal context and a patient within the medical world. Distinct, incongruent, and divergent configurations of space and time mark the nexus of clinic-courtroom, reshaping the relationship of care to investigation, and healing to justice. The on-call nature of forensic practice, which I also experienced as a rape crisis advocate, is characterized by a responsive set of institutional protocols. The report of rape itself activates the technological resources and institutional nexus in which a sexual assault intervention will be staged and engages the professional expertise of police detectives, forensic nurses, and other emergency room personnel. Because many of the experts who are mobilized all work on shifts, picking up "on-call" hours between other tasks or jobs, it also means that sexual assault intervention is often secondary to the careers and daily lives of many of the personnel who respond to these calls.

There is a lively and deeply insightful literature that takes up the politics of naming in victimization studies (Alcoff and Gray 1993; Lamb 1999; Mardorossian 2002). Many feminist scholars argue that the term "victim" is pejorative and ought to be replaced by "survivor," allowing women the opportunity to transcend the disempowered subject position of the victim and move on. I deliberated for some time over what term I would use to describe the men and women I met in the emergency room. As the reader has no doubt already noticed, I chose to use the term "victim," though sometimes I interchange this with the term "patient." I made this choice because I think it is the most accurate given the particular setting in which I conducted research. Legal institutions locate and constitute victims, not survivors, and the forensic intervention, with its therapeutic components, also casts this victim as a patient. In fact, these institutional nodes often deny victims and patients their claims to survival. On the rare occasion I do use "survivor" when referring to a particular individual, it is because in this case the victim referred to him- or herself as a survivor, and is claiming the status of survivor. I also understand victimhood from within an ethnographic context, and hence, describe how victims are not passive, but rather, take on active and participatory roles in the forensic intervention. As they participate in the process of framing themselves as victims, men and women position themselves within the medico-legal nexus. For those who do not actively participate in the sexual assault intervention, there is a risk of being branded non-compliant by the medical and legal staff.

While many studies have rigorously analyzed one particular space, the courtroom (Taslitz 1999), as the most prominent site figuring within sexual assault cases, this book draws attention to the events and processes that must take place as a precondition to prosecution. Very few sexual assault cases reach the level of adjudication, as the strict criteria for prosecution are rarely met. For example, of the Midwestern cases examined by Campbell et al. between 1999 and 2005, 43% of cases were not referred to prosecutors by police for a myriad of reasons, while 15% were referred but not "warranted" (deemed to have significant legal merit) by the prosecutor. Of the 42% that were warranted, 13%

were subsequently dropped or resulted in acquittal, while 29% resulted in guilty pleas or convictions. In the Baltimore emergency room in which I conducted research, logbooks for the years 2002 to 2004 indicate more than 300 sexual assault forensic examinations conducted each year; 2002 and 2003 figures are confirmed by the local rape crisis center's records of emergency room companions dispatched to attend rape victims in the hospital. The Maryland State Police give totals of 179, 208, and 182 rape cases respectively for each year. During this period, forensic examinations could only be conducted with permission from a police detective or a state's attorney; thus, the lower number of cases reported by the police reflects that at least one-third of cases were "unfounded" (deemed to have inadequate legal merit) following the forensic examination. In 2010, media scrutiny and intervention by local and federal government uncovered several factors contributing to police under-reporting of sexual assault in Baltimore.[2]

Whatever stage of legal disposition to which a case progresses, it is still meaningful and meaning-making for those who participate in its pre-trial phases. This book, therefore, focuses on the emergency room, and adjoining sites, such as the police department, rape crisis center, state's attorney's office, and homes of victims as spaces where important legal, medical, and life interventions are made prior to the stage of adjudication. While cases may not reach prosecution, upon reporting they are all subject to a combination of forensic investigation and medical intervention. Drawing on historical material, detailed ethnographic research, documentary artifacts, and interview transcripts, this book interrogates the ways in which medical and legal aspects of the sexual assault intervention are alternately distinguished and conflated. At times, it is individual personnel who may conflate their juridical and medical priorities. At other times, it is the protocols themselves. This volume examines the institutional boundaries of medical and legal practice by focusing on how time operates within both medical and legal registers, ultimately demonstrating that the forensic is not a simple amalgamation of medical and legal components, but a unique mode unto itself. Time, and the way it operates, marking the intervention as urgent and setting various potential future horizons, is a running theme throughout this book as many of the technologies brought to bear are about shaping time, arresting time, and recording time at different junctures of the sexual assault intervention. The forensic, this book asserts, has its own temporal rhythms. Time, expertise, technology, routines, and protocols are all features of the institutional structure that regulates and conscripts the actors who abide within them, whether they are forensic nurses, rape crisis advocates, police and crime lab officials, or prosecutors. By attending to the way individual actors deliver care and justice in the setting of the sexual assault intervention, this book draws attention to how institutional structures can perpetuate cycles of injustice, particularly when the needs of sexual assault complainants intersect with the needs of the criminal justice system. With a detailed and focused ethnographic description, this book brings awareness to the complex dynamics that are unfolding in the course of sexual assault intervention, with the goal of empowering readers to entertain creative and constructive change to the dynamics of sexual assault forensic intervention, whether through policy reform, therapeutic protocols, criminal justice procedures, or as ethnographers of legal and clinical practice.

One of the key institutional features of forensic intervention is its temporal configuration, which focuses primarily on anticipation of the trial. As a privileged site and destination in the idealized sexual assault intervention, the courtroom is present in the emergency room not simply as a space, but as an agency that structures the examination. As anthropologists renew their interest in the role of things as social actors, we have learned to take seriously not only the human denizens of the social milieu, but the non-human (Bennett 2010; Latour 2005; Law and Hassard 1999); in this case, the courtroom is but one of many actants[3] breathing life into the form that suffering, healing, and justice may take. Because the question of consent is at the center of the legal definition of rape, one of the ways in which time takes on prominence throughout the forensic intervention is the perpetual figuring of the courtroom as the inevitable point of arrival; it is within the courtroom that the state bears the burden of convincing a jury that a victim's consent was not offered. While the case under question may not, in fact, reach the courtroom, the courtroom asserts itself throughout the medical intervention. Technological interventions shape the sexual assault victim as a legal and medical subject and produce proof of or against consent. The location of the sexual assault intervention within the emergency room reveals the urgency with which sexual violence is met, and that urgency resonates within both legal and medical logics. Legal urgency is inherent in the challenge of collecting (organic) evidence that is rapidly disappearing or deteriorating while the medical emergency centers on the immediacy of treating the sexual assault victim for physical and psychological trauma, sexually transmitted infection, and potential pregnancy. Here, it is the vital materiality of life itself, in the form of rapidly deteriorating DNA, which demands urgency. Even as forensic nurses aim to act urgently and effectively through an efficient examination rubric, sexual assault victims draw on a range of experiences and relations in making sense of the experience of sexual assault and its aftermath. At present, because so few cases progress to the trial stage (Spohn and Horney 1992; McMillan 2010), we must focus on the intervention itself as the institutional engagement that has the largest impact on victims, their understanding of the process that lies ahead, and their sense of their experience of suffering. Doing so allows us to develop a more ethically responsible and nuanced approach to sexual assault intervention, one that balances the needs of sexual assault victims in relation to the challenges they will face in their recoveries, challenges that go beyond the limited horizon of a potential trial. It also introduces important considerations for thinking about the paths that professionals in the field of sexual assault intervention need to weigh in seeking to develop their expertise and deepen their understanding of what it means to be effective when working with sexual assault victims. What is just another day on the job for a forensic nurse is often a life-changing event for the sexual assault victims with whom they work.

Interrogating Sexual Assault Interventions: Defining the Research Question

The decision to focus my research on emergency room interventions into sexual assault grew out of years of reading about sexual violence in the United States. As a young woman, I had begun to research sexual violence, first reading such classics as Brownmiller's *Against Our Will*, and Estrich's *Real Rape*, in response to the spate of disclosures of victimization that were so common in my social world. Friends, teachers, co-workers, relatives, and mentors began to disclose experiences of sexual violence. "I was raped." "This happened to me." "I was once attacked." The disclosures came from all quarters and were conveyed by speakers sharing their grief, rage, pride, and shame. Concerned—and embarrassed—that I did not know how to respond properly, I tried to learn how to support those whose lives had been touched by sexual violence. As I read over the years, I began to take note of some common features in the available literature. In general, scholarly engagements with rape were often fractured. For example, a psychologist or criminologist might focus on victims or perpetrators. Rarely would both appear within the same framework. Studies that included victims' perspectives or testimonies seemed to share a lot with the sexual victimization self-help literature. A particular uniformity manifested in the common testimonial narratives.[4] Rape narratives seemed to belong to a genre of their own—the tone, narrative features, and quality of the voices did not always reflect the diverse experiences comprising stories of sexual violence. Rape narratives are linked by the act of violence itself. Most narratives inevitably begin with a description of the violent act. The narrator's tone rings with a particular incredulity, while also creating a dire sense of inevitability of the impending rape attack. The anticipatory structure gives way to unavoidable violence. The narratives are written with the benefit of hindsight and the victims know how the stories will end. Narrators also describe the force used to isolate and immobilize them, their protestations, fear, and physical pain. Rape's aftermath always includes utter transformation and discontinuity, though as readers we are dependent on the author to identify these discontinuities, as we know very little about a victim's life prior to the event of rape. Typically, narrators communicate their frustration with the inability of their community of friends, relatives, and colleagues to truly understand the nature of their suffering. Finally, victims depict the insensitivities and failures of law enforcement and medical personnel when they report rape to the police.

This last feature, repeated by scores of rape victims, drew my attention to the issue of rape investigation and prosecution as harrowing ordeals for the victim. My curiosity settled around how rape as a legal category could impose on a victim's suffering by overtaking her access to and expectation of care. When I first accompanied victims during police questioning, I noticed that police scrutiny played a large part in eliciting various details from the victims. These questions were often repeated in the course of questioning, often by different personnel. Thus, it was not uncommon for a uniformed officer, a police detective, and a forensic nurse examiner to ask a victim the same question within a short time span. All three aim to establish an investigative time line, and to identify evidence of a crime having taken place. In the United States, the legal definition of rape rests primarily on lack of consent and the threat and/or use of force, and this definition is always particular to the criminal statutes of the specific state in which the crime took place. The investigative time line, the legal definitions, and eventually, cultural myths about sexual violence produce the rape narrative, and account for the narratives' typical features. The interventions of legal personnel teach many rape victims what matters about rape and what people want to hear. While criticisms of medical and law enforcement personnel and their shortcomings in supporting sexual assault victims are frequently examined in social science literature, the overwhelming institutional stamp on the rape narrative has been largely undercriticized until very recently. The challenge in this book is to demonstrate the intricate means by which sexual violence is defined within a very particular institutional matrix characterized by intertwined projects of juridical and medical intervention.

Historically, Baltimore is like many densely populated urban centers in that the evolution of sexual assault response followed a familiar sequence. After the women's rights movement drew national attention to the issue of sexual violence in the early 1970s (Brownmiller 1975; Griffin 1979), the first sexual assault forensic nursing program opened its doors in Memphis, Tennessee in 1976 (Taylor 2002: S91), the second in Minneapolis in 1977 (Ledray 1999), and the third in Amarillo, Texas in 1979 (Antognoli-Toland 1985). Prior to the advent of more centralized sexual assault intervention programs, states, or even single jurisdictions within a state, would each generate their own medico-legal evidentiary examination, often glossed as a rape kit, and victims could go to any hospital emergency room where the gynecological resident or emergency room physician would conduct evidence collection procedures per the guidelines included with the rape kit (Taylor 2002). Nurses were frequently present, sometimes reading instructions to the doctors who conducted the interventions with the nurse chaperones giving them step-by-step direction. This model did not require any specific expertise on either the nurses' or doctors' parts, but rather just a basic skill set and an ability to follow directions. The lack of specialized competence was itself often devastating for victims, who expected to find themselves in capable hands (Winkler 2002). After victims, medical professionals, and law enforcement all expressed great dissatisfaction with these types of programs, a national movement began to emphasize efficient treatment and efficacious evidence collection. Having witnessed sexual assault interventions in their role as chaperones, nurses were among the loudest critics of the haphazard response and treatment rape victims received in the healthcare system. Nurses were pioneers at the national level, establishing formal training programs, suggesting best practice standards, embarking on more scientific study of forensic practice, and forming a professional association to focus on the skills requisite for effective sexual assault response—the International Association of Forensic Nurses (henceforth, IAFN). The IAFN eventually developed protocols for sexual assault evidence exams, established training and certification standards, founded a peer-reviewed journal of forensic nursing, and also expanded its scope to include forensic nurses working in fields beyond sexual assault response. Experienced nurses may now elect to be tested and receive credentials as FNEs or Forensic Nurse Examiners. As a nationwide movement gained ground, nurses at the local level frequently pioneered the introduction of forensic nursing programs based on their knowledge of the growing field and their dissatisfaction with existing arrangements (Ledray 2001). Under the older systems, advocates, and medical and legal personnel worried that victims were receiving poor care, while evidence was being badly collected and preserved. Thus, between the late 1970s and the present day, a shift ensued in which nurses began to receive training to specifically manage all aspects of victim care. In Maryland, nurses participate in an IAFN-organized course as the IAFN is headquartered in Maryland. The State Board of Nursing also participates in credentialing FNEs. In some jurisdictions, as in Baltimore, a single hospital or clinic claimed responsibility for hiring nurses trained in forensic intervention, and for conducting sexual assault interventions. At City Hospital,[5] nurses had been assisting gynecology residents with forensic examinations for many years. Dissatisfied with the long waiting periods and general lack of compassion from the doctors, who seemed very disinclined to conduct the examinations and even more leery of testifying in court, the nurses at City Hospital heard that nurses in nearby Virginia had completed forensic training and were conducting exams on their own. By 1994, the nurses of City Hospital had established their own program after completing their training and had spread the word throughout the city that all sexual assault victims could be sent to their emergency room based program. The proliferation of training programs and licensing in forensic expertise for nurses corresponded with this call for greater quality of care and higher standards of expertise in sexual assault intervention, though standards for certification and training forensic nurses remain very diverse and vary from state to state, as do the rape kits in use across the country. The International Association of Forensic Nurses reports that there are currently about 590 sexual assault nurse examiner programs in the United States and its territories.

According to Baltimore's current protocol, all victims report to or are transferred to City Hospital, presently the only hospital in the city designated to conduct forensic exams. In the field of forensic nursing, it is notoriously difficult to recruit, train, and fully staff a program so that sexual assault response is available 24 hours a day, 7 days a week, all throughout the calendar year. As noted earlier, sexual assault response is carried out on an on-call basis; thus forensic nurses sign up for a certain number of on-call hours every month, in addition to their primary employment obligations. They are minimally compensated for being on-call, and only receive a regular wage if called in. This puts administrators in a position of constantly covering abandoned shifts when nurses are offered extra shifts through their primary employers, who are more reliable sources of additional income. The pressure of staffing shortages may guarantee that some administrators are willing to keep nurses on the call rotation whose skills may not be up to muster simply because there is no one else to replace them. Often, it is a single nurse administrator who is the last line of defense, filling empty shifts to guarantee that no call goes unanswered and no victim goes unserved. Because of the daunting staffing challenges, many large population centers have transitioned toward a pattern in which only one or two hospitals will have thriving sexual assault nurse examiner programs so that the pools of on-call forensic nurses will be large enough to address the local need. While most jurisdictions in the United States rely on the cooperation of forensic nurses, police officers, and detectives in sexual assault interventions, Baltimore exemplifies this by bringing together the various actors in the common space of the emergency room. Until 2009, a police detective from the Sex Offense Unit interviewed the victim and then determined whether to authorize the collection of evidence, after which the hospital staff paged the on-call forensic nurse examiner. A rape crisis advocate from an independent rape crisis center might also be called to accompany and counsel the victim. Thus, from the outset, the victim would find him- or herself at the confluence of several different institutional processes. While some police, FNEs, and advocates may think they are playing very distinct roles in the sexual assault intervention, the victim may not perceive them to be carrying out distinct functions, or even working for different institutions, particularly because everyone is attending the victim within the same institutional space of the hospital. What's more, as we will see, some police, FNEs, and advocates adopt a cooperative relationship in which they work toward many of the same goals, further fusing into a single entity from the perspective of the victim. As of 2009, compliance with federal law dictates that police can no longer decide when a forensic evidence collection should be undertaken—victims may choose for themselves and they may do so before deciding whether to file a report with the police. While it remains to be seen what long-term impact these new policies will have, many programs, including the one studied in this book, report the immediate effect is the increase in the number of sexual assault victims participating in sexual assault forensic examinations, while scholarship demonstrates very little change in the outcomes of court cases.

These policies unfold at the nexus of two distinctly gendered professional spheres—policing and nursing. As arguably the most feminized of any profession, nursing exemplifies the care work associated with women in the public and domestic spheres (Reverby 1987; Sandelowski 2000). With the exception of nurse practitioners, the typical registered nurse works under the supervision of a medical doctor. The forensic nurse examiners at City Hospital, for example, could only dispense medications under the standing orders of one of the two physicians who provided program oversight. While the nursing profession is

93% female and 7% male, sworn officers in local police departments are about 88% male with a 12% female minority (Health Resources and Services Administration 2010; Langton 2010). While some forensic nurses do become interested in a forensic practice out of a desire to assist victims of violence, nurses also cite other professional reasons for coming to the field of forensic nursing. For many, the field is exciting and the association of working with law enforcement carries great attraction. The training, which is relatively short and does not require graduate education, allows nurses to practice as FNEs with relative independence.[6] While the doctors and nurse administrator may review their charts, the nurse works one on one with her patient and will typically only consult a doctor or another nurse at her own discretion, or participate in peer review with other nurses. As FNEs, nurses' expertise can be acknowledged in its own right.

If the police are most closely aligned with the masculine authority of the state, while the nurses exemplify a feminized force of care, the sexual assault victim occupies the most abject feminized subject position. The flux of gender and power catches all three actors within a relational dynamic in which the FNE, seeking to have her expertise acknowledged, often identifies and allies herself with the police force while appropriating the masculine power of policing. The nurse simultaneously distances herself from the close association with the feminized victim by producing a clinical competence that is professional while not appearing overly empathetic or caring. The FNEs posit that this cool clinical demeanor is a necessity if they are to reliably participate in the criminal justice procedure. Thus, the care they offer victims is often encumbered by its juridical focus.

By focusing on the institutionally constituted subjects of nurses, police detectives, advocates, and victims, this book investigates the agency of institutions at a micro-level. Attending to the interplay between these gendered subjects in the demarcated space and time of the victim-cum-patient's emergency room stay, it demonstrates how multiple and competing imaginaries animate the intervention. It shows how institutional interventions sometimes preclude the consideration of sexual violence within a broader social framework. While the book demonstrates again and again that victims narrate sexual violence within broad contexts, drawing attention to conditions of living, such as race, poverty, work, family life, or the induction of families into foster-care services, these narratives were often subsumed by particular procedures of medical and legal care. Ultimately, this volume draws out institutional investments in notions of appropriately marked bodies and the configuration of sexually violated subjects as constituted by a forensic intervention that is both medical and legal in its modality. It argues that the ethical consequences of sexual assault intervention are borne almost solely by the sexual assault survivor, and brings into view those ways in which different stakeholders in the sexual assault intervention, including FNEs, prosecutors, police, policy experts, and legislators, might challenge the institutional structure to reduce or eliminate such burdens.

Anthropological and Sociological Conversations about Sexual Violence

This work is anthropological in that it is ethnographic, with all of the excesses and surplus that are characteristic of a descriptive enterprise. It is important that some of the narratives, stories, and fragments within these pages do not lend themselves to any one analysis in an easy or simplistic way. Human life is too complex and varied to be easily reduced, and thus the most effective ethnographies recognize these complexities by leaving some things unanalyzed. From time to time, I present details for which I have no definitive analysis, but I hope that readers are empowered to ask their own questions about these interventions and their impact. I approach this material with as much insight as I can bring to bear on it, and thus, this project is a part of many different anthropological conversations. Correspondingly, I have consulted many literatures in crafting my approach to the study. Reading carried me through the many facets of my work, including framing my research question, developing a methodology, carrying out research, sifting through and organizing my data, analyzing my findings, and producing a text. In addition to the rape narrative literature, I looked at a more broadly defined set of literatures on sexual violence, which led me to more specific readings on institutional structures, legal anthropology, clinical practice, and the state. In this section, I discuss only my engagement with the research explicitly focused on sexual violence and how it opened up other literatures and avenues of thought. Where relevant, those subsequent literatures are dealt with in particular chapters.

With its focus on social problems of industrialized urban-centered populations, sociology has taken a systematic approach to the study of sexual assault and sexual violence, particularly since the feminist turn of the 1970s (Rose 1977). Much of this literature has a social constructionist perspective (Chasteen 2001), following the evolving cultural and social construction of "rape" over the past three decades. Significant attention has focused on the proliferation of rape myths, those folk fantasies about rape that persist in the popular imagination no matter how many times they are shown to be unsubstantiated (Andrias 1992; Du Mont and Parnis 1999). These myths, many authors argue, are rampant within police units and other locations within the criminal justice system. Institutional ethnography has also attended to the institutional responses to sexual assault, showing how different actors coordinate their responses in the interests of intervening in sexual violence (Martin 2005).

Sexual assault nurse examiner programs have comprised one of the main professional and institutional innovations in response to the call for better services for sexual assault victims. White and Du Mont[7] have conducted research evaluating the efficacies of sexual assault nurse examiner programs, rape kit technology, legal institutional responses, and forensic evidence (Du Mont and Parnis 2000, 2001, 2003; Du Mont, White and McGregor 2009; Parnis and Du Mont 1999, 2002, 2006; White and Du Mont 2009). The World Health Organization report that they authored suggests that medico-legal evidence has a minor impact on prosecutorial outcomes (Du Mont and White 2007). This finding is echoed in more recent work (Sommers and Baskin 2011). At the same time, a continuing theme in the sociological and criminological literature demonstrates the impact—including psychological—of forensic intervention on the victims who participate in these interventions (White and Du Mont 2009; Du Mont et al. 2009). This careful and rigorous sociological research has continued to shed light on the evolving question of sexual assault forensic intervention, and has opened the door for more qualitative inquiries into medico-legal sexual assault intervention as it is practiced in different geographic and historical settings (Rees 2010, 2011; Crozier and Rees 2011).

Though anthropology has not, historically, been as outspoken on the topic of sexual assault, the discipline frames sexual assault from a different perspective than sociology. Sexual assault has been treated mainly in broad contexts of structural and sectarian violence, and the range of institutions implicated in making sexual assault socially meaningful extends beyond medical and legal institutions. One of the most broad-sweeping and sustained perspectives on violence against women and gender-based violence in anthropology is offered by Sally Engle Merry (Merry 2009). Merry conducted ethnographic research at a number of sites including urban centers in the United States (Merry 2001a, 2001b). Taking a broad view of culture (Merry 2012), Merry has tracked institutional influences as well as the ability of legislative and policy reforms to recast legal subjects through criminal jurisdiction but also through human rights discourses (Merry and Shimin 2011). Her work illustrates the location from which anthropologists are poised to observe, analyze, and critique the intersection of institution, law, and culture as it affects women and men who are victims of gendered violence. Merry's work not only offers a number of theoretical frameworks for analyzing gendered violence, but also helpfully models many different ethnographic methodologies for situating the anthropologist in the field, including attention to historical genealogy in gaining understanding of the anthropological subject (Merry 2003). This historical turn can be noted in some of the other anthropological texts referenced here. Overall, Merry's work boldly suggests how the field might be constituted when anthropologists research violence against women and girls, by positioning the anthropologist at the intersection of law, regulation, institution, history, and culture.

Another long-established voice in the anthropology of sexual assault is Peggy Reeves Sanday. She has addressed the problem of rape in at least three different ways. A comparative study of the configuration of male and female power among 95 Indonesian tribal groups demonstrated great variation in the occurrence of sexual violence in different communities. Sanday then sought to identify what factors contributed to the formation of "rape-prone" versus "rape-free" societies (Sanday 1981). She concluded that a correlation existed between matriarchal governance and lower incidence of rape. She then turned her attention to sexual violence in the United States, focusing on sexual violence in university settings. Building on her prior research, Sanday studied patriarchal power, which she argued was exemplified by the phenomena of fraternities and Greek life on U.S. campuses (Sanday 1990). While her most recent book also grew out of another campus rape case, this time she examined American legal history and turned most of her analysis to the subject of the trial, tying her historical insights to the examination of a set of 1990 cases involving several St. John's College students (Sanday 1996). I found this particular progression in Sanday's research to be extremely helpful in my own deliberations about where to enter into the anthropological study of sexual violence. I read her second study as arguing, if implicitly, that the experience of sexual violence in the lives of the young women she interviewed was primarily filtered through the institution of the university and processes of adjudication. Subsequently, her third study depicted the suffering of another young student, but this time by attributing her sexual suffering to the intersections of the legal and university systems while historicizing the legal technologies available for intervention. Clearly, legal and educational institutional contexts are key sites of shaping juridical and cultural attitudes toward rape. The prison is another site through which cultural imaginaries of perpetration and victimization are articulated. In his anthropological research on mandatory sex offender treatment programs in prisons, James Waldram points to the institutional and disciplinary contexts in which the subject position of "sex offender" is produced. He argues that the treatment profile posits a moral subject who must be habilitated, rather than, for example, an offender who carries out rapes because of patriarchal privilege (Waldram 2012). If the subject position of offender is institutionally constituted, how might the subject position of "victim" be produced within the same institutional contexts?

The autobiographical ethnographies of anthropologists Cathy Winkler and Micaela di Leonardo began to draw in other institutional and social currents that shaped their experiences.[8] For di Leonardo, race was one of the forces cultivating the imaginary by which her case was perceived. Attacked by an African American perpetrator, di Leonardo found herself in the position of dispelling the historically deep popular stereotype that "black on white rape" was the norm (Di Leonardo 1992: 30). Di Leonardo narrates her interactions with the police, including their deployment of particular imaginaries of racial identity and crime statistics. The question of race and crime is a sensitive one, and I was aware, as I did my research, that the statewide coalition of rape crisis centers was conducting a survey-based study on African American women's experiences of the sexual assault intervention (Weist et al. 2009). Rather than turn my scrutiny to the African American experience, I drew on di Leonardo's criticism to think about institutional imaginaries, including the "racialization" of particular problems or bodies. In this book, the racialization of the patient's body plays out within the context of a medico-legal examination heavily informed by nurses' experience in their local professional practices with a largely African American patient population that they associate with particular health issues.

While Winkler begins with the rape attack and then details the horrific circumstances of her own medico-legal examination, a great deal of her study focuses on her interactions with the legal system. Winkler attributes much of what she calls her re-victimization to her entanglements with law enforcement and prosecutors. She also brought her eventual loss of livelihood to bear on her suffering (2002).[9] She is impressively adept in conducting phenomenological analyses of the rape attack, tying her ability to narrate rape to her sensory experiences (Winkler 1994; Winkler and Hancke 1995). She contextualized her phenomenological approach within a broader anthropology of violence and established the tenuous nature of knowledge about violence as it contaminated particular ontological modalities with "suspicious" sensuous ways of knowing. In short, traumatic experiences by their very nature elude description by the narrator who, trauma theorists hold, may not have the language to describe an experience that must remain "unclaimed" (Caruth 1996). As knowledge and memory become unreliable, victims may turn to their sensory knowledge, the sensations of the body, to communicate their experiences with others. In Winkler's experience, law enforcement rejected her sensuous knowledge. I read Winkler as critiquing the precise moment in which a victim's knowledge of self is invalidated by the formal processes of forging justice; this book seeks to explore these moments in the encounters between FNEs and sexual assault victims.

While Winkler experienced the invalidating of her sensual self-knowledge at the hands of the law court, my field research in the emergency room suggested that particular forms of sensuous knowledge were privileged within forensic practice. Forensic nurses were expert in folding the fleshy materiality of the raped body into acceptable forms of evidence that could then be apprehended within and by the court of law. Susan Ehrlich and Greg Matoesian, both noted sociolinguists, treat the linguistic practices of the rape trial with sensitivity and detail, drawing attention to the forms of speech that mark criminal rape trials in an adversarial justice system (Ehrlich 2001; Matoesian 1993). Ehrlich's observation of the dearth of any evidence apart from victim testimony in the two trials she studied motivated me to focus on rape interventions prior to the trial stage as the processes by which material evidence collection occurred were unlikely to make an impact beyond the space of the forensic encounter. Pratiksha Baxi has written about Indian practices of medico-legal sexual assault intervention from an anthropological perspective, suggesting that localized understandings of the sexed (female) body become institutionalized through these practices (Baxi 2005). She suggests that clinical evidentiary procedures produce a raped body that is normalized for the Indian law court, without regard to whether these clinical procedures are grounded in evidence-based practices. In the juridical world, there is no objective knowledge and all expertise is subject to the standards of the court of law, admitted only after being vetted by the court. That doctors and nurses are influenced by their own cultural mores is not a revelation to a medical anthropologist, but Baxi's fine-grained research tracked the specific ways in which forensic practices become standardized, and motivated me to identify these moments among the FNEs with whom I worked.

For linguistic anthropologist Shonna Trinch, the law court also produces the domestic violence and rape victim's voice through an administratively mediated form of listening to domestic violence complaints and rendering the complaints actionable by legal forms of writing (2003: 225–68). These practices are shaped by the formal modes of argument that govern law courts, particularly with respect to rape cases (Matoesian 1993). My emergency room–based research would have to take into account both the places and particulars of the use of touch and the forms of recordkeeping and representation by which evidence was noted and preserved in anticipation of a case's arrival in the court of law.

The court of law exists as part of a complex interplay between various legal sites and techniques that intersect to produce a sexually violated subject. Anthropologist Veena Das has turned her attention to the production of the gendered sexually violated subject, arguing that judicial verification results in a woman's speech being "pitted against her body" (2002: 261). Her work draws attention to the tensions between victim subjectivity and judicial verification, a tension that this book explores by questioning the assumption of the ability of forensic practice to produce a unified body and narrative, and the discrepancies that might arise and be subjected to erasure or rewriting in the course of the forensic examination. Das also analyzes sexual violence at length in her work on gendered violence during the partition of India and Pakistan, interrogating the role of the state in responding to sexual assault (1995, 1996a, 1996b, 2000). Das demonstrates that honor, shame, and family are reconfigured through formally sanctioned state institutions. Survival and suffering are ongoing projects here, and Das's anthropological inquiry poses the question of life "after" violence again and again. What does it mean to survive? What does it mean to choose to re-reinhabit the scene of devastation (Das 2006a)? This book attends to the reinhabiting of the everyday by remaining attuned to the ideas of recovery, healing, and restoration that abound within the sexual assault intervention. Within the sexual assault forensic examination, the circulating imaginations of justice and the successful future varied depending on which actor's perspective one explored. Nurses, victims, advocates, and police detectives often had very different notions of what forms justice and healing might take, and these notions were not stable, coinciding at times, and departing from one another at others. For the victim, the nurse, police, and advocate also represented the state's interests and resources brought to bear on the crisis of sexual assault.

The task I set myself, then, was to think of the institutional investments in healing and justice as deeply tied to several factors. I would have to focus on the state's stake in sexual assault by following the legislation, resources, and sanctions invested in sexual violence. I would have to be attentive to the micro-procedures of forensic practice, and the training of the sensory faculties that constituted forensic expertise. I would also have to look at the technological and representational mediation of evidence—how was evidence produced? In addition, I would have to think about the temporalities at work in the context of forensic practice. My engagement with institutions had shifted to an engagement with instituting. Most critically, I would have to draw out the ways in which victims' understandings of their own experiences of sexual assault and intervention were constituted by the institutional processes in which they participated.

On Methods

I conducted research between January 2002 and December 2006. I began as a rape crisis advocate working in the local rape intervention program. Early on, I decided that I would frame my research by getting involved. From the outset, I abandoned any notion of being a fly on the wall, as this was neither ethical nor desirable in this research setting, committing, instead, to situated knowledge (Haraway 1988). This would help me attain a thorough understanding of how the intervention functioned from within the intervention itself. All stages of my research and writing were carried out with oversight and review from the Johns Hopkins University's Homewood Institutional Review Board and the Marquette University Office of Research Compliance.[10] I chose to become a rape crisis advocate in part to receive the training and learn what stakes I would come to have as a rape crisis advocate. Hospitals are often places full of students. To many of the medical personnel with whom I worked, having an anthropologist in the emergency room was equivalent to having a resident present. Within the cramped confines of the small examination room in which the forensic examination was completed, my presence would be very obtrusive if I was simply to be an observer. As a rape crisis advocate, I hoped to give something back to the community with whom I worked. I contacted the local rape crisis center and shared my research plans and met with the director before being accepted into the rape crisis advocate program. She was supportive of my research goals and held me to the same standards as other rape crisis advocates. With the right training, I was also able to interact with sexual assault victims in what I hoped was a sensitive and ethical manner. I underwent training and supervision, and abided by the rape crisis center's confidentiality clauses. Rape crisis advocates are free to speak and write about their experiences as long as they do not reveal victims' identifying information. In addition, I agreed not to take any notes or ask directed questions during the sexual assault interventions, as the rape crisis center and forensic nursing program did not want me to create an account that might contradict the forensic record. Instead, I wrote my field notes immediately after leaving the hospital. Whether such precautions were necessary or not, I did not want to be in the position of having my research compromise a legal case. Of course, when I began my work, I did not know how few cases advanced to the trial stage. The anxiety my recordkeeping raised retrospectively demonstrates the deeply anticipatory focus of rape crisis intervention among the participating institutional actors.

In the examination room, I focused not only on the interpersonal relationships among hospital and legal personnel and victims, but also on their use and adoption of forensic technologies. The hospital gave way to numerous sites through which a victim's particularly gendered, sexed, and vulnerable body could be given institutional life. Long after the physical evidence of sexual assault had ceased to exist, technologically crafted bureaucratic evidentiary bodies were made to stand in for the victim's sexually violated body. Technology had a place in creating these types of assemblages and assigning them places within the biography of particular subjects and the phenomenal world of their relationships.[11] For example, I observed that victims' bodies were photographed and documented such that they may stand as separate and distinct from the future healed body of the "victim." The recording of evidence as schematic drawing, photographs, and written narrative condensed and encoded rich sensorial encounters between practitioners and victims involving pain, odors, and bodily discharges. These evidentiary records served to construct a body in legal discourse that was able to withstand the passing of time and accrual of duration throughout the juridical process. In the emergency room, I was able to observe the unique administrative features through which a victimized body was fixed in such a way that sexual violation was made legible to a court of law, perhaps at the cost of the victim's own recognition of self.

As a rape crisis advocate, I observed workplace practices, and conducted rape crisis interventions as part of my investigation of the web of relationships created in the institutional environment that had arisen in response to sexual violence. The relationships formed through my work as a rape crisis advocate were valuable for analyzing how others, including forensic nurse examiners, police officers, and victims themselves, were cast in relation to my role as one of many care providers for victims. Though sexual assault cases are a matter of public record with the condition of victim confidentiality, I did not take consent for granted. All research participants took part in the project based on informed consent, and were allowed to withdraw at any time. I took appropriate measures to protect the anonymity of all participants. Field data took the form of recorded and transcribed interviews, as well as field notes, which I was careful to keep secured. Methodologically, I focused on a number of adjacent sites and constituents, including: (1) the emergency room as a space of practice, (2) victims, (3) forensic nurses, (4) detectives and attorneys, and (5) the documents through which their practices are recorded and the technologies used in pursuit of evidence. The emergency room was my primary research site simply because it was here that a sexual assault victim entered the hospital, and interacted with many differently affiliated personnel, all of whom could relate to him or her from different institutional perspectives. Attrition rates are very high following the reporting of a rape complaint; the forensic intervention most typically comprises the victim's only contact with the medico-legal system. Through close observation of interactions during the brief time the victim was in the emergency room, I could identify how specific institutional agendas shaped the process. I concentrated on the way forensic nurses managed what they deemed the contradictory demands of collecting evidence with providing care. I also tracked the uses of various forensic technologies in the examination. I observed 44 examinations during the research period. Following the examinations, I often conducted interviews with forensic nurses, asking them to reflect on: (1) the manner in which they explained their role to the victim, (2) whether they felt they fulfilled the victim's expectations, (3) their relationships with particular detectives and attorneys, (4) their sense of the legal strength of the collected evidence, and (5) their general sense of satisfaction or frustration with the case. In the emergency room, I also observed detectives as they worked with victims and forensic nurse examiners. I paid close attention to what types of questions and concerns manifested in detectives' interactions with sexual assault victims.

In August 2004, following my stint as a rape crisis advocate, I suspended my participation in rape crisis interventions and relocated to the administrative offices of the sexual assault forensic nurse examiner program. In addition to observing forensic nurses carrying out their administrative labors, I gained access to documents I was free to use within the hospital, for example, forensic documentation protocols, and also self-studies the forensic nursing program had undertaken. I was able to use and compile data about these documents when I visited the administrative offices within the emergency room. I have excluded any and all health records from my data in order to protect the privacy of patients. I collected and analyzed the differing types of paperwork and blank forms created for institutional use, as well as the genres of bureaucratic writing used to record the legal case at different stages. These forms and genres are available to document any and all sexually violated bodies, regardless of sex, race, or circumstance. I examined the circulation of texts by following the various forms used as official documentation of the violation and its legal standing, noting protocols, the channels through which paperwork were exchanged, and where they were eventually deposited. I sought to trace how paperwork linked different subjects, spaces, and practices. By collecting these documents, I also compiled an archive that tracked changes and formed wells of institutional memory within administrative procedures.

During this period I also conducted interviews with rape crisis advocates, activists, individual forensic nurse examiners, and select police detectives, crime lab technicians, state's attorneys, and public defenders. I attended and observed monthly staff meetings of the forensic nurse examiners at the hospital, and forensic nurse training sessions, and interviewed forensic nurses in other states by phone to gain a comparative insight. In addition, I attended grand jury orientations each time a new grand jury was seated and received sexual assault training by a member of the forensic nursing staff.

From May to December 2005, I implemented the last module of my research project, recruiting sexual assault victims to interview on a bi-weekly basis. Both the nursing program and the Human Subjects Review Board preferred that these victims were not recruited from among those that I had observed in the emergency room. In fact, they requested that I avoid following up with any of the victims whom I had personally attended as a rape crisis advocate. Again, this concern stemmed largely from the perception that I might become a target of a subpoena in a potential adjudication. A relatively small number of victims responded to my flyer posted in the emergency room. Four of them enrolled in my study and agreed to meet with me on a regular basis. I interviewed each one extensively over a six-month period. I conducted sequential iterative in-depth open-ended interviews with the individuals in this group. Sexual assault cases take six months to one year to go to trial in Baltimore, and I often discussed the potential outcomes of cases with victims. Either law enforcement or the victim might elect to terminate the legal process. Otherwise, the case could end in a trial, or a plea bargain, usually in response to a preponderance of collected evidence. This last outcome was often considered the most "successful" by forensic examiners as it circumvented the courtroom altogether. From the nurses' perspectives, the public did not have to shoulder court costs while victims were not subjected to the ordeal of trial. What's more, the nurse did not have to take time off from work to testify.[12] As institutional structures constructed victims' narratives in such strict terms, I maintained an open-ended format during my interviews so that victims could reflect on the various factors affecting their lives while building their own narrative. Almost all of my interviews were recorded using a digital recorder with permission of the research participant. A research assistant transcribed these recordings. I then edited transcripts for content, erasing all identifying characteristics. By January 2006, I had collected dozens of documents, training manuals, forensic text books, advocacy newsletters, case law notations, and news articles. In addition, I had three thick notebooks full of field notes, as well as hundreds of transcribed pages from the interviews I conducted. A complex rendering of how sexual assault interventions touched many lives emerged from the diverse evidence I collected.

In organizing the materials I had collected and subjecting them to analysis, I used several different approaches. I often searched for repeated phrases or sentiments or frequently occurring questions and coded my notes and transcripts for these themes. Alternately, I scrutinized moments in which tensions arose in encounters between sexual assault victims and forensic nurse examiners identifying all actors, human and non-human, and the attendant structures contributing to the conflict. In part, this was because I refused to take ethical failures for granted. I sought to generate the categories for analysis primarily from victims' and nurses' concerns rather than to take on categories that were ready-made within preexisting literatures.

In addition, I sought to achieve a mode of writing in which the style of rendering reflected the ways in which information and narratives were organized in the course of the forensic intervention. Thus, there is relatively less discourse in the resulting book as compared with a traditional anthropological monograph. Rather, descriptions are offered as they were encountered, in fragments and pieces, with attention to the tone, quality, and inflection with which they were delivered in the telling. These fragments align to reveal the complex workings of the institutional array that organizes the sexual assault intervention. What has emerged is a book in which each chapter focuses on a critical node in which actors, things, and circumstances collide and generate a particular effect or impact on victims and their experiences of sexual assault intervention.

Chapter Descriptions

Each chapter of this book draws on diverse selections from my field research in order to depict a different aspect of how sexual assault intervention becomes a complex lived reality experienced by sexual assault victims. Moving the site of analysis from things to processes to emotions, the book captures how it is that sexual assault intervention is imagined, experienced, and felt. The first chapter begins with a focus on DNA as it takes center stage in forensic intervention, arguing that it, along with the victim, becomes the "patient" in the emergency intervention. Numerous studies have demonstrated that DNA rarely figures in the legal resolution of sexual assault, although it is often the focus of the sexual assault intervention. This book begins by focusing on the single substance that is synonymous with the latest technological advancements in forensic intervention. Chapter 1 argues that victims, nurses, and even perpetrators imagine DNA as a legitimizing feature of victim narratives as well as material validation of the experience of sexual victimization. First, victims often attempt to preserve, transport, and surrender any forensic evidence prior to their contact with law enforcement, demonstrating a keen awareness of the significance of DNA findings. Tales of perpetrators forcing victims to participate in the destruction of potential DNA evidence are rampant within victim narratives. Thus, it is evident that the association of DNA with establishing juridical truth has circulated among both victims and perpetrators. The realities around the discovery and use of DNA in rape cases, however, fall far short of these expectations. While DNA does not, in fact, play a great role in case disposition, nurses reinforce the primacy of DNA evidence in the intense scrutiny and time allocated to the process of collecting DNA in the course of the forensic examination. The examination takes on pedagogical qualities as victims are expected to demonstrate bodily discipline in yielding to the examination practices so that perpetrator DNA can be successfully recovered. Focusing on victim participation in recovering DNA as a form of patient compliance challenges the notion that the ideal victim is utterly passive, as she is expected to be an active stakeholder in the forensic examination process. In the time allocated to the search for DNA, perpetrators are imagined to have expressive, lugubrious bodies, while the ideal victim is curatorial in her approach to facilitating the search for and preservation of DNA evidence. Like a museum curator who orchestrates the encounter between exhibit and public, the victim guides the police and nurse to the evidence on and in her body, evidence that she has often taken pains to preserve.

Chapter 2 describes the ways in which time is worked by the forensic intervention, and how institutional temporality diverges from the ways in which victims narrate their experiences in time. While the search for DNA gives the sexual assault intervention its urgency, there are multiple modes of time operating within the space of the sexual assault intervention. Chapter 2 looks closely at the diverse ways in which time saturates the sexual assault intervention. The problem of documenting medico-legal evidence is frequently a problem of time; by the time a case goes to trial, the victim's wounds, psychological and physical, may have healed. During their examination, forensic nurses capture these wounds through technological intervention, fixing them in time. This manipulation of time in order to overcome the problem of time's forward march is carried out within a particular investigative context in which the victim's narrative is clearly demarcated as having a beginning and an end. This time line of victimization, determined by formal criteria derived from legal statutes, contains within it those elements that are relevant to proving whether a crime has been committed. These elements include indicators of motive, force, and lack of consent. Once the time line is determined, nurses work to produce evidence that populates the time line in dense increments. This process takes the form of a forensic interview, and in the course of this interview, victims struggle to describe the event of victimization through their own meaningful frameworks. Victims' narratives of suffering do not have the same start- and end-points as the forensic narrative. The forensic interview becomes a series of interruptions in which victims tell their stories and forensic nurses stop them with questions in order to craft a forensic narrative. This struggle over the most meaningful way of telling about sexual assault is largely driven by the different anticipatory structures in which the participants are enmeshed. For the nurses, it is the court of law that is the ultimate point of arrival, and for the victims, it is a return to the everyday that forms the future horizon.

Chapter 3 shows how truth-seeking criteria are instilled in forensic nurse examiners. It argues that forensic nurse examiners rely on criteria abiding within institutional structures and drawing on legal frameworks. These modes of reasoning and evaluating evidence are particularly marked when nurses are challenged by intense emotion. This chapter turns to how the sexual assault forensic examination, with its focus on violence resulting in bodily and genital injury and the recovery of organic substances, is an intimate and challenging encounter; sexual assault intervention requires generous resources in managing emotional distress, and it is not simply the victim who is vulnerable in the course of intervention. Nurses must have strategies to conduct themselves appropriately, even when the case under investigation tests the limits of their comfort. Drawing on scholarship around emotional labor, disgust, and training, this chapter looks at the pedagogical techniques through which affective expertise is inculcated into forensic nursing staff. It shows that emotional mastery is taught through ostensive lessons, rather than overt instruction, by drawing on three areas of ethnographic research that highlight nurses' strategies and the moments in which their motivations become opaque to victims: (1) observations of nurses conducting forensic examinations; (2) interviews with nurses about their personal intervention style; and (3) observations of forensic nurse training programs. Through these sources, the chapter reveals the spectrum of facial expressions, gestures, and utterances that make up the affective expertise of forensic nurse examiners, and how this affective register orients the forensic nurse toward the question of truth. The cases in this chapter illustrate how, time and again, nurses respond to situations that they find personally alarming by mobilizing criteria of credulity. In essence, trainers teach them to put aside their emotional responses and adopt legal criteria. Rather than sort through their complex feelings, nurses become practiced at deferring their emotional responses by focusing on the credibility of the case they are building. This training has a strong impact on nurses' "bedside manner" and accounts for the cool, clinical affect that confuses and, at times, dismays sexual assault victims seeking a kind word or a more warm and supportive demeanor.

Chapter 4 begins with the case of emergency contraception, a therapeutic technique, to probe the relationship between sexual violence and reproductive violence. A forensic nurse examiner's orientation to victims' future possibilities and potentialities is heavily framed by legal criteria, while victims draw on very complicated relationships and histories of violence, and frequently structure their own narratives around issues of livelihood. While nurses are struggling with their own complex emotions, victims struggle with a range of issues and concerns of their own. Like the struggle over the "time" of the narrative, this is in contrast with the information and themes elicited and recorded by the forensic nurse as she constructs a forensic narrative of the victim's experience of assault. Reproductive and productive concerns are frequently victims' primary worries. Many of the victims are economically vulnerable, and managing the threat of pregnancy and securing work were common concerns in reclaiming control over one's body and life. Thus, it was typical for victims to accept the emergency contraception offered by the nurses. In addition to concerns about reproductive health, victims continually articulated their worries about sexual assault related to their ability to make a living, and discussed the return to work and the securing of income as a sign of healing. This was a major theme for the victim population I worked with, but one that was frequently ignored or subverted in the medico-legal intervention. Victims were literally interrupted and asked to provide other details unrelated to their concerns about livelihood in order to propel the forensic interview forward. If participating in prosecution interfered with the ability to work, the women with whom I worked frequently chose to petition the state's attorney to withdraw charges. Without the resources to guarantee their economic security, victims had to weigh their own participation in the prosecution against their other interests.

Chapter 5 takes the example of photography as a legal technology, showing how the medical and legal are materially linked though forensic photography. In particular, photography is used to deal with and erase the problem of duration. High-quality images are achieved by balancing victims' needs with the court's demands, and the visual artifacts that emerge are uniquely forensic rather than a simple amalgamation of medical and legal components. Effective forensic photography is heavily dependent on victims' active participation. The chapter shows that forensic photography, while anchored in both obstetric and criminological photographic traditions, is not a simple combination of both, but rather unique in that they take pains to break the photographic plane with the victim's gaze. This defies obstetric conventions in which the viewer never sees the patient's face, let alone meets her gaze. The intersection of gazes during the forensic examination itself functions such that the victim can communicate her pain to the forensic nurse. Other visual conventions overcome the healing of wounds over time by capturing forensic findings so that they are fixed in time and therefore accessible for viewing by the jury long after they have healed. Thus, while the photos are purportedly for documenting wounds, they actually serve to document affect. Examining the visual component of sexual assault intervention illustrates the ways in which technology impacts interactions between nurses and victims, and also defines forensics as something more than the knitting together of distinct legal and therapeutic components.

Chapter 6 turns from visual documentation to focus on other forms of documentation and paperwork. While sexual assault forensic protocols produce visual images, these images are contextualized by other forms of documentation that serve as a repository of institutional memory and imagination of sexual assault. These documents transmute individual cases by subjecting them to a process of aggregation that retains and reproduces gendered stereotypes about rape that individual nurses and doctors are typically sensitized to and seek to avoid. Chapter 6 also analyzes the ways in which technologies of documentation sustain particular gendered imaginations of victim and perpetrator. While nurses may be well trained and oriented toward sexual assault as a form of violence that impacts men and women, the paperwork they use has built into it gendered assumptions that cast women in the role of victim and men in the role of perpetrator. The writing and reading practices associated with documenting examinations, and the audit practices for reviewing forensic documentation, also reveal the gendered assumptions with which the documents are encountered by practitioners. These documentary structures and reading practices reproduce stereotypical understandings of sexual assault rather than affording victims the opportunity to disclose and document their unique experiences of victimization. As a result, nurses' own sensitivity to the unique elements of each victim's experiences is erased while documentary requirements sustain and institutionalize stereotypical accounts of perpetrator and victim behavior and identity.

Chapter 7 analyzes the way forensic medicine configures the home as both harmful and healing. The techniques of forensic intervention are not limited to reshaping the image of the victim and her wounded body in the forensic photograph or documentation, but rather extend even to reworking the victim's sense of her home and her family, and the process through which this transformation of home is achieved is at the center of the chapter. Sexual violence most often involves a victim and a perpetrator who know one another, often through the same kinship network. While statistics bear out this pattern, forensic protocols view home as both the place of risk and the place of healing. Even as a perpetrator from within the kinship network is frequently named as the party to be investigated within the forensic documentation, as the case progresses and nurses prepare to discharge the victim, the victim is frequently commended back into the care of the family members who are suspected of creating or contributing to the conditions of victimization in the first place. Within the course of the forensic examination, forensic nurses achieve this effect through a micro-localization of the crime scene to the victim's body rather than locating the crime at a set of geographic coordinates. By insisting that "the body is the scene of the crime," nurses can divorce home as the site of the attack from home as the site of return and healing. Tracking the complicated family negotiations that emerge among members of a victim's kinship network as the forensic intervention unfolds, this chapter demonstrates the family's awareness of itself as a potential source of comfort and healing, as well as betrayal and harming.

Chapter 8 looks at the idea of patient compliance as it migrates from nursing practice and medical intervention into forensic intervention. While it is tempting to condemn law for its co-optation of medical procedures, medicine is deeply implicated in shaping legal sensibilities within the sexual assault forensic examination. This chapter looks at how forensic nurses draw heavily on their nursing practice in their work with sexual assault victims. As most Baltimore nurses who become forensic examiners are largely from emergency medicine backgrounds, sensibilities formed within emergency medicine practices often inform their forensic practice. In particular, nurses mobilize ideas about patient compliance in their forensic practice. Understanding patient compliance as a recent invention of modern medicine (Greene 2004), the chapter shows how patient compliance emerges to account for uncertainty in the forensic intervention. Generally referring to the expectation that patients will follow medical orders, patient compliance is often called into question when treatment regimens fail. Thus, nurses are skeptical of victims who show signs of drug use or reveal an HIV-positive status in the course of the medico-legal intervention, as these statuses are stigmatized as indicators of risky behavior. Victims' complaints about pain may be ignored or deflected in these contexts as nurses identify pain complaints as drug-seeking behavior. HIV-positive status puts patients outside of the purview of prophylactic therapies, and with medical and health status always legally discoverable, a patient with an existing history of a sexually transmitted infection could potentially be seen as less credible to the jury. In addition to illegal pharmaceuticals, victims with complicated diagnoses and unusual prescription medication scripts may further be suspected of non-compliance, thus compromising credibility. While forensic intervention purports to speak to the facts of the case, it has become a new way of telling old stories about victim credibility in the court of law.

Overall, these chapters enumerate a number of themes, which are discussed in the conclusion. First and foremost, the ethnography paints a picture of a newly emergent professional field—that of forensic nursing. Each chapter highlights a different aspect of the proficiencies and capabilities comprising the skill set of forensic nurse examiners. Altogether, this book depicts the richly layered conception of expertise produced throughout the stages of sexual assault intervention, fostering insight into where experts, and victims, too, might offer meaningful and creative resistance to the structures that encumber the delivery of care for sexual assault complainants. An understanding of forensic expertise suggests the underlying imaginary of the rupture of sexual assault, and the state's place in repairing this injury. Thus, sexual assault emerges as a temporally bounded, highly specific, legally defined sequence of events that are characterized by a densely populated time line. The forensic nurse produces material evidence with which to inhabit the time line.

Additionally, the nurse and police investigators together aid the victim in producing the narrative features that will provide the descriptive force of the time line for purposes of prosecution. In the emergency room, the technological resources wielded in the name of evidence collection and therapeutic intervention drive the criteria defining consent. The sexual assault victim is constituted as a particular legal subject through his or her intersection with the appropriate technological intervention. She must make her body available to forensic scrutiny without complaint. Even as the forensic nurse examiner investigates the sexually violated body, she manages the victim's potentialities and possibilities. The cooperative victim and the compliant patient intersect within this institutional matrix.

This book provides many descriptions of circumstances of sexual violence as told to me by different men and women.[13] Their pain and concern encompass a wide range of experiences—the common feature binding these accounts is their unfolding within and intersection with forensic intervention rather than grounding the analysis within the moment of violence itself. In taking this approach, the book raises doubts as to the neatness of the category of "rape" and invites readers to the conversation rather than paralyzing discussion by producing a tone of horror. In many ways, the legal system materializes a rape allegation and significantly shapes the experience of victims as they seek to make sense of the violence that has intruded in their everyday lives. Increasingly, the law operates by deploying therapeutic technologies with trained medical personnel within hospital settings.

Forensic nurse examiners, police investigators, crime lab technicians, attorneys, and rape crisis advocates strive to institute uniformity with the legal and therapeutic regime through which the intervention is staged. Victims thoughtfully fold sexual violence into a range of events, trajectories, and concerns, framing its significance through diverse engagements with life, love, mourning, and oppression. At times, these map easily onto the frameworks instituted by the legal and medical goals of sexual assault intervention. Inevitably, their accounts and experiences encompass surpluses, excesses, and uncertainties that do not lend themselves to medico-legal definition. The pages of this book capture these realities as victims give voice to them, showing where they are woven into the institutional fabric of legal and medical intervention, and where those narratives, often painfully and singularly autobiographical, move away from the institutional grain, confounding the "one size fits all" model of care offered in the forensic intervention. I hope that this ethnography captures the multitudinous reality of sexual assault, the actors that shape that reality, and the disruptive tremors that impact and unsettle victims' lives in a myriad of ways. Gathering this information, attentively parsing through it, and listening the way only an ethnographer can, we might begin to imagine a way to challenge existing models and introduce more ethically informed modalities of intervention that better serve the needs of victims, nurses, prosecutors, rape crisis advocates, and even the state.

1

"The Hand of God"

DNA and Victim Subjectivity in Sexual Assault Intervention

Wherever he steps, wherever he touches, whatever he leaves, even without consciousness, will serve as a silent witness against him. Not only his fingerprints or his footprints, but his hair, the fibers from his clothes, the glass he breaks, the tool mark he leaves, the paint he scratches, the blood or semen he deposits or collects. All of these and more, bear mute witness against him. This is evidence that does not forget. It is not confused by the excitement of the moment. It is not absent because human witnesses are. It is factual evidence. Physical evidence cannot be wrong, it cannot perjure itself, it cannot be wholly absent. Only human failure to find it, study and understand it, can diminish its value.
—Paul L. Kirk, *Crime Investigation: Physical Evidence and the Police Laboratory* (1953)

DNA is like the hand of God pointing down and saying, "It's you!"
—Emma, forensic nurse, quoting *Forensic Files*

When we think about forensic intervention in this day and age, what most frequently captures our imagination is DNA—that fragile, ephemeral, and reliable key to many mysteries, both scientific and criminological. DNA is the key to justice, and efforts such as the Innocence Project, which seeks to exonerate those wrongfully convicted often in relation to DNA-related findings, reinforce this popular notion.[1] Our common wisdom holds that if a rape victim submits to the scrutiny of a forensic examination, and organic substance is recovered, subsequent tests will reveal the DNA hidden in the evidentiary depths, and the identity of a perpetrator will be unambiguously indicated, putting justice more easily within reach. Locard's exchange principle, a theory in forensic science which several nurses explained to me, holds that a perpetrator always leaves a trace of him- (or her)self at the crime scene, just as the crime scene will leave a trace of itself on the perpetrator (Saferstein 2006, 101). In a sexual assault case, the victim's body is treated as part of the crime scene, and thus, forensic nurses must find the evidence using the right techniques and expertise. In a 2003 interview with a forensic nurse examiner, here called "Emma," the significance and presumed capacity of DNA identification as a magic bullet in rape investigations was conveyed through Emma's sharing a quote from one of her favorite on-air forensic profilers from the reality television show, *Forensic Files*. Emma quoted this line to me, a line she often repeated to other nurses and medical personnel who were often under her proctorship during their training: "DNA is like the hand of God pointing down and saying, 'It's you!'" This was said with a dramatic emphasis and an accompanying gesture in which Emma's hand was transfigured: tense, strong, and pointing at a hypothetical rapist invisibly hovering before her and no longer able to hide. The gesture was arresting, especially to me, as I occupied the seat of the hypothetical called-out rapist being accused by Emma's pointing finger.

Emma's confidence in the power of DNA to establish a much sought after juridical truth did not necessarily stem from her experience as a forensic nurse and sometimes legal witness. Of the more than 300 evidentiary examinations she had performed in her 11 years as a forensic nurse examiner, she was subpoenaed fewer than five times, testified perhaps three times, and did not know (or remember) the outcomes of those trials. The state's attorney did not communicate with her regularly, and though she had a very good relationship with the head of the local crime lab, she received only very intermittent follow-up. There is a wide gap between the confidence forensic nurse examiners place in the DNA evidence they collect and the reality of what happens to DNA evidence in the United States. In 2009, the rape kit backlog was brought compellingly into public discourse by a Human Rights Watch report documenting the backlog in Los Angeles County, citing in excess of 12,669 untested rape kits as of November 2008 (Tofte 2009:

3). The release of the Human Rights Watch report prompted numerous local investigations by journalists, who showed that the rape kit backlog was not limited to Los Angeles alone, with some media attention given to similar findings in many states. What is more, research also demonstrates that the impact of forensic evidence on case disposition in U.S. sexual assault investigations is minimal, as most cases of sexual assault are between parties known to one another, and thus, identification does not play a part in case resolution (Peterson et al. 2010; Sommers and Baskin 2011; Du Mont and White 2007). Where DNA identification of an unknown assailant may be the cornerstone of a case in which the victim and perpetrator are strangers, in cases where they are not, DNA identification is often irrelevant. In these cases, the defense does not deny that sexual contact has taken place, and typically argues that sexual intercourse was not assault because it was consensual. DNA findings do very little to resolve questions of consent.

Despite the skepticism of many scholars as to whether DNA has a part to play in sexual assault case disposition, our collective interest in DNA in U.S. popular culture (as attested to by any number of forensic-focused television series) and the intensive pursuit of DNA in the forensic intervention itself, do suggest that DNA matters, whether or not it is tied to legal outcomes. As reliance on DNA within U.S. and English legal regimes has increased, scholarly attention to the vagaries and complexities associated with the introduction of DNA into our search for juridical truths has been carefully parsed by scholars (Lynch et al. 2008). At a minimum, Emma's oft-repeated declaration that DNA is the hand of God attests to the complicated imaginaries attached to the ephemeral substance. Emma's claim calls forth the image of her own hand, doubling as this God's hand, as she and other forensic nurse examiners use their hands to work over the bodies of sexual assault victims, tweaking, trimming, scraping, swabbing, tweezing, manipulating, positioning, and documenting their findings during a sexual assault examination. It is in this body work that transformation takes place: an experience that more and more American women and girls (and a significant number of men and boys) will have in the years to come as forensic intervention becomes more commonplace and federal legislation dictates that victims of sexual offenses, no longer subject to the discretionary decision-making of police and prosecutors, can elect to have a sexual assault forensic examination without police involvement. Unique to each state in the United States as it is guided by state crime statutes and a host of other variables unique to local geographies, the intervention itself consists of an evidentiary examination, as mentioned before, also called the rape kit, and a therapeutic nursing care intervention carried out under the oversight of a physician's medical authority though the physician is most often absent and therefore represented through standing orders, periodic case review, or both.

For many sexual assault victims, it is the forensic nurse examiner with whom they spend the most time, and who represents their entree into the criminal justice system. Forensic nurse examiners in Baltimore, Maryland, like those across the country, expend a great deal of their energy and resources collecting evidence that will never be processed. DNA collection and wound documentation account for most of the forensic examination, an ordeal lasting a minimum of two hours for those sexual assault victims reporting to law enforcement. This chapter ethnographically illustrates the way DNA plays a part in shaping victims' subjectivity, that is, their understanding of their suffering, rather than focusing on the role of DNA in sexual assault prosecutorial processes. While forensic technology may well serve as a primary "technology of repair" in juridical projects (Wagner 2008), it is equally important to attend to that which these technologies simultaneously re- or unmake. Because of the salience of DNA in our popular imagination (Brewer and Ley 2010; Shelton, Kim, and Barak 2006), nurses easily reinforce the emphasis on the importance of DNA evidence with the intense scrutiny and time they allocate to the process of collecting DNA during the forensic examination. As nurses perform the examination, victims experience it as a form of embodied training. This is largely affected because victims are expected to demonstrate corporeal discipline in yielding to the examination practices so that perpetrator DNA can be successfully recovered. As the victim's and perpetrator's (absent) bodies are interpellated into the forensic regime, what emerges is far more complex than a simple dichotomy of victim-perpetrator, active-passive, expressive-receptive, or male-female. Here, the term interpellation derives from anthropologist Malathi De Alwis, following Louis Althusser, as she deploys it in her descriptions of Anglican missionary work among Sinhala women in nineteenth-century Ceylon (De Alwis

1997). De Alwis argues that while the missionaries were unsure as to whether they had successfully converted Sinhala women to Anglicanism because they could not see whether the women were truly ideologically committed to Christianity, they could produce an embodied subject who took on the corporeal and material aspects of a committed Christian. The forensic examination serves as another type of institutional interpellation in which its subjects, both victims and perpetrators, are interpellated into an idealized configuration of these roles. By delving into the intersection of nursing protocols and victim experiences of forensic examination, particularly those protocols and experiences linked to the pursuit and recovery of DNA, this chapter gives an account of the social, material, and representational practices that contribute to the contingent configuration of the victims' and perpetrators' bodies and subjectivities within forensic intervention (Taylor 2005: 742).

Because the majority of sexual assault cases I observed were not prosecuted during the time frame within which I conducted my research,[2] it became apparent that the forensic intervention itself played a central role in victims' perceptions of their own subject position, and that the conception of DNA was densely invested with meaning for all of the stakeholders participating in the intervention. Victims almost always came to the hospital for forensic examination with the expectation that DNA would be collected. Nurses spent most of the forensic examination collecting DNA-based evidence, demonstrating to victims through the examination procedure the apparent importance of this evidence. The victim's participation in the forensic examination is tantamount to participation in a corporeal training process in which the importance and primacy of DNA are reinforced. In addition, victims' descriptions of sexual victimization often include stories of how assailants attempted to destroy or "disappear" DNA evidence. Thus emerged a sense of the expressive, secreting bodies of perpetrators, frequently imagined as male and eager to cover their tracks, while the victim, ideally, recognized her own victimization as it unfolded, and facilitated the preservation of evidence in an active and curatorial mode.

As mentioned previously, the program upon which the research in this book is based is located within an emergency room, which is one of the most common models for sexual assault intervention in the United

States.[3] If we think about a sexual assault intervention as an emergency and question the source of urgency that calls for an emergency intervention, it becomes clear that there are two objects of care: the patient herself, and the fragile organic matter that may yield DNA. The timing and resources of the sexual assault intervention are deeply invested in both stabilizing and treating the traumatized patient, and reducing the vulnerability of the organic evidence being collected. The victim is expected to facilitate this process by tolerating pain, discomfort, hunger, cold, and shame, and perhaps delaying her need to urinate or defecate. For the sustenance and preservation of perfect evidence, a victim must be willing to offer herself up to the forensic nurse examiner's scrutiny and ministration.

In the initial moments following sexual assault in cases where victims choose to report to law enforcement, caregivers and law enforcement collaborate in assisting victims to regain their safety and security. They are accompanied to the emergency room by a uniformed officer who notifies a detective from the sex offense unit of a new case. The detective will frequently meet the victim in the emergency room. Prior to January 2009, the detective would have to authorize collection of evidence, at which point the forensic nurse examiner would be paged and would have 45 minutes to respond.[4] Multiple factors contribute to the urgency here: first, the sexual assault victim must be treated with prophylactic antibiotics in case she has been exposed to sexually transmitted infections; second, the victim has 120 hours in which to be treated with emergency contraceptive medicines if she so chooses; third, evidence on the victim's body may wash away or otherwise be lost if efforts are not made to collect evidence before such ephemera are unattainable; and finally, organic evidence may putrefy and decay if it is not collected within a narrow time frame, thus proving useless for purposes of isolating and potentially identifying DNA.

The course of the intervention may unfold as follows. The example of a case involving a woman, here called Kendra, is illustrative. Kendra's journey to the emergency room began with a 911 call. She was taken to the hospital following a night out at a club during which she had been drugged and raped. Awakening the next morning in an unfamiliar private home, naked, she quickly dressed and fled the scene. She found a pay phone and called the police, who she tells me answered her call within 20 minutes. A passerby noticed her distressed and disheveled appearance and offered to wait with her for the police officer to arrive. When the officer arrived, he took an initial report, helped her into the squad car, and drove her to City Hospital. On route to the hospital, he radioed the case in to the Sex Offense Unit, and they dispatched two detectives to meet Kendra in the emergency room. The two detectives interviewed Kendra for more than an hour, taking a detailed report, at which point they declared her case "founded," their language for legally meritorious, and asked the hospital to page the forensic nurse. Shortly after the nurse was paged, the hospital also paged the rape crisis center, and I was subsequently dispatched to attend this case.

As Kendra waited for the nurse who would conduct her examination, she complained that she had an urgent need to urinate. The registration clerk directed her not to use the facilities, as the forensic nurse examiner would want to take the urine sample for the rape kit. When I arrived, Kendra was standing in the middle of the crowded waiting room holding a sealed collection cup in a clean plastic specimen bag, searching for the forensic nurse. When she had complained to the registration clerk a second time about her need to urinate, the clerk had relayed Kendra's complaint to the forensic nurse administrator who, though present, was not on call to conduct the examination. Emma had agreed to allow Kendra to pee after she was convinced that Kendra "really couldn't hold it." She instructed Kendra in how to collect the urine, and then told her to wait for the arrival of the forensic nurse who would conduct her exam.

When the second nurse, Crystal, arrived, she rushed into the exam room and commenced setting up the space for the examination. She noted that the kit had already been opened and that the urine sample had been taken. She consulted with Emma about this turn of events, all the while making "tsk-tsk" noises, and proceeded to prepare for the rest of the examination. Crystal's "tsk-tsks" and accompanying head shakes indicated that she found the circumstances of the pre-opened kit less than ideal. In preparation for conducting the exam, Crystal opened all the remaining packaging of the rape kit, organized the swabs in a holder so she could grab one after the other. She set out dropper bottles of water as well as toluidine dye, and lined up envelopes in another rack so that dry swabs could be repackaged and sealed when they were prepared. She also printed numerous patient labels ahead of time so that the envelopes would be marked and time stamped. Finally, she made sure the videographic photo printer was loaded and ready for use. She then went out to the waiting room to greet Kendra and bring her back to the examination room to begin the exam.

Kendra and I had been going through some of the handouts and pamphlets the rape crisis center provided, and discussing what the exam would be like. Given the choice to have me accompany her, Kendra quickly agreed, smiling shyly and saying, "I'm not so good with the exam stuff—it will be good to have a hand to hold." When Kendra came into the exam room, she saw a small space, one corner of which was dominated by a gurney identical to the exam table one sees in any doctor's office, complete with retractable stirrups for pelvic examination. Behind the table was a wall-mounted coat rack with a clothesline strung between two of the hooks in the rack. Clothespins hung from the line and were used for hanging any wet clothing. A table fan located on the counter on the wall perpendicular to the clothes hook could be used to speed the drying process. Wet evidence cannot be stored until it has been dried thoroughly, lest it rot and putrefy. Swabs are also dried before packaging, though they are placed in an enclosed dryer that protects them from contamination as they are dried. The box dryer also sits on the same counter space as the table fan. In short, there is as much, if not more, space dedicated to the potential evidence as there is room for the patient herself, and we might read this allocation of space within the clinic as the spatial governmentality of forensic intervention (Merry 2001b).

In the United States, there are about as many sexual assault evidentiary exam protocols as there are states. The Maryland State Police Victim Sexual Assault Evidence Collection Kit consists of 17 distinct steps. Of these 17 steps, 16 are focused on locating and collecting DNA evidence. While the steps are listed in one sequence, different nurses carry out the examination in different orders, some following the sequence as it is recorded in the forms, and others following an order of their own designation. Many nurses cite the "crown to toe" preference, as nursing exams often begin with the head and travel down the body. The exam steps are not laid out following this logic. Individual nurses tend to be very consistent once they set up a comfortable practice for carrying out the examination—having established the order in which they will conduct the examination, they will not stray from it if at all possible. In addition to carrying out the 17 steps of the examination, forensic nurses will also collect an additional swab to test for sexually transmitted infections, administer an antibiotic, offer and administer emergency contraception with victims' consent, and provide referrals for mental health, HIV testing, and gynecological follow-up. Some of these steps are interwoven into the forensic examination.

The first part of the examination is a forensic interview—this is officially recorded in both steps one and two of the rape kit. This may take anywhere from 15 to 45 minutes. Here, the nurse will use the crime lab paperwork to collect detailed information about the rape attack. The questions that the forensic nurse asks during the forensic interview establish two things: (1) an account of the attack in the victim's words, which is recorded on the blank note page; and (2) the probable location and state of evidence and injury on the victim's clothing and body. The victim's narrative guides the nurse's scrutiny, indicating where she should direct special attention. If, for example, the victim reports that she was forced to perform oral sex, the nurse may elect to take extra oral swabs. If the victim reports that the assailant ejaculated on a particular part of her body or on her clothing, the nurse will again collect the relevant evidence and note this in the narrative.

While steps 1, 2, and 16 revolve around documentation on forms that record the patient's narrative, medical history, and physical examination findings, steps 3 through 15 all involve collection of either the victim's DNA or potential DNA evidence from the assailant. The first step following the interview is collecting the victim's clothing, even if she has changed since the time of the assault, as forensic evidence may have transferred from her body to the textile. The victim must undress over a paper sheet in the middle of the floor so that the nurse can monitor whether any debris falls from her body. When the victim is fully undressed, the forensic nurses will inspect the clothing and the victim's body with an alternate light source which makes otherwise unseen organic matter visible to the naked eye. This is helpful to show bruising or ecchymosis under the skin, particularly in cases of strangulation, as blood pooling below the epidermis will often show up with use of the light source. Otherwise, the light is used primarily to find organic matter, such as blood, semen, vaginal secretions, and saliva, which may yield DNA evidence. After this step, the victim is dressed in a hospital gown and the examination continues. When Kendra carefully undressed over the sheet, she gently embraced herself, commenting on the goose bumps rising on her arms as she shed her layers. The exam room thermostat was typically set to lower temperatures—heat might contribute to rotting; the nurses treated the exam room like a de facto refrigerator. While this was perhaps optimal for the preservation of DNA, it was not optimal for addressing the victim's comfort. Kendra was relieved to slip on two hospital gowns: one opening to the back and one opening to the front as a type of robe. While some nurses might offer an additional sheet or blanket straight from a warmer, Crystal did not leave the room to fetch a blanket, moving ahead with the examination in the name of efficiency.

Once clothing has been collected, nurses will also take a blood sample from the victim, scrape under the fingernails, and pull head and pubic hairs. The four swabs taken during the pelvic examination, while only comprising steps 10 and 11, often take the longest when compared to the other steps of the examination. The buccal swabs, marked as step 6, are oral swabs taken from each cheek inside the victim's mouth; some nurses begin the examination with this step so that they can offer victims something to eat and drink. Other forensic nurse examiners, as I mentioned earlier, wait until step 6, following the interviews, the clothing and underwear collection, debris collection, and taking bite mark and licking swabs, before taking the cheek swabs. For victims this can mean bearing thirst or hunger for many hours in some cases. As stated earlier, victims are discouraged from urinating prior to the forensic examination, including the genital swab collections undertaken during the pelvic examination, lest they wash away or destroy potential evidence. The pelvic examination is often prolonged by both swabbing and photographing. It is conducted with the aid of a speculum, and victims must endure this extra discomfort while nurses insert swabs, visualize the cervix, and inspect the genitals for any signs of injury.

All of these steps require the victim's cooperation and, ideally, her consent. She must hand over her clothing, expose her body to the forensic nurse's scrutiny, and tolerate exposure, pain, and discomfort. Of the three- to four-hour interview and examination, the nurse spends almost all of the time on evidence collection, and a maximum of 20 minutes on what we might consider the caregiving aspects of the examination. The victim suffers the majority of the discomfort for the purpose of evidence collection. As she is interpellated into the forensic regime, the victim is subjected to the priorities of the forensic examination—she must relinquish her body to the forensic intervention for the good of collecting evidence that may yield DNA.

At times, the victim's consent may not be requested at every step of the examination. For example, hair pulls from the head and pubic area are required from the victim. While Kendra did not fall into this group, many sexual assault victims may fall in and out of consciousness during the course of the sexual assault examination, either due to exhaustion, shock, or, as is often the case, recent drug use resulting in a stupor that is frequently recognized as coming down from a high. I saw at least two victims awakened from their stupor screaming as a result of the pubic hair pulls taken from their sleeping bodies. The pubic hair pull is preceded by the pubic hair combing, which I have seen a few nurses approach with attempts to alleviate the awkwardness by being playful or joking. One nurse would frequently ask her patients how they wanted their pubic haired style, grinning and saying, "Bet you didn't think anyone would ask you THAT this morning." Kendra, who was awake and sober throughout her experience of being examined, was building a rapport with Crystal that was sharply interrupted in the moment that Crystal took her pubic hair pulls. Kendra's smile turned to surprise and then pain. Her eyes filled with tears as she glared at Crystal and said, "You hurt me!" The room was silent for a long moment before Crystal explained matter-of-factly, "I had to." Kendra questioned whether any of the subsequent examination would be as painful and Crystal paused to consider before responding, "no—we'll take it slowly with the pelvic exam, but I think that is the worst of it." The subsequent examination was largely conducted in silence, punctuated by my frequent questions to Kendra as to whether she needed anything or had any concerns—to which she responded by asking that I continue to distract her. As the pelvic exam ended, Kendra asked Crystal what she had seen. Crystal evaded giving a direct response to Kendra's question, and Kendra turned to comment, "I think I understand why rape victims don't call the police some time."

Pain management is a delicate business during the sexual assault examination—pain is frequently an indicator of injury. It is not always a simple matter for a victim to communicate her pain to the forensic nurse examiner, in part because she is lying down on a gurney and her gaze may not meet the forensic nurse's gaze, an issue more fully explored in chapter 5. Often, it is the rape crisis advocate who notes the grimaces and winces that flit across the victim's face and communicates the patient's discomfort both to the victim and to the nurse. The nurse may then adjust her technique, and simultaneously apply more scrutiny and focus to the area of discomfort lest a wound is revealed. Nurses and rape crisis advocates also speak of and prepare for the olfactory aspects of sexual assault examination—as one nurse characterized her work, "it is stinky and swampy." Nurses consider bad smells to be indicators of human organic material and processes of decay, requiring attention and collection if possible. In short, smells are frequently regarded as evidence of evidence—in other words, those victims who smelled the worst were often thought to be "telling the truth." Bad smells, as it were, is how the evidence sometimes speaks to the nurses—the victim does not have to tell the nurse where to focus, as the putrefying material invites the nurse's intervention directly. By suggesting that evidence speaks directly to them with its odors, and applying their techniques for recovering and preserving this evidence and arresting it from putrefying further, nurses cast DNA as the object of their intervention apart from that of their original patient, the victim. These smells are not recorded in the forensic documentation, so here, the material efficacy of the smell is located in how it engenders a shift in the nurse's behavior, eliciting from the nurse a commitment to find what remains hidden.

In narrating their experiences, many of the sexual assault victims with whom I worked demonstrated or mentioned a few ways in which preserving evidence became a concern during or following the attacks against them. Of the 44 cases I observed within the emergency room, 13 victims brought a change of clothing with them to the hospital, indicating an expectation that the clothing they wore would be collected as evidence. In addition, 12 victims brought evidence beyond what they were wearing to the forensic intervention. Of those twelve, eight brought the clothes they had been wearing at the time of the attack since they had subsequently changed. Three brought a napkin or paper towel with which they had wiped themselves after being attacked. The clothes, paper products, and towels were sometimes brought to the emergency room in plastic or paper bags (seven plastic, one paper), or simply folded and placed in a purse or shoulder bag (in four instances). The prevalence of plastic bags suggests, again, a pop cultural referent for "bagging" evidence as forensic practice actually employs paper bags for evidence since plastic does not allow the flow of oxygen and, again, promotes rotting or degradation of evidence. The twelfth victim brought neither her clothing nor a paper towel, but all of the dishes, glasses, and flatware that the perpetrator, a co-worker she had invited into her home, had touched. Filling three bulging plastic bags with these effects, Laura hauled all these items to the hospital with her. The next section describes Laura's account of victimization, and the way in which she focuses on the collection of evidence even as she struggles to affirm the certainty that she has been the victim of sexual violence.

Laura's Story

Laura came in to the hospital two days after she was raped by a co-worker. She told me that though she walked around "in a haze" following the attack against her, unsure of how to proceed, she knew that she had to preserve the signs that the man she accused of rape had been in her home. On the night of an early fall thunderstorm, Alfredo, who worked with Laura in a retail store, claimed he was locked out of his car and could not wait for a locksmith and then make the long commute home in the heavy downpour. He asked Laura if she would be able to put him up for the night. Though she did not know him well, Laura agreed to his request. "I had a second bedroom, and I wanted to be a nice colleague because I was really depending on this job." The next chapter will attend to the circumstances of Laura's biography and professional life in greater detail. Laura also told me she felt as if a co-worker was not a stranger, so though she considered him no more than a professional acquaintance, she was not afraid of Alfredo.

On the way to her home, Alfredo insisted he was hungry, and asked that Laura stop at a restaurant so he could order a meal for dinner. Laura told me that Alfredo rebuffed her suggestions to stop at a restaurant on the way to her home, insisting they go out of the way to a restaurant he liked. He asked Laura if she would come in with him, but Laura, annoyed with his insistence that she drive him to this particular restaurant, told him she would wait in the car and asked that he order his meal to go. Alfredo placed his order and came out with his food some 30 minutes later. Laura was even more upset with the delay at this point; she wanted to get home quickly since the rain had intensified and it had grown dark. Her dog had been in the house all day and she was anxious about taking him out.

Upon arriving at her home, Alfredo asked Laura if she had anything to drink. She showed him what she had in the refrigerator and told him he could help himself. After looking in the refrigerator, he asked her if she had any alcoholic beverages, at which point she showed him the wine rack and her liquor cabinet. Alfredo began helping himself to the alcoholic drinks. He also helped himself to Laura's china, transferring his restaurant food onto her plates and eating and drinking at her dining room table. Laura told me she had not joined Alfredo during his meal, but instead went upstairs to make sure that the guestroom had towels and fresh linens, and then took her dog outside to be walked in the rain. When she returned to the house a short time later, Alfredo called out to her from upstairs. Laura went upstairs to see what Alfredo wanted, thinking he was going to ask her for toothpaste or some other item a guest may require from a host. Instead, he was standing in the guestroom bare to the waist with a towel wrapped around him. Laura was confused and backed away, but did not want to be rude. She said that Alfredo grabbed her arm and pulled her into the guest bedroom, struck her hard across the mouth, and threw her down on the bed.[5]

As she cried out in alarm, her dog rushed upstairs and began barking frantically. Laura told me that Alfredo kicked the dog hard, grabbed it by the scruff, and tossed it from the room before slamming the door shut. He held Laura down and forced her to have intercourse while the dog continued to bark and whimper outside of the door. If she struggled, Alfredo punched her in the head. She told me she quickly quieted down and told him not to hurt her. "I just wanted it to be over, and I wanted to survive. I didn't want him to hurt me so bad I might die, and I was worried that he had really hurt my dog."[6] After about a half hour, Alfredo threw himself down on the bed and went to sleep. Laura was confused by his behavior. It was clear to her that the sex had been nonconsensual, but his apparent calmness made her doubt herself. Afraid that he was merely pretending to sleep, Laura did not dare move for what seemed like an hour. When she felt certain he was asleep from the rise and fall of his breath, she quietly left the guestroom.

"I remember grabbing my dog, my purse and my car keys, glancing down to make sure I was dressed, and rushing to the car." With no destination in mind, Laura drove the car until she felt safe enough to stop. She then checked her dog to make sure he wasn't injured, and then kept driving around town, not stopping and never settling on a place to go. She drove until the sun came up, and at about 10:30 a.m., she decided she had to return home. "I was afraid I would come back and he would still be there, but I couldn't just drive around. I had things to do and places to be and I needed to go home in order to get through the day." As Laura unlocked the front door of her home, she feared that Alfredo would still be there. Bracing herself as she went up the stairs, she quickly found that he was gone. Unsure of what to do next, Laura turned to cleaning up, as she would do after any visitor's overnight stay.

In the kitchen and dining room, she found herself running her eyes over every dish, plate, cup, and bowl that had been left out from the previous evening. She carefully lifted each thing she thought Alfredo had touched and put it into a plastic bag, including wine bottles, stemware, plates, a few spoons, forks, a knife, a salt shaker, and numerous other kitchen and dining items. "When I finished, I had three bags full of things." Laura then went upstairs to gather the bed sheets. Laura reflected that though she was still not sure what to do at that point, she knew she had to gather evidence that Alfredo had been in her home.

In those moments following the attack, Laura's life became a living embodiment of Locard's exchange principle, as those quotidian household objects are transfigured into evidence of a crime. Alfredo's presence in Laura's house and the fact that the site of the house was a crime scene had given rise to a new lens through which Laura regarded her things. It is Alfredo's mere presence, the materiality of his incursion into her home, which Laura sought to evidence in the gathering of the everyday effects that had been transformed by Alfredo's contact with them. While Laura projects her sense of Alfredo's physical incursion outward onto her household effects, gathering them together to submit to the police, she later submitted to a forensic examination so that the physical traces of Alfredo's crime may be recovered from her own person.

Assailants

EMMA: We've had . . . I can remember several cases when the perpetrator had the victim shower, and he would watch them to make sure that they washed themselves good. I mean, they're getting smart, too. We're educating the public and we're educating the bad guys.

S: Even wearing a condom—

EMMA: Everybody knows what DNA is now. They're not quite sure what it is, but they know they can leave it behind and go to jail for it.

It is not only victims who come to forensic interventions with preconceived ideas about DNA and forensic evidence. There is evidence of Emma's assessment of assailants' attitudes toward DNA evidence in the accounts of victims. When they recount their ordeals of being sexually violated, victims also frequently refer to things that the assailant said or did in the course of victimizing them. A pattern of assailants' concerns with obscuring or destroying DNA-based evidence emerges from victims' accounts. Laura, for example, went to recover the bed linens from her guest bedroom, where she had been attacked. When she reached the room, she saw that the sheets were gone. At first, Laura was puzzled and wondered if Alfredo had stripped the sheets and left them somewhere else in her house. She did not find them in the laundry room, any closets, or the guest bathroom. She noticed that the towel Alfredo had used was also missing. Laura told me, "At that point, I realized he had taken the sheets and the towel, and I realized that even he knew he had done something wrong. That's when I picked up the phone and called a friend to tell her what had happened to me. She told me to call the police and that I had to go in to be examined."

To Laura, Alfredo's theft of the bed linens indicated that he was cognizant that he had raped her—and it was this disappearance of evidence that prompted her to act on her feelings and reach out for help. It bears mentioning that all of Laura's compliant cooperation, and her care to collect all of the evidence involved, amounted to no formal charges or legal outcome following the forensic examination. In Laura's case, the police detectives expressed their frustrations to her and affirmed their belief that she was a crime victim. They stated their hands were tied as Alfredo had claimed diplomatic immunity, and they urged Laura to concentrate on moving on. Laura's case is unique in that there was a positive identification of an assailant the police were fairly certain had committed the crime of which he was accused. She is not unique in that her case resulted in no conviction. Nor was she the only victim who reported some evidence taken or otherwise tampered with by the assailant themselves.

Nia, Angela, and the Destruction of Evidence as a Feature of Victimization

Nia was one of two victims I saw in the emergency room who was forced to shower after an intruder broke into her home and raped her. After he assaulted her, the intruder told Nia to get out of bed and go to the bathroom. Her assailant carried a gun, and Nia feared that he would kill her. He then ordered her to climb into the bath tub, turn on the water, and rinse herself off with soap. As she recounted the series of events, Nia hugged her arms around her chest and dropped her eyes. Nia told me that the assailant kept the gun trained on her the whole time, and forced her to wash a second time when he thought she was not scrubbing herself vigorously enough.

Angela, unlike Nia, was not forced to shower, though the assailant forced her to spit onto a tissue and then proceeded to wipe her chest and neck with her own saliva. "He wiped me wherever he had kissed or licked me," she explained. "I guess he thought my spit would cover his or something. I don't know." The accounts of these Baltimore victims resonate with other accounts reported on in popular media: a 43-year-old rape victim forced to clean herself in Los Angeles, a 16-year-old in Tottenham, England doused with caustic chemicals after she was gang raped, and a Florida woman and her son gang-raped and sexually abused by three assailants who then forced them into a tub filled with vinegar and water to which they added hydrogen peroxide and nail polish remover. These are only a few examples of the accounts which can be found in newspaper reports from all over the world. When reported to the police, these acts often alert detectives to several possibilities: that the reported assailant is a repeat offender who has experience with DNA-based evidence,[7] or, more likely, that the criminal act is premeditated, as the assailant takes care to destroy evidence. In Baltimore, however, this is not enough for a detective to request that the rape kits are processed. Without an arrest, they may not ask for the crime lab to test the DNA samples to see if there are matches in the DNA database.

Accounts like Nia's and Laura's indicate that perpetrators place stock in the importance of DNA evidence. Though the lengths to which they go to destroy such evidence do not always result in the obliteration of DNA, victims enfold the act of evidence-tampering into their narratives of forced sex. During the rape attack, assailants take pains to send the message that victims will not be able to participate in prosecution because they will be without evidence. The suggestion of a lack of access to justice disempowers the victim, who also invests in the efficacy of DNA in cases of sexual assault, and rapists are willing to use force or the threat of force to effect the destruction of evidence. Nia was forced to wash with soap and water at gunpoint. In cases like that of the victim in Tottenham, the assailants' desire to destroy evidence resulted in serious bodily injury. Assailants, like forensic nurse examiners and sexual assault victims, invest DNA with power and the potential to associate them with their own crimes. They manipulate what they perceive as genetic evidence to lessen their chances of being caught and prosecuted, often forcing victims to participate in these processes and further disempowering victims. As they disempower victims by suggesting that evidence will be destroyed and result in a diminished chance of attaining justice, they reinforce victims' high investment in genetic evidence.

Pedagogical Persuasions

The opening of this chapter states that the forensic intervention plays a pedagogical role. Throughout this chapter, the reader can see how the forensic intervention trains victims by subjecting them to physical ordeals like tolerating cold and pain, and managing bodily needs, very much in the same way children's socialization and development is frequently associated with bodily discipline, as we train children to continue to master their needs to urinate and defecate as a gatekeeping threshold that marks their entry into wider social circles (Lacan 2007). In the case of sexual assault victims, the physical commitment and discipline required from the victim serves as a type of forensic mirror that interpellates the victim into a social regime in which she comes to see her fragmented self as it is constituted by the world-making forces of forensic intervention. It is because of the intense discipline and even self-mastery that is required of the victim that the subject position is not one of pure passivity and reception. The victim must actively resist the desire to react to her sensations and emotions, while conscientiously working to remain aware of her pain and discomfort as they may be signs of the presence of evidence. Meanwhile, she does not necessarily refuse the challenge of revisiting memory as it works itself over the haptic receptors of her skin, creeping and crawling as she struggles to recall the violent events that have propelled her into the present setting, lest her chills and involuntary recoil serve, again, as a sign of contact with the perpetrator. In this sense, the victim takes on a curatorial role, guiding the nurse across her body from crown to toe as the exam moves through its stages.

Where women's bodies are frequently cast as overflowing and porous (Grosz 1994; Kristeva 1982), in the forensic encounter it is the male body that is expressive and secreting, while the female body becomes a medium upon which bodily signs of sexual incursion can be grafted—the victim's body may hold perpetrator semen, saliva, and hair, perhaps secretly, and all rapidly disintegrating and "dying" as the nurse works quickly to locate, collect, and preserve these secretions in as optimal a state of vitality as possible. The nurse's hands, firmly manipulating the victim's body in search of signs of the perpetrator's body, shape the emergent subjectivity of the victim within the experiential node emerging at the intersection of sexual violence, forensic intervention, and everyday life. What, then, does the victim "learn" about her experience and her subject position as a result of her participation in a forensic sexual assault intervention? Among some of the things that she discovers, she learns that the work of care extends not only to her personal well-being, but to the precious organic evidence itself. She learns that her own physical needs and desire for safety may be delayed in favor of the institutional agendas of the criminal justice system. She learns that DNA matters, despite the fact that it will remain very unlikely to impact the outcome of her case, and that by demonstrating her full commitment to DNA's recovery, she has demonstrated her full commitment to participation in the criminal justice system (Corrigan 2013a). This level of cooperation is the minimal requirement of the compliant patient.[8] Within this context, the epistemology of victimhood constitutes and shapes deeply embodied and personal experiences of sexual suffering for the ranks of women, men, and children who participate in forensic intervention as the beginning, and perhaps ending, of their search for care and justice.

The reverent tones and breathy excitement with which the forensic nurses related Locard's principle of exchange to me seem to vault the principle from the forensic into the mythic and perhaps the metaphoric. The collision between the victim and the perpetrator results in the physical interchange of material. This physical evidence is granted its own efficacy within the forensic intervention, for it "bear[s] mute witness against [the perpetrator]. This is evidence that does not forget. It is not confused by the excitement of the moment. It is not absent because human witnesses are. It is factual evidence. Physical evidence cannot be wrong, it cannot perjure itself, it cannot be wholly absent. Only human failure to find it, study and understand it, can diminish its value" (Kirk 1953). Whether or not the search for these materials comes to fruition in the form of positive identification of DNA evidence, moot in cases in which the parties are known and simply dispute the consensual nature of a sexual encounter, the expectation that such evidence will be present, and can be destroyed or obfuscated, animates the victim's experiences of assault, and the ensuing progression of intervention. In this sense, DNA proves to be the hand of God, acting through the nurse's hand, manipulating the victim's body and shaping the victim's subjectivity as she is interpellated into the forensic intervention and oriented toward a particular expectation of what healing or justice may follow.

This chapter has attended to the central role of DNA within the sexual assault forensic examination, the popular imagination, and even as an element of the narratives of victimization that sexual assault victims describe in the reporting of sexual assault. As forensic nurses work with sexual assault victims, they might question the lessons they impart in this work. What do victims perceive as the priorities of the sexual assault intervention? Is the emphasis on DNA-evidence collection warranted, or can we achieve a better balance of the needs of victims with the needs of the criminal investigation? Taking these dynamics into consideration, we must remember that such lessons are not inscribed through a disembodied pedagogy, but rather are etched on the "canvasses" of victims' bodies and spirits.

2

Making Time

Temporalities of Law, Healing, and Sexual Violence

Clocks slay time . . . time is dead as long as it is being clicked off by little wheels; only when the clock stops does time come to life.
—William Faulkner, *The Sound and the Fury*

Bad luck comes in threes.
—"Laura," interview

A sexual assault forensic intervention is not a single process characterized by a single mode of time, though many things happen in a single space. The various processes that are set into motion in response to sexual violence all engender the ways in which sexual assault becomes storied. These stories, how they are told, and the experiences that they validate, are critically important for the victim, as well as to the criminal justice proceedings that take place. A legal narrative unfolds, discrete events strung together like beads on a thread. The criminal justice personnel will investigate each link in the chain of events. A therapeutic narrative unfolds simultaneously, in which the nurse assesses the victim as a patient, determining her health status, and setting a regimen for her future recovery. And concurrently, struggling to emerge from the uncertainty of her recent past, the victim shapes her personal narrative, grasping at the threads of meaning at the edges of her frayed tangle of experiences. While there are several events that are common to these narratives, namely sexual violation and the initiation into the relevant institutional processes, the narratives flow together and come apart at various points, unified by events, outlooks, and sometimes, emotion. Where the narratives diverge is in their working of, with, and in time.

There is no shared sense of duration, no shared horizon in the future, and no singular moment that sparks all narratives to life. Law, healing, and biography are thick with their own temporalities.

This chapter investigates the multiple modes of time operating within the space of the sexual assault intervention. It opens with a quote from novelist William Faulkner, who describes a clock as slaying time, noting that only when the clock stops does time come to life. Rather than thinking of the time of the clock and the time of the stopped clock (the time of life), readers can linger over Faulkner's gentle phrasing. Time comes to life when the clock stops, he states, implying that life itself is devoid of time until the clock stops and time, held apart from life, may now return to it. As time returns to life, so life regains its texture, density, and flow. Though it is a simplification, the time of the forensic intervention was clock time—metric, linear, and bounded. There is little vitality in its operation. The autobiographical strands of the story, of the event of violence and its aftermath, however, are animated and vital, thick with experiences drawn from all recesses of life.

As described in chapter 1, the diminishing life of DNA is but one of the forces driving the tempo of the unfolding legal intervention. Along with the DNA, the problem of documenting medico-legal evidence is frequently one of time; by the time a case goes to trial, the victim's wounds, psychic and physical, may have healed. During their examination, forensic nurses capture these wounds through technological intervention, fixing them in forensic time so that they may endure and extend into the time of the trial. This manipulation of time in order to overcome the problem of time's forward march is carried out within a particular investigative context in which the victim's narrative is clearly demarcated as having a beginning and an end. This time line of victimization, plotted on criminal time, is determined by formal criteria derived from legal statutes, and contains within it those elements that are relevant to proving whether a crime has been committed. These elements include indicators of motive, force, and lack of consent. Once the time line is determined, nurses work to uncover evidence that populates the time line in dense increments. This process takes the form of a forensic interview, during which victims struggle to describe the event of victimization through their own meaningful frameworks. Victims' narratives of suffering do not have the same start- and endpoints as the forensic narrative. The forensic interview becomes a series of interruptions in which victims tell their stories and forensic nurses ask questions in order to craft a forensic narrative. This struggle over the most meaningful way to relate a sexual assault is largely driven by the different anticipatory structures in which the participants are enmeshed. For the nurses, the court of law is the ultimate point of arrival, and for the victims, a return to the everyday is what forms the future horizon.

One of the most common temporal approaches to violence is to treat it as rupture and a break from the everyday; casting violence solely as rupture privileges one particular temporal arc that defines a narrative of sexual assault as a disruption which begins at the moment of rape and continues forward on a unified trajectory. What is missing cannot simply be called "pastness," but rather the restructuring and reorientation of a victim's life around the event of sexual assault and the various ways in which life histories and experiences can be reorganized to indicate a temporal framing of the sexual assault and its unfolding, not forward into the future, but as tremors that travel outward into life.

In my years as a rape crisis advocate accompanying sexual assault victims during forensic exams, I have often heard the eerie litany of rape narratives. While the individual circumstances of each victim's story are quite different, the narratives themselves seem to be recounted within a particular institutional genre. Whether written (Raine 1998; Winkler 2002) or orally recounted, these narratives carry a particular institutional signature: there is a cataloguing of horrors, always including statements of anguish and disbelief, a victim's acts of resistance, and an accounting of her lack of consent. My ethnographic experience brought me to focus on the institutional processes associated with sexual assault interventions as generative of modes of telling. The narrative that is elicited by police scrutinizes the aspects of sexual assault that will hone in on establishing that there is enough evidence to satisfy the legal burden of proof. These "signs" that the law was, indeed, broken are then incorporated into the victim's narrative—she is led toward a mode of voicing sexual assault through the dialogic process of her many encounters and interviews with various different personnel involved in the intervention. Unfolding in clinical space, narration is a dialogical process constituted by the encounter between clinician and patient (Mattingly 1994, 1998). Like many truth commissions, forensic investigation requires a highly disciplined narrative in which the standards for victimhood are demonstrated as having been met and surpassed while conforming to culturally normative gender regimes (Ross 2002).

This chapter argues that what is at stake for the victim is more than the words and ways in which she gives voice to her narrative of suffering. The institutional protocols produce a rape narrative that begins in an unremarkable everyday, is punctuated by disruption, which leads to suffering. This tripartite narrative is perhaps too simplistic for many victims, particularly those living at the economic and social margins of urban life. Regardless, the victim is framed through her induction into the institutional form of sexual assault, and she adopts a standing language previously unavailable to her. In navigating this standing language, the victim comes to understand the available trajectories of her suffering. The "vocabulary" of sexual assault interventions indicates a particular sensibility or a sort of landscape upon which a victim must find her footing. This landscape reveals not only suitable expressions with which to engage, but also particular temporal markers indicating the appropriate time line for suffering sexual assault.

While I, as a researcher, struggle with the problem of defining sexual assault, this is not an open-ended question when it is posed to a forensic nurse examiner, a police detective, or a state's attorney. As the principal personnel attending sexual assault victims who elect to participate in the legal process, these actors have a clear sense of what a sexual assault is and how it must be documented. Practically, of course, this is a necessity as it supports a legal rubric in which these transgressions can be prosecuted. Sexual assault interventions, as this book has thus far demonstrated, are not simply the purview of the criminal justice system. Rather, the investigative processes are coupled with therapeutic components. For example, the interventions are carried out in a hospital emergency room, officers of the law are trained to be sensitive to victims' needs, and forensic exams are carried out by nurses who also ensure that victims receive medical care, therapeutic referrals, and, sometimes, a rape crisis advocate to provide support and counseling during the hospital visit.

One Sunday morning on a crisp fall day, I was dispatched to the hospital as the rape crisis advocate for a sexual assault victim who had returned in the morning after walking out in the middle of the night before her exam. When I arrived at the hospital, there were, in fact, not one, but three sexual assault victims waiting in the emergency room, and the case for which the rape crisis dispatcher contacted me turned out to be the last I dealt with rather than the first that day.[1] As the rest of this chapter illustrates, the circumstances that brought these three women to the hospital were different. As I spoke with each one, accompanied them through their forensic examinations, answered their questions, and offered resources for future support, I witnessed the web of institutional processes begin to draw them in, and the resistances that these women offered. This chapter concentrates on the struggle over time and narrative, though later chapters will turn to the contested notions of home and even images of suffering.

It is productive to characterize the series of interviews the victim goes through as her initiation into the formal processes that will guide her for the duration of the legal case. The first interview is conducted by a uniformed officer who answers the 911 call. The second interview is carried out by a sex crimes detective and delves into much greater detail than the initial report taken in the first interview. Interviews conducted by the detective can last anywhere from 45 minutes to three hours and sometimes longer. Until 2009, it was the detectives who authorized the collection of forensic evidence by a forensic nurse examiner. The nurse examiner was often the third official to interview the victims. In the forensic interview, very detailed questions are asked about the assault in order to structure the processes within the forensic examination. All three interviews ask overlapping questions—where was the victim? Who assaulted her? What happened? And how did she indicate her lack of consent?

One shared goal of all of the interviewers is establishing a clear time line, and it is the police detective assigned to the case who is generally charged with producing the highest level of detail. "Every second, every minute, must be accounted for," a detective sergeant told me seriously. "If the story is airtight, we have more to go on and we know we are going to do better when it comes to court." With a detailed time line of sexual assault, detectives anticipate the exacting rigor of a good defense attorney. The narrative also guides their investigation as crucial details point investigators in the right direction as they search for evidence. This time line emerges in the mode of criminal time.

Next, forensic nurses collect evidence that corroborates or contests these narratives, and in doing so they also initiate the beginning of another temporally marked process: evidence collection itself. Examinations take place under rigorous rules of chain of custody. Thus, every piece of evidence collected is labeled with its time of collection, as well as the name of the collector. Security guards witness the placement of evidence into police lockers, and detectives sign and note the time when they collect evidence kits and drop them off for storage. Forensic nurses know that they must carry out the forensic exam within a reasonable time period, as defense attorneys will question the validity of evidence collected if it is tainted by prolonged exposure to the elements, or worse, unaccounted for time lapses. In a few cases where nurses have taken "too long" to complete exam reports and place them in the evidence locker, they face the fear that defense attorneys will imply that hospital personnel have tampered with evidence. This regime can be marked as forensic time.

My role as a rape crisis advocate placed me at the victim's disposal throughout her hospital stay. Between and during all of the steps that a victim undergoes at the hospital, one-third of her time may be spent waiting—waiting for the detective to show up for the interview; waiting for the forensic nurse to arrive; waiting for the exam room to be prepared; waiting for lab results, medications, or a ride home. It is during these times that I tried to carry out the charge of my intervention, to support the victim and follow her lead, and make sure that she understood the full range of her choices. This could take the form of sitting in silence or engaging in whatever conversations the victim would have me share with her. In these interstices, other modes of narrating life emerge. This book characterizes these modes as biographical times, maintaining the plural as each victim may engage multiple biographies in her narration. All these modalities of time, biographical, forensic, and criminal, emerge as non-synchronous in the cases that follow.

Laura

Laura, whose case I described in the previous chapter, was the first woman with whom I spoke that day. In the last chapter, I relate how Laura made her way to the hospital bearing all of the household goods she viewed as evidence. Here, I recount how she described her life circumstances in our conversations, and how she connected these circumstances to her present plight. When I met Laura, she told me that she was relieved to have someone with her, as she was currently waiting in the emergency room alone. Some friends of hers, doctors who worked at the hospital, had driven her there and were waiting to take her home. In the three hours we spent together, Laura shared with me the enormous bad luck that had followed her for the past ten years of her life. "I thought I was getting back on my feet and then this happened!" "This" was a sexual assault that had taken place two days earlier in Laura's home. After a difficult divorce that left her with very little in the way of financial assets, Laura had started over, moving to Baltimore and leaving behind an abusive husband. A physical therapist, she worked at two hospitals over an eight-year period before losing her job because of budget cuts. Now she was working retail to make ends meet. "I can't believe it, I just can't believe it—it's one more thing, just one more thing," she repeated at many different points during her hospital stay. "I hope it is the last thing, because I can't take any more," she told me. In these short utterances, Laura voiced a sense of her suffering as a long, slow series of hardships rather than the sharp interruption plotted on criminal time.

As I described in the previous chapter, Laura carefully collected bags full of "evidence," including all of the household implements the attacker had touched, drank from, or eaten out of. "I didn't know what to do with it, who to give it to, or who to call, but I knew I had to keep it." Later, as mentioned in the previous chapter, she glanced into the guest bedroom where the attack had taken place and was surprised to see the sheets had been taken off of the bed and were nowhere to be found. "When I saw that he had taken the sheets, I realized that even he knew he had done something wrong," she told me, "and so then I called a friend who told me 'Laura, you have to call the police.' My friend was a nurse and knew which hospital I would have to go to for the exam, so I called friends who worked at that hospital and they brought me here this morning." She described the 36 hours between the sexual assault and her arrival at the hospital as a complete blur.

Because of her status in the local medical world as a physical therapist, Laura knew quite a few people who worked at the hospital, many of whom recognized her in the emergency room. At every encounter, she was very forthcoming about her reasons for being in the hospital. The exact words of her friends' responses varied, but their sentiments did not: "Oh Laura . . . and after everything you've been through!" or "Laura, that's terrible. How can that be, after everything else that has happened?" or "Oh, sweetheart, I really hope this means you have used up all of your bad luck." Her friends recognized the streak of bad luck that Laura herself had described as coming to an end with the third instance of bad luck in the form of a sexual assault. The first and second unlucky events that she described were her abusive marriage, and then the loss of her job as a physical therapist. As she was in the process of the sexual assault intervention, Laura gave voice to the violence of her past marriage, and her economic vulnerability following her job loss.

When Laura went in for her forensic exam, the forensic nurse examiner asked her to describe what had happened. As the nurse asked the required questions originating from the documents included in the medico-legal examination, the lulls during which she was writing down Laura's responses on the form were filled with Laura's ruminations about her situation, her awful luck, and her hopes that this terrible event would mark the end of the unlucky period in her life and better times ahead. As soon as she had finished writing a response to each question on the form, the nurse would interrupt Laura with the next question. In this way, after telling her friends, the police, and me, Laura's fourth turn describing her attack was interspersed with her own understanding of the significance of this rape, its place in the life she had been living these many years, and its indications for the future. The official narrative entered into the nurse's records would have no mention of these circumstances, and the recommendations the nurse provided: "Make sure you follow up with therapy; these things can be very hard to get through," seemed not to engage with the grain of hope planted in Laura's longing for the end of her streak of bad luck and the possibility that fates, or a creator, or a universe, or cosmic force would not be so cruel as to allow her to continue suffering. When the exam was over, Laura expressed her relief, both at having the forensic procedure behind her, and at running into so many of her friends in the emergency room. She found assurances in their overwhelming support of her and their recognition of the injustice of this monumental transgression in her life. "I'm so glad I came in," she told me. "It has to get better from here on out."

Laura's complex narrative hinged on her sense of herself as being terribly unlucky. There was no place, however, for the broader temporal frame in which she felt she had suffered, no matter how many times she reminded the nurses or the police about her years of suffering. This story could only bubble up in the interstitial spaces between the formal questions in the forensic interview, heard only by me and recorded later in my field notes. Laura's personal sense of her suffering, and its emplotment[2] over a long duration in which it came to have meaning, could not be acted upon by the legal system. For the court of law, the beginning of Laura's misfortune was the moment in which her co-worker stepped into her home. For Laura, this could not be the case as it would not yet allow for the possibility of the end of her suffering. Rather, she was expected to muddle through and do the best she could until her case did or did not come up for trial. The forensic nurse and the police officer could not acknowledge that she had already imagined one path into the future.

Keisha

The struggle between the forensic framing of sexual assault with victims' own practices of meaning-making and vastly different senses of urgency became more apparent as the day continued. The next victim I attended, Keisha, was a young girl who had been raped by her father that very morning. From the hallway outside the family waiting room, I could hear an animated chorus of dissenting voices. Expecting a heated discussion, I knocked on the door and entered the room to find Keisha surrounded by eight female family members of varying ages. Though the conversation reduced in volume, it continued steadily. I quickly identified Keisha, however, as she was the only silent person in the entire room. A woman sitting across from her quickly sprang up and introduced herself as "the mother," then ordered Keisha into the hallway to speak with me privately. This "private" exchange included the mother, however, and though I addressed myself to Keisha directly, including offering to leave if she found my presence overwhelming, it was her mother who spoke for her. When the nurse insisted that

Keisha's mother should not be allowed in the forensic examination with her daughter, Keisha's mother became very concerned that the nurse would offer her daughter a "morning after" pill without consulting her.

Though her mother was not allowed to accompany her, Keisha first spoke to me to indicate that she wanted me to accompany her during the forensic examination. In response to my offer to accompany her during the exam if she desired, she said, "Yes, can you come with me? I don't want to be by myself." I assured her mother that the nurse would not give Keisha a contraceptive pill without Keisha's consent. "I heard that stuff can keep you from having babies ever," Keisha's mother frowned. Though she did not insist on being present at the examination, Keisha's mother insisted that the forensic nurse provide further information about the morning after pill before administering it, a message I passed on to the nurse before the examination started, saying simply, "The patient's mother seems very concerned about the side effects of emergency contraception. She may have some questions for you." As we walked to the examination room and away from her mother, Keisha broke her silence for the second time and initiated a conversation about not wanting to be pregnant or sick.

Four or five minutes into the forensic interview, the nurse asked Keisha if she could identify the perpetrator in her case, and whether or not she knew him. Keisha wrinkled her nose in surprise at the nurse's question and answered directly, "Did I know him? Yea, he was my father!" While the family members had been discussing this fact quite openly in the waiting room, the nurse did not ask about the perpetrator's identity until she was well into the forensic interview. In response to Keisha's disclosure, the nurse gasped, then immediately recomposed her face and said, "Well, he wasn't acting like a father now, was he?" Perhaps the nurse's surprise reflected her orientation toward a rape narrative as a single disruption, one contrasting with the prosaic time of the family. In this case, the perpetrator was a family member, a common enough statistical pattern. Keisha's family time was, in part, marked by a long history of violence, and a failure of her caretakers to protect her. Thinking about Keisha's return to home, I asked her whether she felt safe returning there. She was surprised when I asked this question— "I hadn't thought about that, but actually," she seemed to be testing out a few possibilities, "he's been arrested for violating his parole with what he did to me, so I guess, yea, I'm alright cause he's gone straight to jail. He just got out yesterday after four years for something he done to me before." Keisha's vulnerability and her future safety were part of a long history of her father's offending. His removal from the home was immediate as he would be re-imprisoned for violating his parole. Soon after the exam ended, Keisha's mother was invited into the examination room. The nurse recommended to her that both of them seek therapy, handing them several brochures and phone numbers for counseling services.

When I walked back to the waiting room with Keisha and her mother, another one of Keisha's family members jumped up, hugged Keisha, and asked to speak with me in private. "I'm Alecia, Keisha's aunt," she told me in the hallway while shaking my hand. Alecia identified herself as the one who had called the police since Keisha came to her first. "I want to know what we have to do now. I don't think it is a good idea for only—one person to have the instructions." The one person to whom Alecia referred was obviously Keisha's mother, and by indicating that Keisha had placed her confidence in Alecia rather than her own mother, Alecia signaled that Keisha did not necessarily trust her mother. At that moment, I realized the heated conversation that I had overheard when I first walked into the room to take Keisha for the forensic examination was around Keisha's mother's reasons for letting the father into her home after he was released from prison. Keisha's grandmothers, aunts, and cousins were upset that the man had been allowed into the home after his previous abuse of his daughter. I, like the rest of her family, found it unsettling that Keisha's mother had allowed her child's father back into the home after he had already abused their daughter. Alecia attributed all of the mother's apparent concern for Keisha to be outward manifestations of her guilt.

Tonya

The third victim I accompanied was Tonya, the woman who the rape crisis advocacy coordinator had originally dispatched me to see in the morning. Exhausted from being awake all night, Tonya was allowed to sleep in a spare bed in the emergency room while the other two victims were examined first. When it was her turn (at 5:30 in the evening) she was first admonished for having walked out of the emergency room the night before. Her departure was an interruption of forensic time. "I had to see my baby girl!" she replied unapologetically, invoking the never-ending obligations of maternal care. "But you might have lost evidence!" the nurse told her. While delivered in a lecturing, reproachful tone, the nurse's admonishment was meant to convey a sense of care, though, as I have argued in the previous chapter, it may well be the DNA evidence and not the patient who is the object of care here. Tonya, having endured a harrowing and horrific night prior to coming to the hospital, had little patience with the nurse's chastisement and seemed to experience it as forensic discipline. Whenever the nurse adopted this tone, Tonya's frowning face indicated that she was not necessarily receptive to this form of care and discipline.

The previous night (or early that morning), Tonya had been making her way home in a cross-town hack.[3] Because it was 1:00 a.m., she had flagged down a passing hack rather than call a taxi or known hack driver with whom she regularly secured transportation. While there are many stories about unknown hacks attacking female passengers, it was not the driver who assaulted Tonya. Rather, trying to pick up extra fares, the hack driver stopped and pulled over for two more riders, both male. Tonya became annoyed when the other riders insisted that the driver take a detour to a convenience store, and she complained that she should get dropped off first. The other passengers, however, offered the hack driver cocaine if he made their stop first. Directing him to a parking lot behind a dark convenience store, they dragged Tonya from the car and proceeded to assault her. The driver fled, and Tonya was left alone with the men. After assaulting her, they attempted to strangle her and break her neck several times. Tonya blacked out three times and finally decided that the next time they tried to break her neck, she would pretend to be dead. This ploy succeeded, and the men ran off, leaving her for dead in the parking lot. Tonya told me that the only thing getting her through the fearful ordeal was thoughts of her baby girl. "I couldn't leave her without no momma, so I just thought, please God, get me through this so I can take care of my baby." After she was sure that she was alone, Tonya pulled herself up and walked back to the street, where she was able to flag down a passing patrol car.

Tonya's examination took the longest because of the overwhelming amount of evidence to be documented. As she had been strangled, she had petechiae (burst blood vessels) in her eyes, and her throat, as well as fingerprint-shaped bruises behind her ears. Throughout her examination, Tonya talked repeatedly about revenge. The nurse raised an eyebrow at every mention, telling her to take it easy because, "I better not read about you in the news." "I don't care, the police better find these guys before me because if they don't, I am going to shoot them. They better protect that [hack] driver, too." After crashing into a parked car, the hack driver had been stopped by the police, who found him to be under the influence. He immediately told the police that he had witnessed a sexual assault, and Tonya's speculation was that his cooperation had secured him immunity from prosecution for drug possession. This infuriated her as she was in doubt over whether the hack driver had intentionally conspired with the attackers in exchange for the cocaine. The driver had not come to her rescue, allowing the assailants to drag her from the car and then fleeing the scene as they attacked her.

After being brought to the hospital in a patrol car, Tonya had begun to worry about her daughter, a three-year-old who was in a neighbor's care. "I was supposed to get her after work—and my neighbor has to go. What was I going to do?" The nurse told me that Tonya had announced that she had to leave the emergency room, striding out into the night less than an hour after arriving. When Tonya had returned that morning after picking up her daughter and leaving her in the care of her boyfriend, the nurse was surprised. "I was so glad she came back! But when she left, there was so much evidence, it could have been lost! But I called the detectives and told them that she was back and we were going to do the kit and they told me to take my time." The nurse had found a bed for Tonya to rest in while she saw Laura and Keisha first, and then had awakened Tonya and started her examination. The nurse was able to give Tonya time to rest within the space of the hospital. When Tonya had been "missing" while retrieving her daughter, there was no time to spare.

Toward the end of the examination, Tonya began to talk about her daughter, finally asking me if I could check on whether she had arrived in the emergency room yet. She was expecting her boyfriend to meet her at the hospital with her daughter. When I came back and told her that yes, her daughter was waiting for her, Tonya began to talk spiritedly about going home, holding her daughter, taking a bath, and then curling up with her daughter and going to bed. When the examination was over, Tonya brought her daughter back to meet the nurse and me. She left walking hand in hand with the little girl, who talked animatedly as they left the hospital. While I understood the nurse's frustration at Tonya's leaving the evening before, the urgency that compelled Tonya to walk out and check on her child seemed to have served her well. Though she had put forensic time on hold, she could not suspend her own caretaking. Accounting for her daughter's well-being had drawn her world into the space of the hospital, allowing her to participate in the examination and the police investigation. I understood her shift in conversation from vengeance against the perpetrators who had assaulted her to looking forward to seeing her child as a shift in her expectations for the immediate future.

Unraveling Time

Though the details of each of these cases are quite selective and abbreviated in this account, it is precisely because I witnessed all three cases within such a short time frame that I became sensitized to the ways in which the criminal justice process had demanded one framework for the narratives of sexual assault, allowing for a singular time line for all three women, erasing the ways in which sexual assault had reverberated in their lives in radically different ways. For Laura, this was through the frame of bad luck, for Keisha it was in her sense of her family as alternately the source of both threat and safety, and to Tonya, rape had unfolded as she caught a hack, a routine event for her as she had no car and could not afford regular public transportation. Yet the solutions all three women were presented with, the temporal trajectory that the forensic intervention demanded they anticipate, dictated the same destination for all three. The hospital served as the space in which to build the case and collect evidence, the court of law was the site of justice, and a therapist's office was their means to recovery. Yet each voiced very different concerns about their circumstances, and the comforts and reassurances that they desired.

The picture of time within which the sexual assault intervention process worked presented the hospital as the stage in which the action would unfold, and the women as actors waiting in the wings, just out of our sight. Homogeneous and scripted, the stage assumes that the victims' narratives can be captured in contemporaneous and coincidental structures. In this understanding, the action is understood as taking place only within the frame of the stage, and the space offstage or out of frame as Teresa De Lauretis might describe it is of little or no consequence to the audience's understanding of the sequence of events (1984). What happened off stage is not of consequence—it can only be imagined and thus is labeled "rape" or "sexual assault." To stretch the metaphor, the stage itself binds the actors through conventions of set design, lighting, and sound effects. While the physical location of the victims in the same space—the emergency room—coincides, the (temporal) texture of their experiences during their stay can be so markedly dissimilar as to render their subjective experiences of the intervention quite diverse. Even the hospital stands in their subjective landscapes as a distinctive location.

To take examples from these three cases once more: for Laura, the hospital was a familiar and comforting place, one where she could reunite with colleagues whom she did not hesitate to call on for support. Keisha, in contrast, found the hospital a place where she had been brought on an involuntary basis, where she was passed from one person to the next and where family members voiced their opinions about her future without listening very intently to her own desires. Despite, or perhaps because of, the alienness of the hospital, Keisha seemed to find respite in the company of strangers, as she thought differently about the context of her family. The hospital perhaps tracked with Keisha's experience of home in some ways: a contradictive space in which her body was subjected to processes in which she did not wish to participate or was given little say, and the simultaneous location of directive nurturance.

Tonya, unlike the other two women, thought of the emergency room as a place that one was free to walk away from and return to, although the nurses and emergency room personnel were not especially happy about dealing with her stance as they worried she had compromised the evidence she carried on her body. As stated earlier, Tonya had returned to the emergency room at 7 a.m. after walking out in the middle of the previous night. The hospital had served her as a place of rest and safety.

With the knowledge that her daughter was safe, Tonya was free to succumb to her exhaustion and to slumber so that she might be prepared to endure her examination.

Of the three victims, Tonya was also the only one who was told that there had been three cases that day. When she asked the forensic nurse why she had been allowed to sleep for so long, she was informed that there had been two other victims in the emergency room at the same time and that they had been examined before her to give her more time to rest. "Three victims at the same time?" she asked during the forensic examination to no one in particular. "That's sad; that's really sad."

In contrast to the temporal framing of the theater stage, we might also consider time in its metric and topological incarnations. Spatializing time might help us to explore its potential. For example, one might contemplate Michel Serres's explanation of time as a handkerchief:

> If you take a handkerchief and spread it out in order to iron it, you can see in it certain fixed distances and proximities. If you sketch a circle in one area, you can mark out nearby points and measure far-off distances. Then take the same handkerchief and crumple it, by putting it in your pocket. Two distant points suddenly are close, even superimposed. If further, you tear it in certain places, two points that were close can become very distant . . . As we experience time as much in our inner senses as externally in nature—it resembles this crumpled version much more than the flat oversimplified one. Admittedly we need the latter for measurements, but why extrapolate from it a general theory of time? (Serres 1990)

In this passage, Serres distinguishes between what he considers a metric of time from topological time. Metric time is the clear delineation of a time that moves progressively forward and backward in "straight" lines. The "crumpled" version of time is the proximity of metrically distant points on the handkerchief as the fabric is folded in the hand such that they become proximate. This is the model of time that perhaps best reflects the way violence is made meaningful within the lives of those who suffer it. For victims, who render their experiences meaningful within the complex and autobiographical topologies of their own life circumstances, the soteriological narrative is one that may reach back to any number of events or moments in time, while its futures race ahead on many paths that flow from its anchoring into the heterogeneous biographical narratives. The institution, however, requires that the time of sexual assault can be measured and plotted, resembling the flat metric time with which Serres contrasts topological time. For Serres, metric time is the way that an institution can impose its method (45). Because the institution, in this case the forensic practice and the criminal justice system in which it is embedded, must produce a narrative that can be investigated and assessed in a juridical process, the twists, folds, tears, and crumples of the topological narratives that sexual assault victims voice during the intervention are subsumed under the metric narrative solicited and preserved in the dialogical relationship between the nurse and victim. The nurse, working by the clock and calendar, drains the vitality from the life narrative the victim works through in the aftermath of violence. Only when the clock, or the interview, stops, does time come to life as the victim is allowed to speak and tell the nurse and the advocate what matters to her.

An emergent tension arises in the warp and weft woven by the institutional temporality of sexual assault and the narratives offered by Laura, Keisha, and Tonya. Differences in sequencing and duration are immediately apparent. A "metric" understanding of sexual assault would plot the beginning of the experience of suffering squarely at the moment of the sexual assault itself. The three women all offer diverse starting "points" for their narratives of suffering, none of which definitely mark sexual assault as a bounded event that begins the trajectory of their experience. The very processes of establishing a time line of events and protecting the evidentiary chain of custody are metric functions. These techniques use time to measure and mark linear processes, and these processes ultimately serve as legal measures themselves.

These metric tools produced the narratives that stood in contrast to more topological narratives generated by the victims. Laura folded the attack into a triad of misfortunes that included her divorce, job loss, and the sexual assault, noting again and again, with relief, that bad luck comes in threes. Within this triad, the sexual assault was placed sequentially at the end rather than the beginning of her misfortunes. Keisha, on the other hand, was dealing with a long-standing situation in which her family relationships were the source of her susceptibility to violence. Imprisoned once for an earlier incident, Keisha's father had escalated his violence toward her only one day after being released from prison, while her mother had aroused the suspicion of the entire family by inviting the abuser back into her home. Yet the intervention with which she had been presented framed the moment of sexual assault as the first betrayal in Keisha's life, and thus, the protocols blinded the nurses such that they saw no problem in directing Keisha to rely on her mother and seek therapy for the assault, a turn of events to which I return in chapter 7. For Tonya, the event of sexual assault was intimately tied to her economic disadvantages. Without dependable public transportation or access to a car, hacking was a daily mode of conveyance and, thus, a source of vulnerability. The attackers' ability to buy the cooperation of the hack with cocaine further signaled the social universe that Tonya was forced to navigate. Furthermore, Tonya had done something quite unusual in leaving the emergency room and returning after checking on her daughter and arranging childcare. The standard expectation of the hospital procedure as uninterruptible once initiated had been pierced by Tonya's urgent desire to see and care for her child. Forensic nurses were quite used to victims storming out as a result of unbearable mounting pressure. But they were completely unaccustomed to victims who returned after storming out.

In all three cases, the assembling of significant events or moments that comprised a certain picture of the risk and suffering encompassing the experience of sexual assault was decidedly non-metric. Drawing on moments strung together not through their temporal sequencing but through their affective connections, sexual assault had, indeed, initiated tremors in the lifeworlds of the women who suffered from it. Like a spreading ink stain, the center or originating point of the event of sexual assault grew less distinct and locatable as it took on unexpected shapes and proportions, settling into an opaque and asymmetric blot.

Within the process of the sexual assault intervention, very little leeway was granted Laura, Keisha, or Tonya to voice their suffering within their own frame of understanding. Rather, they quickly engaged with the standing language of sexual assault made available to them through a medical and legal intervention. The parameters defining the form of comfort offered to them were drawn from emerging forensic processes rather than the lifeworlds suggested by each woman.

These three women and their cases form a triad that introduced its own topology to my ethnographic research. How to enfold within one process three distinct actors from different socioeconomic and racial backgrounds, of different ages, professions, and family positions? The advantage of ethnography is that Tonya, Laura, and Keisha's narratives need not run together, but may remain distinctive. The forensic nurse, with her charge to produce forensic evidence, did not have the luxury of leaving these three women's stories as they were narrated to her, structuring them within a linear metric, smoothing away the nubs and the uneven textures to produce a uniform evidentiary artifact in her report.

Through the grammar of time introduced by forensic nurses, sexual assault victims experience the reframing of their suffering and its emplotment along particular trajectories that lead to specific destinations—legal, medical, and therapeutic. What is at stake is not simply the successful outcome of a court case. The institutional process that guides the developing legal process also shapes the victims' paths and potentials to negotiate their own lives. This process must take place within a weave of life that positions the victim in relation to her own temporally textured experience in relation to sexual assault such that she can begin to make sense within this web of meaning while perhaps seeing her way out of it. As it stands, the narrative arc of disruption in which the moment of assault is taken as a radical redirection of an otherwise unremarkable life does not encompass the complex ways in which victims understand the violence that has occurred in their lives. Neither does this narrative leave room for acknowledgment of the vulnerability and danger of poor women and men who navigate an everyday in which violence is not a singular occurrence.

3

On Truth and Disgust

Managing Emotion in the Forensic Intervention

We as nurses basically working in the emergency room prior to 1994 were very, very concerned with how the victims of sexual violence were treated. And I'd been around long enough to know—and saw firsthand—that they were not treated very well. They were not treated well by law enforcement; they were not treated well by the healthcare system. And we as nurses were never trained how to talk to rape victims, how to address their needs, and as a result many of these women who came in as victims were very much like ourselves, in the same age bracket, and I think a lot of the nurses, including myself, were very uncomfortable with dealing with sexual assault survivors. And as a result, what happened, sometimes, was that the patient was put into a room, given a box of Kleenex and a blanket. Then the door was shut. [pause] Now I'm not saying that happened all the time, I'm just saying that that was somewhat typical.
—"Emma," interview

This excerpt from an interview with Emma, one of the directors of the Forensic Nursing Program at City Hospital at the time of my research, contains in it one version of the origin stories of her program in its present form. In addition to introducing a clinical paradigm to the sexual assault intervention, the advent of the forensic nursing program marks a shift in the professional sphere in which nurses work and the skills and expertise they require to be effective. Individual professional fields often have unique standards by which vocational expertise can be ascertained (Latour and Woolgar 1986; Mitchell 2002; Rabinow 1996; Weber

1946: 129–56). Emma highlights the poor treatment and lack of support for emotionally distressed sexual assault victims; she critiques the treatment of sexual assault victims as both a lapse in the ethics of care and as a professional failure, two mutually constitutive directives in this case. Treatment refers to more than aspects of medical care. Emma's statement draws attention to the act of "treating," an act that Emma ties to qualities of emotion—how to feel and how to attend to the feelings of a suffering sexual assault victim. In their inadequate attempts to provide comfort, hospital staff members leave victims in a room with a box of Kleenex and a blanket. Before the existence of the Forensic Nursing Program, "we as nurses," states Emma, "were never trained how to talk to rape victims." Talk, Emma suggests, might be the one therapeutic tool that can enhance the work that forensic nurses do, extending beyond the rudimentary material technologies of comfort afforded by tissues and a blanket.

With just cause, there is great focus on lessening the burden of emotional distress on sexual assault victims in the design of the sexual assault intervention (Crowley 1999: 12). Victims' emotional expression is also of interest in the prosecutorial context: juries attribute credibility to victims who display particular emotional states (Konradi 1997: 30; Sanday 1996: 64–65).[1] Emma's description, however, also draws attention to forms of emotional distress and control experienced by the nurses themselves. She hints that she and her colleagues often identified with the victims, as they were "very much like ourselves, in the same age bracket." Later in the interview, she continues to talk about how the Forensic Nursing Program came into existence:

> We as nurses got together one time and said, "There's got to be a better way for victims of sexual violence. There's got to be a better way." And one nurse said, "Well, I've heard that nurses in Virginia are doing their own exams," and said "why doesn't somebody call them and see what's going on?" So one nurse did call, and they said, "Yes indeed, we're doing our own [forensic] exams. We've got special training. We have started a program called a SANE [Sexual Assault Nurse Examiner] Program," and she said, "As a matter of fact, we're having a training program in about two months. Why don't you send any nurses that may be interested?" So City sent about 12 nurses down there. They stayed for a week, they got intensive training—Ann R. is one of those nurses—came back

> and they were all excited, and Ann sort of took the helm and started the program. Prior to nurses doing the exams in 1994, residents—GYN residents—would do the exams. And they did not like doing it. As a matter of fact, they hated it. They didn't like going to court, and they did not do a very good job. Not to mention the fact that they had absolutely no kinds of training whatsoever. And my big issue—complaint was that they came down here [to the ER] with an attitude. You know and I'm thinking being sexually assaulted probably ranks up there as one of the most traumatic things that is ever going to happen to you in your life, and to have a resident walk in with a major attitude is exactly what they did not need. And one time I remember literally reading off directions to the resident as he collected the swabs. (Interview, September 10, 2004)

In this excerpt, Emma narrates a series of events through which a set of gynecological residents are replaced with newly trained forensic nurse examiners. Pedagogical structures and strictures reveal the ways in which competence and expertise are evaluated within the healing professions. In referencing the presence of a gynecology resident, Emma reminds us that hospitals are not simply therapeutic in purpose. They are also places where medical and nursing students come to complete their training (DelVecchio Good 1988; Luhrmann 2000). As residents are ostensibly in the emergency room in a learning capacity, Emma implies that they learn at the expense of sexual assault victims. In her words, the training deficit of the gynecological residents manifests in two ways. First, they are unfamiliar with the correct procedures for conducting forensic examinations, a shortfall well documented in other ethnographic writing about sexual assault examinations (Winkler 2002: 44). Their second failing lies in the distasteful "attitude" they display when conducting examinations, an attitude that Emma characterizes as exactly what the victims do not need.

The criteria by which competence in forensic care can be judged emerge from Emma's description. Within the medical vocations, standards of professional competence vary across fields. As DelVecchio Good argues, questions of competence are often tied to regulation by the law (DelVecchio Good 1988). In her example, malpractice suits become the grounds upon which medical practitioners are deemed competent. The relationship of the law with regard to the competence of forensic nurse examiners, however, does not hinge on the malpractice suit. Rather, forensic nurse examiners are considered competent based on prosecutorial outcomes of the cases they investigate.[2] Beyond the legal litmus test, there are other criteria by which forensic nurse examiners earn a reputation for competence among their peers. A well-trained forensic nurse examiner is familiar with the procedures and techniques for collecting evidence. She does not have to read the instructions on the rape kit in order to carry out the examination. Her training also extends to her demeanor and attitude. How is the correctness of attitude demonstrated? Gestures, words, and facial expressions are among the criteria of a "correct" attitude. "The social (as well as the professional) constructions of nurses, in a way, forbid the verbalization of emotions such as disgust and repulsion. The caring nurse," Dave Holmes and his co-authors write, "is supposed to be able to sublimate negative feelings in order to maintain ethical standards, but behind the appearance of tolerance and calm, nurses may experience dramatic personal responses when they come into contact with particular groups of clients or particular nursing care situations, such as in public health, community health, and forensic settings" (2006: 310).

This chapter explores the methods by which forensic nurse examiners are trained and accrue experience in what might be characterized as emotional labor (Hochschild 1983). Hochschild has described emotional labor in one's profession as emotional expressions that workers come to recognize as appropriate or inappropriate to particular situations that are likely to arise in the work setting (2003: 74–76). With time, a worker internalizes the emotional structure of the work environment; that is, an ideal fit is one in which the worker is not suppressing his or her emotional responses, so much as the employee experiences only emotions and sensations that are appropriate to the workplace (ibid.). There is ample literature discussing emotional labor in both legal and medical fields (see Martin 1999; Pierce 1995; Segal 1988; Zimmer 1987). An important vein in the literature specifically addresses the gendered nature of emotional labor (Pierce 1995).

While research participants were often reticent regarding the gendered nature of their forensic labor, gender is often obliquely invoked in their talk about the work they do. In the two interview excerpts I have included here, Emma twice uses the phrase "as nurses." In my recorded interviews with forensic nurses, only one has ever used the phrase "as a woman," and here she was demonstrating how she spoke to the victims with whom she worked (Interview 1/21/05). More common was the understanding that the category "nurse" was often interchangeable with or inclusive of "woman." Another nurse stated, "I think as a provider, as a nurse, I'm going to give the kind of care that I'd want, or that I'd want for my mother or sister or friend" (Interview 11/16/04). In addition, Emma refers to forensic examiners intervening to improve conditions for rape victims as "Nurses looking out for other women" (Interview 9/10/04). Nurses look out for other women and consider what they'd want for their mothers, sisters, and friends. The forensic nurses explain their stakes in forensic intervention through tropes of professionalism, invoking care through kinship relations. The gendered nature of nursing emerges in the muddled trope of kinship as it is through the relational categories of mother, daughter, and sister that care is invoked.

How do nurses learn to control the range of expressions and impressions that govern their professional lives? Rather than through explicit instruction, forensic nurse examiners experience ostensive forms of pedagogy through which they learn to discipline their expressions and emotional experiences with what I call criterial thinking. Rather than succumb to sensory or emotional excesses, a forensic nurse examiner is trained to overcome her feelings of discomfort by substituting them with the question of legal criteria. Recall, once more, that nursing itself is a deeply feminized field, and that the lure of forensic nursing for many nursing professionals is its affiliation with the criminal justice process. Here, the criminal justice process may be considered a masculinized force. The criterial thinking of nurses is therefore a way to navigate the boundary between the feminized role of the victim and the masculine role of criminal justice. The practice of falling back on a default mode of criterial consideration is manifest when forensic nurse examiners face the "threat" of such sensory and emotional excess, particularly those excesses marked as disgust.[3]

On Disgust

The threat of disgust is a constant professional hazard for forensic nurse examiners and other service providers participating in the sexual assault forensic examination. My use of disgust follows Carolyn Korsmeyer and Barry Smith's explanation of the term in their introduction to Aurel Kolnai's 1927 essay "On Disgust":

> Disgust is a powerful, visceral emotion. It is rooted so deeply in bodily responses that some theorists have hesitated even to classify it as an emotion in the fullest sense, considering it more akin to involuntary reactions such as nausea, retching, and the startle recoil. Like these it is an aversive response and belongs among the body's protective mechanisms. Disgust helps to ensure the safety of the organism by inhibiting contact with what is foul, toxic, and thereby dangerous. But for all of its engagement of bodily responses, disgust is also an emotion that is at work in creating and sustaining our social and cultural reality. It helps us to grasp hierarchies of value, to cope with morally sensitive situations, and to discern and maintain cultural order. (Korsmeyer and Smith 2004: 1)

During my field research, I frequently participated in conversations about how to manage both the emotionally and physically "disgusting" aspects of rape intervention. Bad smells, grotesque wounds or physiology, and accounts of violence and abject poverty were among the topics of conversation. In training, both nurses and advocates were warned about the high likelihood of being disgusted. At a rape crisis advocates training I attended in early 2002, the program director cautioned the rape crisis advocates in training that one might be overwhelmed by "bad smells" and "unpleasant sights" when accompanying patients during forensic examinations. The advice for what to do in such situations suggested the level of self-mastery expected among the rape crisis advocates. Rather than look directly at genitalia, the trainer encouraged advocates to focus on making eye contact with victims. Another suggested strategy was to stand near the victim's head rather than at the foot of the examination table.

It was not simply the sight of the body to which advocates were vulnerable. The scientific and literary discourse on smell explores the links of the sensory experience to intense emotional sensation such as fear, passion, and desire (Chen 2002, 2004; Herz and Cupchik 1995; Süskind 1986). As mentioned in chapter 1, bad smells might originate from putrefying human secretions and unwashed bodies, and the threat of experiencing an offensive odor was quite real. The trainer advised us to step out into the hallway and take a "breather" if the odor proved overpowering. Disgust should never register on one's face as this may further dismay or shame the sexual assault victim. What's more, the rape crisis advocate trainer also suggested that we advocates should similarly excuse ourselves if we felt tearful or if we might cry. Neither the advocate nor the nurse, it was implied, should show such strong emotions. Rather than responding with any strong show of emotion, the rape crisis advocate was trained in a crisis intervention model designed to reflect and identify the sexual assault victim's emotions and feelings (Dattilio and Freeman 2007: 278).[4] I raise these features of sexual assault intervention in order to introduce two points. First, it is not disgust alone, but all powerfully motivated emotional expressions that are discouraged and avoided by rape crisis advocates and forensic nurse examiners. Second, where rape crisis advocates receive explicit training on the management of their emotions and the emotions of sexual assault victims, such direction is not part of the curriculum for training forensic nurse examiners.

To say that disgust was one of many expressions to avoid in the context of the sexual assault intervention is not to say that it is necessarily avoided for the same reason. Putrefaction and bad smells were not simply objectionable because they elicited a strong personal reaction, but because they might indicate the degraded nature of organic material. The "hierarchy of value" being ascribed is the quality of evidence. For example, when learning how to preserve and package forensic evidence, forensic nurse examiners are given the example of a victim who brings the clothes she was wearing during the attack to the hospital with her (Crowley 1999: 113, 137). In this case, the victim has packaged the clothing in a plastic bag. Forensic nurse examiners are taught to remove the clothes from the plastic container, air dry any articles that are wet, and to repackage the clothes in a paper bag. As one nurse told me, "If you leave the clothes in a plastic bag, by the time someone in the crime lab unpacks them to analyze them, they will be smelly and rotten and covered with all kinds of stuff, and the DNA will be lost" (Field Note 3/24/2004).

Both forensic nurse examiners and rape crisis advocates often regaled each other with stories of the worst or most challenging cases in their experience. In the course of my interview, two rape crisis advocates and one forensic nurse examiner all described cases in which an unusually bad smell raised the specter of disgust. All three stories contained the suggestion that the bad smells were indicative of some human secretions, and that such cases tended to point to a phenomenology of truth in which bad smells verified the allegations of sexual assault victims.

These suggestions are but one instance in which the encounter with disgust, one of many emotionally intense sensations a forensic nurse examiner may experience in the course of the sexual assault forensic intervention, is aligned with the question of truth and falsehood. "So strong is the revulsion of disgust," write Korsmeyer and Smith,

> that the emotion itself can appear to justify moral condemnation of its object—inasmuch as the tendency of an object to disgust may seem adequate grounds to revile it. At the same time, the fact that the emotion is quick and reactive may serve to cancel out these grounds by inducing one to reflect on the reasons why disgust is aroused. Thus the experience of disgust both grounds moral perspectives and casts doubt upon their validity. (2004: 1)

Disgust itself invokes the threshold between veracity and suspicion. It becomes the epistemic ground "for truth and falsity, warrant, [and] justification" (ibid.: 11).

Purity, Danger, and Abjection: Averting Horror, Averting Failure

Pollution, abjection and the human body constitute well-trod territory in anthropology and feminist philosophy (Douglas 1966; Grosz 1994; Kristeva 1982). Mary Douglas's classic *Purity and Danger* subtly traces the modalities through which theologians and anthropologists understood purity and uncleanness in relation to the sacred. Her broad-ranging analysis begins with linguistic differentiation and moves on to conceptions of purity and danger in ritual. Interestingly, among the many figures with whom the text begins is St. Catherine of Siena, who nursed the ill and chided herself for her revulsion of wounds and took powerful measures of self-reproach (1966: 7).[5]

Forensic nurse examiners face the additional danger of pollution and abjection[6] when carrying out procedures that focus on the human body and its orifices and secretions. In particular, danger of pollution is introduced when the work involved requires the collection and preservation of the fluids cast off by the human body. For Kristeva, the encounter with the location of fluids in places and circumstances under which they should not appear, outside of a body, comprises a terrifying psychic event in itself (1982: 19). Here is semen putrefying outside of the body because it is unwanted; it cannot be destroyed or removed until it has been preserved as evidence. Kristeva's theory builds on Douglas's and teases apart the place of the abject in the dangers of liminality. The claim of sexual violation propels the body into dangerous liminality. The rape victim indicates a disturbance of "identity, system and order" (Kristeva 1982: 4). In her description of the phenomenology of abjection, Kristeva characterizes the rejection that one feels as shielded from shame; shame, she tantalizingly relates, is tempered by certainty (1982: 1). A quality of certainty emerges in forensic encounters with the abject; the pedagogical regimes through which certainty is given foundation animate my analysis.[7]

Healthcare professionals are trained to accept and mitigate the risk of infection in their encounters with potentially infected bodies. Many of the nurses with whom I worked reported taking the course of preventative pharmaceutics for HIV following accidental exposure to needles or infected blood (Field Note 8/13/2002).[8] Tolerating potential exposure to the risk of infection is part of the daily world of the nursing profession and is not limited to the forensic nursing specialty. While the nurses may be accustomed to encountering misplaced body fluids, for the victim, the substances may be doubly alien—her own secretions are no longer a part of her once they are expelled from the body, and the secretions of the rapist, at times intermingled with her own, were never a part of her body in the first place. For the nurse, the victim and the unseen perpetrator are the sources of any organic material in question. The procedures of forensic intervention sometimes reveal or confirm the presence of these secretions. A seemingly dry leg may fluoresce under an alternate light source. A microscope can reveal the presence of sperm and ejaculate on a victim's person. In response to carefully posed questions, a victim can reveal where saliva, invisible to the naked eye, may be found on her neck, chest, or face. Attunement to the abject state is brought into being through the revelatory nature of the forensic encounter.

When encountering the abject in the course of sexual assault intervention, forensic nurses often shift from registering their disgust to an assessment of the criteria of facticity. In May 2002, this seemed to be the case for the forensic nurse examiners who treated a victim I call Amanda. The following is an excerpt from my field notes describing my impressions of Amanda:

> She has obvious injuries, including a dramatic choke mark on her neck, and she is walking with a limp.[9] I comment on her appearance and her apparent injuries, asking her if she is in pain. She tells me she is really hurting, especially "down there."
>
> "You see, she says, I am on my period and I had a tampon in, and now it is stuck up there. I would take it out myself, but they say it is evidence, so I have to wait." This is said in a very matter of fact tone. Throughout the next couple of hours, she will repeat this statement in a variety of tones, with escalating urgency and upsetness.
>
> I ask her if she was given any pain medication [at the previous hospital], to which she answers that they gave her some Motrin, but it is wearing off. I tell her the nurse will take care of that and I will see if she can be given something soon. I note that she sits very gingerly, trying to avoid putting any pressure on her pelvic area by slouching backwards and side to side so that the base of her spine takes most of her weight.

Amanda had first presented in another hospital emergency room, and had been transferred to City Hospital after the police instructed the first emergency room staff. Her growing agitation and grief evoked a strong response in me as her rape crisis advocate and I felt duty-bound to address her concerns. She had been sitting in the emergency room waiting room for many hours. The forensic nurse who was on-call to do the examination had still not arrived, though Emma was on the floor doing administrative work that day and handling two other victims who had come in while she had been on the earlier shift. When I arrived after being dispatched by the rape crisis center, I alerted Emma to Amanda's distress. Amanda was very upset. After suffering through a rape, she literally sat on the edge of her seat expressing her irritation and pain. She was unhappy that she had to wait in the hospital, and when I asked if I could do anything to alleviate her discomfort, she asked me to notify the hospital staff that she was menstruating and had been wearing a tampon when she was sexually assaulted. She was both uncomfortable and deeply concerned that the tampon was menacingly lodged within her; waiting for the on-call nurse delayed the removal of the tampon, which added to her tension and dismay. As she spoke about the tampon, one sensed that she was growing increasingly distraught. With a twinge of fear in her voice, she insisted, quite reasonably, that the tampon should be removed immediately.

Hearing about Amanda's predicament, Emma agreed to speak with her as soon as she completed examining the victim who had come in before Amanda. She, too, was affected by Amanda's agitation and escalating horror and immediately agreed to extract the tampon prior to the forensic examination. She nodded sympathetically as Amanda tearfully explained her discomfort. In addition to comforting Amanda and contributing to her sense of control over the unfolding situation, Emma knew that a tampon properly removed, prepared, preserved, and packaged by a forensic nurse examiner could potentially yield valuable legal evidence. Thus, Emma accompanied Amanda to an exam room. Ten minutes later, Amanda burst out of the room visibly red-faced and angered. She marched up to me and announced that she wanted to leave and did not wish to wait for the arrival of the on-call forensic nurse any longer. Emma trailed tentatively behind her, asking Amanda if she was sure she wished to leave the hospital. "If you leave, we won't be able to collect the evidence; it's now or never," though Amanda kept up a stream of salty invective and refused to cast a glance at Emma. Protocol demanded that we had to respect Amanda's decision to refuse forensic examination and leave the emergency room. I procured a taxicab voucher from one of the hospital social workers and called a car to come and fetch her. We waited outside for 20 minutes. I listened to Amanda voice her objections, and made sure she had phone numbers and contact information for counseling referrals. I asked her if she might reconsider the forensic exam or if her mind was made up. Amanda claimed she was sick of waiting, and referred only obliquely to what happened in the examination room with Emma. She was tearful and angry, but calmed down a great deal while we waited for the taxi. Even when the edge of her anger seemed to have worn off, she did not wish to stay in the hospital: "I don't think the nurse believes me, and after what I've been through, I don't fucking need this."

When Amanda had left, I went back to the forensic examination office to speak with Emma and to complete the prerequisite paperwork.[10] Emma had contacted the forensic nurse who had been called to come in to do Amanda's evidence collection and informed her that her services would not be needed for now. The victim had, as she put it, "voluntarily left the emergency room." Returning the phone to the receiver, Emma turned to me with eagerness to talk over Amanda's dramatic departure. "What did she say to you when she left?" she ventured curiously. When I responded that Amanda had told me she was upset about waiting for the on-call nurse and had, additionally, felt that Emma did not believe her, Emma continued. "Did she tell you that when I went to remove the tampon, there wasn't one? The tampon she was complaining about WASN'T THERE. There was NO TAMPON." I asked Emma what she thought had happened. Was Amanda mistaken? Was she in pain and confused about her physical sensations? Or, as Emma seemed to imply, was she lying? With a shrug of her shoulders and a knowingly arched eyebrow, Emma replied, "All I am saying is there was no tampon. That's all I am saying." With that declaration, Emma returned to the paperwork on her desk.

It was obvious that Amanda's fear of the tampon in her body had initially affected Emma and me—it was hard not to feel a mixture of concern and revulsion on Amanda's behalf. By deciding to remove the tampon prior to the arrival of the on-call nurse examiner, Emma had subtly modified the examination protocol. This course of action would provide Amanda with much-needed relief while promoting the integrity of potential forensic evidence. When the examination unfolded in an unexpected way, Emma did not spend a long time pondering the absence of the tampon. She was not open, as I was, to some other explanation in which it might be reasonable to feel a sensation that did not yield to a physical reality. Emma simply pointed out that she had not found a tampon. To Emma, Amanda's sharp insistence that a tampon was causing her pain was unfounded in a reality that rested on legal criteria. While other explanations could respect the pain as real in its psychic dimensions, the veracity of Amanda's physical pain was under suspicion. Once Emma had shifted from sympathetic certainty to the refusal of making narrative space for a less secure story, Amanda interpreted the nurse's withdrawal as professional disbelief, possibly disdain, and reacted in defense of herself and her narrative. Neither woman, respectively representing the strict evidentiary protocols and the recourse to a convincing narrative of personal suffering, was prepared to negotiate potential alternative explanations of pain and trauma.

"What Kind of Victim . . . ?"

I now turn to a case that reveals what stakes might be invested in the practice of maintaining composure as a forensic nurse examiner, particularly under circumstances that challenge one's own sense of propriety and comfort. In this encounter, a question posed by a sexual assault victim who I call Sierra drew my intention to the potential of professional failure. The question posed was and remains a difficult one to answer, but it is a provocative heuristic. The convergence of several factors leads to the circumstances under which the question emerges, and there are difficulties inherent in satisfactorily answering the question. Sierra's question is, "She hates me because I am black, right?"

It was an afternoon on the Sunday following Thanksgiving and the "she" in Sierra's question was Kelly, the [white] forensic nurse examiner treating her and conducting her forensic examination. Kelly had left the examination room briefly to transport Sierra's urine sample to the hospital laboratory. Sierra's question was not out of context—she was trying to figure out why Kelly had begun behaving very brusquely toward her. To be sure, Kelly had been rather clipped that day—she was usually very warm and friendly, but coming in on a holiday weekend had soured her mood. When Sierra had responded affirmatively to Kelly's question, "Have you showered since the assault?" Kelly had expressed frustration over the compromising of serological evidence—all that blood, saliva, and semen literally down the drain. Still, Kelly had remained professional and patient until Sierra refused the emergency contraception that Kelly had offered her. The offer is standard to every sexual assault intervention.[11] Sierra's response was not standard, it seems. Out of a total of 44 examinations I observed, Sierra was the only woman I ever saw refuse the emergency contraception, though many were wary of it and engaged in long deliberative processes. She followed the announcement of her decision by expressing her desire to bear a child and become a mother. For one split second, an expression of repugnance flitted across Kelly's face. Then it was gone.

Kelly's change in attitude did not go unnoticed by Sierra, nor was it very subtle. Kelly stopped smiling at Sierra or making eye contact. The tone of her voice changed accordingly. Sierra felt the prickliness and had voiced her curiosity about its origin, and its possible relation to racial prejudice. Why would a forensic nurse examiner, charged with care for and examination of a sexual assault victim, treat an already suffering victim coldly? When Kelly and I were out of Sierra's earshot, Kelly voiced her objections very vocally. "What kind of victim wants to get pregnant?" As I have stated, among those I observed, Sierra was the only sexual assault victim with reproductive potential who refused the emergency contraception. While other victims readily reject the possibility of pregnancy and assent to emergency contraception in a manner that is interpreted as properly expressing revulsion and disgust (Hoyson 2009), Sierra separated the possibility of maternity from the conditions under which conception might have occurred. By refusing emergency contraception and telling the nurse that she had been thinking of having a child for some time now and so she "wouldn't mind" getting pregnant, she did not adequately express disgust and refusal in a way that was, perhaps, recognizable to a hypothetical jury. Sierra's admission that she had been contemplating motherhood before the incident of sexual violence indicated that for the moment, she would not allow rape to serve as an interruption to her prior life trajectory and her desire to become a mother. By implying an insistence that the sexual assault had not wholly transformed her into a differently desiring being, she had not sufficiently demonstrated the role of wounded victim. Moreover, Sierra's refusal muddled classic categories like love and hate, while her leaving open the possibility of pregnancy cast her in the role of nurturance rather than one of abjection. The forensic nurse voiced the expectation that Sierra's desire to become a mother should have been transformed into a desire to take all possible measures to avoid motherhood in the present circumstances. This seemed the only appropriate shape for the psychic wound that Sierra should bear if she were to properly embody the role of rape victim.

As I've already indicated, Kelly reacted quite strongly to Sierra's decision, telling me, "I just don't believe her. What kind of victim wants to have a baby?" The forensic nurse examiner had now expressed her suspicion with regard to the veracity of Sierra's claims. What are the conditions of possibility for the introduction of suspicion in this interaction? Was this, in fact, a lack of sympathy based on a racial prejudice (i.e., a nurse perceiving a black woman expressing a pathological desire for single motherhood; doubly pathological as the wrong kind of "father" figures in fulfilling this desire)? Furthermore, what is the relationship of the fleeting expression of disgust on Kelly's face and her movement toward an assessment of suspicion? I interpret the sequence of events as follows: the proximal following of one set of expressions (those associated with disgust) by another set of expressions (those conveying suspicion and weighing the facticity of Sierra's case) demonstrated a learned forensic professionalism and expertise.[12] I now turn to one scene of instruction in which instructors teach forensic nurse examiners, among other things, how to respond to one type of emotional input by deliberately overwhelming them within a classroom setting.

Criterial Thinking: Ostensive Demonstrations

The scene of instruction that I describe is set in the classroom in which a one-week forensic nurse examiner certification course was held in August 2005. There is an entire and vast literature on emotional labor that refers to many scenes of instruction itself, for example, Hochschild's flight attendant who sits in an auditorium making a note to "smile" because the instructor tells all of the flight attendants in training that smiling is their greatest asset (1983). This is not the model of learning in training forensic nurse examiners. There are never such explicit instructions on how examiners should compose their features, or how they should feel in relation to particular experiences or scenarios. How, then, do they learn that this (particular) feeling goes with that (particular) turn of events?[13]

On the fourth day of the weeklong forensic nurse examiner training, Sergeant Raymond was the day's instructor. The first three days had focused on intensive genital anatomy, and forensic examination techniques (with heavy emphasis on documentation and paperwork). Sergeant Raymond had been asked to teach the part of the course on the police perspective on sexual assault, and the relationship of police work to forensic investigation. An educator at the police academy and a seasoned police detective, Raymond asked us, as a class, whether or not we thought a man could break down a door, sexually assault a woman, and leave the house all within five minutes. "If that was the time line that you were asked to give your professional opinion on in court, could you say whether or not it was possible?"[14] Many of the nurses present shook their head, and a few murmurs of "five minutes is not a lot of time" passed through the classroom. Sergeant Raymond asked us for a show of hands. Most of us, it seemed, were of the opinion that it was not possible or highly unlikely.

"I am going to play you a tape of a 911 call my department received a few years back." This was as much preparation as we received before hearing a recording that truly unsettled us by provoking a very severe emotional response in response to the presentation of a raw and violent reality. The cassette was a recording of a call from a woman as a man broke down her front door, her bedroom door, and raped her all while the phone was still connected to the emergency operator. The tape started with the woman frantically telling the operator that someone is trying to break down her door. The caller's voice is thick with fear and panic. The sound of the crashing of the front door is followed by panicked screams and quick and heavy footsteps coming up the flight of steps. There is a loud crash as the bedroom door is kicked in. The woman shouts "he's in the room!" and the phone drops from her hand (we hear the thud), but the line is still connected. The caller is screaming—she continues screaming and sobbing for the duration of the call. At first, the operator calls out, "Ma'am. Ma'am, are you there?" but the operator quickly falls silent. After 90 seconds of the caller screaming and sobbing (and the qualities of those screams and sobs change, inviting us to imagine what is happening to the caller's body to change her voice), sirens sound in the distance. The footsteps retreat and the screaming stops, but the sobbing does not subside. It is, obviously, a difficult tape to listen to—now as we listened, Sergeant Raymond narrated the set of events that we heard taking place on the cassette tape as it played in the thick, dense stillness that had settled over the room.

> "He's breaking down her front door."
> TWENTY SECONDS LATER: "He is breaking down her bedroom door."
> "Now he is raping her."
> THIRTY SECONDS LATER: "Now he has turned her over and is raping her anally."
> "Now he is leaving."

The call itself was, indeed, less than five minutes in duration—in fact, it was closer to three minutes. When Raymond stopped the tape and turned to us to deliver the pedagogical message that the victim, in fact, had accurately reported the assault as having lasted under five minutes, we sat stiffly in stunned silence neither making eye contact with one another nor with him. I noticed that the other two trainers had left the room. Sergeant Raymond went on to tell us that the assailant in this case had been apprehended and sentenced and was serving a long prison term, and so on and so forth. Though welcome, this news hardly mitigated our individual and collective responses.

Nurses milled uncomfortably in the hallways in the break that followed the session. I located Ryan, one of the two trainers, to ask her about Raymond's lesson. Ryan told me she always left the room when Raymond played the tape because she did not like to listen to it. He had been using the tape for years—she thought it really impacted the nurses strongly. "They hear what it is really like out there." Still, she did not want to hear the tape after her first time, and had slipped out of the room knowing what was to come. Other nurses talked with one another in small groups in the hall. Many nurses commented on how terrible the call was. A few expressed their desire to be warned of the content; some argued that such a warning would have made the tape less powerful. These concerns were not voiced in the space of the classroom or in the presence of the instructor, though they were elicited by the "exercise" of listening to the tape. While it was an implicit lesson of the day, the issue of managing stress and emotionally intensive or draining work was foregrounded by the tape. The lesson does not suggest that emotions are to be buried or avoided; rather, they are to serve as the basis of action.[15] If I take Raymond's framing of the tape as a suggestion for how a forensic nurse examiner should manage the challenge, I can think of him as introducing a set of criteria with which to consider the recording. These criteria turn on the factuality of the narrative driving the investigation. Is the victim's report true? This instruction, unlike the example of the flight attendant, is communicated without being framed as a directive: "Don't think about how sad or hurt this person is. Don't think about how sad or hurt you are. Don't think about how you feel at all. Think about whether this is true or false."[16] Rather, it is introduced by framing the recording as an example of what is possible or not possible. The "answer" to the initial question of possibility is that, yes, the narrative is truthful. The criteria that guide the forensic approach to the evidence of the 911 recording introduce a scale of trust and suspicion—it is veracity that is under question.

The Problem of Child Victims

All throughout my fieldwork, I have discussed other concerns around stress management and "emotional labor" with forensic nurses. Sometimes I would raise the issue; sometimes they would bring it up. I was frequently told that most cases were not emotionally challenging, but every once in a while, a nurse examiner would handle a case that really "stuck with her." Different nurses had very different strategies for how to manage these difficult cases. These techniques involved either or both some general reorientation toward all of the cases a nurse encounters, or established specific categories of cases around which a nurse would maintain a heightened awareness, either avoiding or practicing a technique of mindfulness in order to remain calm and professional throughout. An example of what I characterize as a "general" solution to emotional sensitivity was one nurse's experience with desensitization therapies, an experimental hypnosis-based technique, which she claimed had helped her immensely. She also commented that the child sexual assault cases were especially difficult for her as she was mother to a daughter, so she ceased doing examinations of child victims. This represents a specific tactic of avoidance of a class of cases.

In accordance with Maryland state statutes, pediatric and adult victims are examined differently, and the Board of Nursing requires forensic examiners have special credentials to handle pediatric cases.[17] In Baltimore, child and adult victims are seen at separate hospitals; the program I worked with at City Hospital only saw adult victims. The legal statutes stipulate that any victim 13 years or older is treated as an adult.[18] Thus, what I refer to here as child forensic examination programs see those victims under the age of 13, while those programs deemed adults-only conduct interventions with all victims age 13 and up. The forensic nurse who states that avoiding child examinations entirely is an efficacious solution for reducing stress, and emotional sensitivity must strictly adhere to the criteria for discerning a child from an adult. That is, the forensic nurse examiner must see, or rather feel, invested in a meaningful difference between a 13-year-old and a 12-year-old if she is going to accept the prospect of examining the 13-year-old.

Polly is a forensic nurse examiner who began practicing in a child forensic nursing program and then shifted to the adults-only program. It was not any special sensitivity to or challenge of caring for child victims that caused her to shift her practice to an adults-only program. Rather, she cites her frustration at the low numbers of cases requiring sexual assault intervention in the children's program—she would have been unable to maintain her certification as a forensic nurse examiner because she could not complete the five required annual cases.[19] In order to gain more experience and ensure a steady flow of cases, she moved to the adult sexual assault intervention program at City Hospital. Polly's move protected her professional interests. To accrue evidence of her competence, Polly must continually accumulate experience. Though the concerns that necessitated her shift from a child to an adult program were associated with professional concerns, I asked Polly if she experienced any difficulty when examining 13- and 14-year-olds in the adult sexual assault intervention program at City Hospital. She replied that 13-year-olds in Baltimore City were "just as sexually experienced as 30-year-olds" (Field Note 9/16/2004). This formulation is indicative of Polly's professional investment in the criteria by which the law discerns a difference between adults and children, though it does not necessarily reveal Polly's personal feelings. Later conversations between Polly and me suggest that her understanding of the division between adult and child may not be as neat as her first response indicates. Polly concedes that younger victims are "posturing" or "don't really know anything" or "pretend to know more than they actually do." This, she says, becomes clear over the course of the examination process, though it may not be apparent in the early encounter.

In Polly's responses, we see the variable permeability of the age boundary between adults and children in the world of forensic nursing. Polly can reliably invoke and realize the age line—her experience tells her that 13-year-olds are just like 30-year-olds. The age boundary, however, is not fixed or permanent. Polly concedes that the sexual maturity of the 13-year-olds can evaporate or fall away in the short duration of the forensic examination. The age line proves a meaningful criterion without permanently applying to all moments of Polly's life. It is also paired with other criteria, in this case, locality, in order to operate with specificity. Not all 13-year-olds are like 30-year-olds; only those from Baltimore are identified in this way.[20]

One final note on Polly's response to my question: when I asked her if she found child examinations more difficult than adult examinations, she understood my question to be inquiring about the emotional challenges of conducting forensic examinations on children. She did not interpret my question to be asking her about the technical challenge of examining children. Discussions about the efficacy of examining children and young adults were not uncommon among forensic nurse examiners (Suggs et al. 2001: 153). Examiners need to master a specific set of techniques in addition to those needed to examine adult sexual assault victims. Additionally, detailed anatomical knowledge is necessary, particularly concerning sexual development. A forensic nurse examiner who is able to identify and record the child victim's stage of sexual development, often using the tool of Tanner Stages (Crowley 1999: 145–46; Girardin et al. 1997: 111–13), provides a valuable standard for gauging the passing of time in a juridical system in which prosecution may unfold over long durations. Forensic nurse examiners consult illustrated and photographic charts in order to accurately identify the Tanner Stage (or Tanner Scale) of the body they are examining. The scale, which differentiates the stages of sexual development of males and females, is based on secondary sexual characteristics. This includes the appearance and size of the breasts in females, and the growth and density of pubic and body hair in both males and females. The assessment that forensic nurse examiners must make with regard to sexual development circumvents the potential dismay of viewing a child's sexually violated body. Child victims, potentially entering the courtroom as adults, are fixed as children within the well-documented evidence collected during the sexual assault intervention. As legal subject, the child's incapacity to consent is more firmly demonstrated when the developmental criteria of childhood are introduced in the court of law.

Though Polly does not emphasize the technical differences between child and adult sexual assault cases, many of her colleagues brought the singular aspects of the two types of sexual assault interventions to my attention. Certification requirements for forensic nurse examiners suggest an appreciation of the additional expertise of child sexual assault examiners. In order to be certified to conduct child and adolescent examinations, a forensic nurse examiner must first be certified and hold her license for adult practice (Code of Maryland Regulation 10.27.21.05). Within the sexual assault forensic intervention, the categories of "adult" and "child" denote distinctive technical requirements, biological development, social and sexual maturity, and legal subjects.

Legal Frameworks

Returning to the encounter between Sierra and Kelly, Kelly expresses her discomfort with Sierra's decision to refuse emergency contraceptive measures, which led her to doubt the veracity of Sierra's allegations. Here, it is the significance of the refusal in light of its legal implications that emerges as the realm in which criteria will be applied. Indeed, it seems appropriate that a forensic nurse examiner should be concerned with establishing evidence consistent or inconsistent with the allegation a crime has occurred; this seems the very exercise of the investigation and trial itself. But how is Sierra's decision to accept or refuse emergency contraception salient to a legal case? Why doesn't it simply fall within a therapeutic discourse? To understand why a decision about contraception can be seen to support or detract from a legal case, one must understand the legal criteria operating in criminal investigations. Each of the legal definitions establishing the criteria of sex offenses under the Maryland Statutory Law hinges on the absence or presence of consent. The statutes name six different sex offenses: Rape (First Degree), Rape (Second Degree), Sex Offense (First Degree), Sex Offense (Second Degree), Sex Offense (Third Degree), and Sex Offense (Fourth Degree). The statutes each differ in the particular type of sexual acts they address, but all pair the description of a sexual act "against the will and without consent" of the alleged victim (see table 3.1). That is, an individual is a victim of sexual violence if and only if the sex act in question was carried out against her will and without her consent. If the individual is not understood to have withheld (or withdrawn)[21] consent, she is not a victim, but a consensual party to the sex act.

In addition to being the basis for participation in political life (Pateman 1980), consent is notoriously difficult to document, and there are various impassioned (and long-standing) arguments for and against the inclusion of consent as the crux of statutory governance of sex offenses (see Harris 1976; Remick 1993). At one end of the intellectual spectrum, some feminist scholars argue that the deep patriarchal structures undergirding social life make all sex coercive and generate an impossibility of women freely consenting to (hetero) sexual intercourse (Reitan 2001: 44). There is little agreement over what constitutes consent, and how one determines whether or not consent was given, refused, or withdrawn, particularly in typical cases in which there are no witnesses other than the alleged perpetrator and victim (Harvard Law Review 2004). Hence, Kelly's suggestion that willingness to bear a child is indicative of Sierra's consent to participate in a sex act, perhaps even if only retroactive consent, materializes the fact of consent for the purposes of the law.

Table 3.1. Maryland Sex Offense Statutes

Crime	Class/ Maximum Penalty	Maryland State Statute	Description
Rape First Degree	Felony/Life	Art. #27 Sec. 462	Vaginal intercourse with force or threat of force against the will and without consent, and (aggravating factors) · Uses or displays a weapon, or, · Inflicts injury on victim or anyone else, or, · Threatens victim or anyone known to victim, or, · Commits or threatens kidnapping, or, · Is aided by one or more persons
Rape Second Degree	Felony/20 Years	Art. #27 Sec. 463	Vaginal intercourse with force or threat of force against the will and without consent, or victim is mentally incapacitated, mentally defective, or physically helpless, or victim is under 14 years and the person who performs the act is 4 or more years older (persons under 14 do not have the right to consent)
Sex Offense First Degree	Felony/Life	Art. #27 Sec. 464	Sexual act, i.e., cunnilingus, fellatio, analingus, anal intercourse, or object into anal or genital area for gratification with force or threat of force against the will and without consent, and (aggravating factors) · Uses or displays a weapon, or, · Inflicts injury on victim or anyone else, or, · Threatens victim or anyone known to victim, or, · Commits or threatens kidnapping, or, · Is aided by one or more persons
Sex Offense Second Degree	Felony/20 Years	Art. #27 Sec. 464A	Sexual act, i.e., cunnilingus, fellatio, analingus, anal intercourse, or object into anal or genital area for gratification with force or threat of force against the will and without consent, or victim is mentally incapacitated, mentally defective, or physically helpless, or victim is under 14 years and the person who performs the act is 4 or more years older (persons under 14 do not have the right to consent)
Sex Offense Third Degree	Felony/10 Years	Art. #27 Sec. 464B	Sexual act, i.e., intentional touching of victim's anal or genital areas for sexual gratification (does not include use of penis, mouth, or tongue) against the will or without consent and (aggravating factors) · Uses or displays a weapon, or, · Inflicts injury on victim or anyone else, or, · Threatens victim or anyone known to victim, or, · Commits or threatens kidnapping, or, · Is aided by one or more persons

To continually demonstrate her lack of consent, Sierra must reject the possibility of conceiving a child from the encounter. I return to Sierra's case with respect to reproductive violence in chapter 4. Of course, the process of securing Sierra's informed consent in the course of the intervention has not included a discussion of the future-oriented rules. Thus, Sierra's decision breaks these rules even as she is unaware of them.

Because the legal instrument divides sex offenses into six different types of crimes, forensic nurse examiners are not simply working to establish whether a sex offense occurred or not. Different charges encompass different physical acts, and carry different penalties. Their examination must also take into account what sexual contact took place and which body parts were involved (table 3.1 provides a detailed list). The injuring, use or display of weapons, verbal threats, and presence of one or multiple individuals during the attack are the legal criteria by which use of force is established. Utterances can be acts within the bounds of these legal definitions. In addition to addressing the question of physical force, forensic examiners also assist in documenting whether victims are "mentally incapacitated, mentally defective or physically helpless" (see table 3.1). Forensic nurse examiners can establish and record whether victims are mentally or developmentally challenged.[22] The category of "mentally incapacitated" individuals also includes those who are heavily intoxicated or inebriated. Forensic nurse examiners may establish a victim's level of intoxication through a number of factors. A blood alcohol level, observation of the victim's current mental state, and victim's account of events may all play a part in establishing mental (in)capacity.

Within the statutory guidelines, childhood also becomes a meaningful legal category. In the guidelines describing second-degree rape, a felony charge with a maximum sentence of 20 years, the crime is described as:

> Vaginal Intercourse WITH Force or threat of force against the will and without consent OR Victim is mentally incapacitated, mentally defective or physically helpless, OR Victim is under 14 years and the person who performs the act is 4 or more years older (persons under 14 do not have the right to consent)

Individuals under the age of 14 do not have the right to consent. The statutes draw a hard line at a particular age. Though the statutes distinguish between individuals age 14 and those who are older, forensic examination programs split their practices into adult and child using age 13 as the point of separation. The legal set of distinctions does not necessarily map easily onto the distinction made by the forensic nursing program. While the legal criteria invoke childhood in terms of an individual's "right to consent," a feature that forensic nurse examiners consider in their work, forensic medicine additionally draws distinctions based on anatomical differences between children and adults. Tanner stages, detailed descriptions of the victim's primary and secondary sexual traits, would be described in the medical narrative to fix the identity and age of the victim within the forensic record.

Other Criterial Norms

Distinguishing between child and adult sexual assault victims is not the only way in which criteria are put to work in the sexual assault forensic examination. Once again, I turn to Polly for an example of yet another completely different set of criteria, which is drawn from a more general set of medical referents within the world of nursing. In an interview, Polly told me:

> I've had to tell parents that their kid committed suicide, or walk out and tell family members—or be there—when they were told, or walk the family members back into shock trauma to see their mangled—we fix them up as best we can. That to me, on the "oh shit" scale, it can't even be compared, really. I kind of put sexual assault survivors on the scale of someone who's been through really nasty chemo or cancer therapy, and they're in remission, and every day is a goal, one more day is good. You know, I feel for you. I hope it never happens to anybody.

Here, Polly introduces what she cheekily dubs the "oh shit" scale. While this type of comparison appears to disrupt the particular reverence typically accorded to sexual assault intervention, it is a comparison invited by the recruitment of nurses into forensic intervention and by the overlapping space of forensic and medical practice in the emergency room. Though they do not compare the experience of sexual assault to medical crises, Laura (introduced in earlier chapters) and Terry establish their own wider framework of casting sexual assault in relation to their personal encounters with suffering. Laura spoke of rape in a triad with the experience of domestic violence, followed by loss of her job and economic security. In her words, rape was third in a series of misfortunes she had experienced over a ten-year period. Another sexual assault survivor I interviewed many years after she had been raped, Terry, told me the following:

> I was raped once. It was bad, but it wasn't the worst thing that ever happened to me. The worst thing was being in a very bad car accident . . . because you could tell a rapist not to rape you, but you couldn't tell a dense hulk of metal twisted around your body and immobilizing your body to let you go.

Terry's assessment of the experience of sexual violence relies on criteria of suffering graded by her own life history, sense of agency, and her own personhood. In effect, Laura and Terry produce their own "oh shit" scales; this tactic is not Polly's alone.

I place the examples of Terry and Laura beside Polly's to draw a few similarities and differences. There is a danger here in glossing all of these emergences of particular criterial structures as elaborate rationalizations or psychological resistances. In fact, at a conference where I presented this material an audience member once suggested to me that Laura's folding together of three instances of bad luck is actually a form of denying the pain of sexual assault. I am not interested in diagnosing Laura's "real feelings" because the anthropological goal lies in examining the underlying social structures and technologies through which Laura's narrative is nurtured or suffocated. What's more, in the anthropological discipline, people are not considered crystalline containers in whom true thoughts can be deciphered as if some type of text. I have only Laura's account of herself and her utterance through which to understand that, in the moment of our encounter, a meaningful set of criteria emerged through which she could have some insight into her experience of violence. Similarly, I am not suggesting that forensic nurse examiners, faced with the pain of managing the suffering of sexual assault victims, resist feeling by automatically replacing emotional criteria with "rational" ones. Rather, my argument is that forensic professionalism requires forensic nurse examiners to bracket one set of assessment by applying other standards, and that these criteria are ostensibly demonstrated in the course of forensic examiner training. Considering Terry's and Laura's observations alongside Polly's may deflect accusations of insensitivity. There is, however, an important difference to note amid the criterial scales by which the three individuals qualitatively gauge the experience of sexual violence. This is based on referents by which a scale is configured. While Terry recalls accidents, and Laura instances of bad luck, Polly's criteria for establishing an "oh shit" scale draw on her experiences as a registered nurse, and are not simply limited to her practice as a forensic nurse examiner. This store of medical experience is one of which registered nurses are frequently reminded during their forensic nurse examiner training and certification processes. In this manner, they are trained to distance themselves from the emotional labors of caring for rape victims in part by relativizing suffering vis-à-vis other forms of pain and misfortune encountered in nursing practice.

The eye that weeps and the eye that sees may be one and the same,[23] but the forensic nurse will, analogically, defer or submerge her weeping because she retreats to a position from which she may only discern her own eye as one that sees for the law. The moment that Kelly feels unsympathetic toward Sierra because of Sierra's decision not to take an emergency contraceptive, she falls back to the question of whether Sierra's statement is true or false. The opening question, of whether Kelly dislikes Sierra because she is black, is still unanswered. I end with it because Sierra discerned Kelly's regard of suspicion and mistrust for her. This suspicion and distrust may be grounded in forensic practice precisely because of its legal (and not medical) investment in establishing whether a statement is true or false. This is but one way in which the legal and medical are conflated as both discourse and practice, producing a uniquely forensic mode. The forensic strategy is also staked in replacing one set of criteria with another as a strategy for overcoming the challenge of one's own emotional distress and moving on with the task at hand. In this exchange, the delicate apparatus through which a moment of misunderstanding emerges is evident. The institutional structure of the sexual assault intervention, and its location at the juncture of law and medicine and within the particular geographical and historical contours of Baltimore as a locality, introduces a number of different conditions that comprise the possibilities that then generate misunderstanding, hurt, and allegations of racism. When sexual assault victims put the name of racism to their sense of oppression within the forensic encounter, they are marking the structure of feeling that has emerged in the distilled residue of the organization of forensic intervention over and above the institutional and ideological organization of the intervention (Williams 1977: 126–27). An affective gradient characterized by racial prejudice certainly emerges as a facet of the structure of feeling of forensic intervention. It is neither a product of explicit forensic pedagogy, nor attributable to a single structural feature. Rather, the experience of racism is generated by the convergence of a number of factors, and it is neither real nor imagined, but dispersed and refracted through institutional and pedagogical intersections (Jackson 2007). While the law is alleged to be universal and color-blind, the affective gradient of forensic intervention includes an extra-legal surplus to which racially marked supplicants have potential recourse.

Forensic nurse examiners face daily difficulties in their chosen vocation. They are evaluated on their technical expertise, which they openly seek to maintain and improve and for which they receive pedagogical support in the form of mentors, course proctors, and funds dedicated to their annual re-training. They must also manage the stress, excitement, and agonized aspects of the career—to be a forensic nurse is to have a particular emotional mastery and control. Emotional mastery is more surreptitiously "learned" in the course of practical training. By focusing on establishing juridical truths in the forensic encounter, forensic nurse examiners can often sidestep the unsettling nature of the cases they see on a daily basis. In emphasizing juridical criteria, sexual assault victims are made to feel that forensic nurses either trust or distrust their statements, and this can contribute to easing or tensing face-to-face relations between victims and examiners. When learning how to expertly treat sexual assault victims, ostensive lessons instill an emphasis on juridical criteria and juridical truth when faced with accounts of violence, allowing forensic nurse examiners to avoid the question of trust altogether. The emphasis on fact does not necessarily free sexual assault victims from experiences of pain or fear, as they are encumbered by the consequences of the violence, as well as the burden of recounting events for legal posterity, and feeling as though they are found worthy or unworthy juridical subjects.

4

Re/production

Articulating Paths to Healing and Justice

If the law always demands the production of a body and this body is already constituted as a socio-legal subject (Das 2006b: 95), rape trials are particularly exacting in their stipulations for the constituting of the sexually violated body. The legal subjectivity of sexual assault victims depends on a narrowly bound imagination of a reproductive future, which the victim must subsequently enact by the adoption of a particular attitude toward conception and contraception. Studies of mass rape have clearly established a link between sexual violence and reproductive violence. Sexual assault emerges as "occupation of the womb" (Fisher 1996: 91); "biological warfare" (Allen 1996: 42); and "genocidal" (Mackinnon 1993, 1994).[1] Women's bodies appear as one more theater of war, and reproductive violence jeopardizes the futures of large collective entities, such as tribes, nations, ethnic and religious communities. How is the future at stake in cases of "individual" or "peace-time" rape? When reproductive violence appears in the literature on rape, it tends to focus only on reproduction as parturition. The politics of reproduction is addressed through lively and rich conversations within anthropological literature (Ginsburg and Rapp 1991, 1995). Reproduction describes a range of topics, including "parturition, Marxist notions of household sustenance and constitution of a labor force, and ideologies that support the continuity of social systems" (Ginsburg and Rapp 1991: 311). As this chapter demonstrates, all of these understandings of reproduction figure within the sexual assault intervention.

For sexual assault victims in the emergency room, engaging reproduction as a question of livelihood produces an understanding of the reproductive future that may be disrupted by sexual violence.[2] In part, there is also a legal future at stake, and forensic nurse examiners must manage victims' reproductive potentials and possibilities in order to bring the victim into being as a legal subject. In rape cases, this relates largely to the question of consent. The forensic examination produces proof of non-consent through technological intervention. Marilyn Strathern has written about the proliferation of technologically mediated reproduction, such as in vitro fertilization, as the reproduction of desire (Strathern 1995: 354–55). In sexual assault intervention, technological mediation in the form of emergency contraception tracks victims' desires. As in the case of Sierra in the previous chapter, to refuse emergency contraception is to invite a forensic nurse's distrust.

My encounters with victims in the emergency room were striking in that they revealed that the violence of rape in their lives often built on the preexisting everyday violence of their intimate relations. Practitioners and scholars often treat sexual violence, like other violent traumas, as a singular event characterized by massive rupture of social relations (Brison 2002; Hirsch 2007). Unfortunately, sexual violence can occur frequently and repeatedly in the lives of many men and women in Baltimore, Maryland. While my research was based in Baltimore, this dynamic extends across other social and economic margins in the United States. Victims' framing of the event of sexual assault in relationship to already fragile, meaningful relationships suggests that they do not necessarily experience an absolute break between life before and after sexual violence. Rather, sexual violence unfolds into many ruptures and repairs. In the struggle to make and secure a life within a set of delicately nested relationships, victims face the potential of sexual violence to disrupt reproductive regimes. Sexual violence and subsequent interventions into sexual violence may wreak havoc on tremulous kinship relations while they interrupt access to livelihood. Consequently, victims consider the possibility of re-knitting or stabilizing already delicate social relations when deciding whether to participate in or withdraw from the legal process.

Emergency Contraception and the Consenting Subject

While medical science has progressed in its understanding of the mechanism through which conception takes place, the possibility of pregnancy continues to adhere to notions of consent to sex in the sexual assault investigation. The attitudes toward victims' ready acceptance of emergency contraception call to mind sixteenth- and seventeenth-century notions about rape and pregnancy in U.S. rape statutes (Hambleton 2001). Both popular belief and legal statutes held that no woman could become pregnant without mutual orgasm, and that orgasm, being of the mind and the body, was achieved only during consensual sex.[3] Thus, women who became pregnant after accusing men of rape were, in fact, seeking to preserve their honor and hide the fact of inappropriate or non-socially sanctioned consensual and pleasure-inducing sex. In contemporary sexual assault interventions, the contraceptive technology of the day has modernized this older shadow tradition of judging female consent by establishing the horizon for demonstrating a rational measure of withheld consent. The window for demonstrating that one has withheld consent extends from the moment of sexual assault to 72 to 120 hours into the future. Ovral and Plan B, the most popular forms of emergency contraception administered in sexual assault interventions, have been proven to work up to this long from the instant of introduction of sperm into the vaginal canal (Rodrigues, Grou, and Joly 2001; Von Hertzen, Piaggio, and Ding 2002). Despite the difference in time span in which a victim can indicate non-consent as a result of available contraceptive technologies, in general terms, the earlier formula holds: women who become pregnant have consented to sex.[4] Those who have truly expressed non-consent demonstrate their non-consent by opting to take emergency contraception.

With the development of new evidentiary technologies, has the ability of the forensic examiner superseded previous practices of analyzing the victim's character to surmise and judge the truthfulness of her accusation? Harriet Baber notes that "in the past, the burden of proof has been placed wrongfully on the victims of rape to show their respectability and their unwillingness, the assumption being that (heterosexual) rape is merely a sexual act rather than an act of violence and that sex acts can be presumed to be desired by the participants unless there is strong evidence to the contrary" (Baber 1987). While the burden of proof in rape trials has theoretically migrated from the question of the victim's (and assailant's) respectability to that of forensic practice and material evidence, available contraceptive technologies have reshaped consent. Within this regime of consent, locating indicators of the victim's respectability in her choices during the forensic examination has replaced the questioning of the victim's character by publicizing her sexual history.

Forensic nurses are alarmed and disapproving when victims assert their desires by opting out of emergency contraception or even simply deliberate for too long before taking the pills. Forensic nurse examiners act as and on behalf of the state; their concerns are the state's concerns. The intervention functions on several levels. First, it prevents the lives of children born from violence. It also serves to preempt a future marked with difficulty and stigma for such children and their mothers. In cases where women wish to prevent pregnancy, it restores rape victims' embodied sense of reproductive autonomy. Simultaneously, a rape victim's desire to take emergency contraception indicates her nonconsent; a refusal to take the pills may threaten the state's case against the alleged rapist. Thus, under the rubric of care, forensic nurses act as first-line arbiters of state interests.

The nexus between patient, medical authority, and emergency contraception generates an imagination of the opportunity for nurses to educate patients, even with respect to issues appearing outside of the bounds of sexual assault intervention. In her testimony against making emergency contraception available without prescription, Susan Crockett stated, "As an OB-GYN I'm going to go down kicking and screaming before I allow somebody to break that relationship between myself and my patients, because I value the education component so much in the relationship I have with my patients" (Wynn and Trussell 2006: 304). For forensic nurse examiners, the sexual assault intervention serves as a venue for educating the victim into the appropriate legal subjectivity. Willingness and enthusiasm to take emergency contraception crystallize one's lack of consent and materialize the appropriate regimes of desire.

In both the clinic and the emergency room, patients are subjected to numerous conditions in order to access emergency contraception. With reference to women who must access emergency contraceptives from their healthcare providers, Lisa Wynn and James Trussell conclude:

> Prescription status for [emergency contraceptive pills] reinforces medical authority in several ways: by making the health care provider the

> ultimate arbiter of a woman's access to the drug, by mandating the doctor as a principal beneficiary in the economy of the health care transaction (because a woman does not pay just for the drug but also for the prescription, which usually costs more than the drug itself); and by requiring the woman to submit to any additional procedures (ranging from a pregnancy test to a pelvic exam to a pap smear to STI testing) and expert advice (from a discussion about ongoing contraceptive use to a discussion about sexual risk taking to one about mechanism of action of [emergency contraceptive pills] and their potential effect on a fertilized egg) the doctor decides to impose. (2006: 305)

The battery of procedural interventions is even greater in the case of sexual assault victims, whose willingness to submit to other examination procedures further consolidates their credibility. Because victims of sexual assault are also consumers of healthcare, forensic nurse examiners sometimes voice suspicions that allegations of rape may be a ploy to access free emergency contraception. Other forensic nurse examiners insist that while they never assume that a would-be victim would fabricate rape allegations for this reason, they fear that the defense attorney may do so. By subjecting sexual assault victims to a succession of invasive procedures, many of which are unpleasant, inconvenient, painful, or humiliating, forensic nurse examiners guarantee the veracity of the patient's status as victim. As outlined in chapter 1, full cooperation may include ingesting bad-tasting medications, eating and drinking food only when sanctioned to do so by the forensic nurse examiners, providing urine samples or resisting the urge to use the toilet, tolerating the pain and discomfort of hair plucking and a speculum examination, and enduring the cold of the examination room. These measures constitute the conditions under which emergency contraception must be administered in order to produce a credible sexual assault victim (Corrigan 2013a).

Preventing Pregnancy, Foreclosing the Reproduction of Violence

In addition to its role in the production of credibility and the corroboration of non-consent, emergency contraception functions to foreclose the production of children born from the violent encounter of rape. These stakes are as real in the state imaginary as are the burdens of shame and suffering that rape victims may actually feel in relation to potential pregnancy, not to mention the additional risks of sexually transmitted diseases and HIV/AIDS. As Veena Das describes the state policies with regard to unwanted women and children on both sides of the freshly drawn Pakistani and Indian border following partition, national honor demanded a practical approach to kinship such that national agendas came to be aligned with personal shame and honor (Das 1995). The state attempted to recover "abducted" women regardless of these women's desires, and while the nation received them and their children, there was no possibility to place those "recovered" citizens with their families where they were no longer deemed marriageable. These realities gave rise to new institutional arrangements where unwanted women and children could reside, having survived their "successful" repatriation.

One need not look to large-scale postwar historical examples to understand that being conceived as a result of sexual violence introduces many complications to one's social life. Sierra's case in the previous chapter is one indication that there is something distasteful to the forensic nurse examiner in Sierra's desire for maternity. Sierra's maternal aspirations and her expression of bodily autonomy in her desire for pregnancy do not operate to offset the violence of paternity. The fear of paternal violence also echoes in the concerns of a couple dreading the day when their adopted child might demand to know the identity of his biological parents. Would they disclose the fact of his parentage, that his father raped his mother, in response to the child's query (Goodfellow 2002)?

In chapter 2, I discuss the case of Keisha, whose mother expressed grave misgivings over the nurse administering the emergency contraception to her daughter. The mother was specifically concerned that taking emergency contraception would impair her daughter Keisha's future reproductive capacity. Her tone and specific concern did not seem out of place in the context of the depth and living memory of African American patients' distrust of medical practitioners in Baltimore, particularly in relation to involuntary sterilization of African American women (Roberts 1997; Terrel et al. 2004). In this particular case, however, the perpetrator was Keisha's biological father. In the nurse's view, the horror of incest and the burden of a child impregnated by her biological father outweighed any concerns that the mother might have. For the mother, neither horror diminished the other: subjecting Keisha's already violated body to the further damage of uncertain medical technologies demanded serious deliberation. Under Maryland statutes, the decision regarding emergency contraception, along with the decision to participate in the forensic examination, was left to Keisha alone while her mother was proscribed from attending the forensic examination or being present when Keisha made the decision to take the emergency contraception. When the nurse offered Keisha emergency contraception, she immediately indicated her wish to take it.

Keisha's assent to the forensic nurse examiner's offer of emergency contraception reveals the future she and the forensic nurse examiner wish to avert. In the immediate future, Keisha would return to her mother's home, the site of chronic sexual abuse. Perhaps in Keisha's deliberation, being pregnant and being a teenager herself in her present household carried with it the threat of introducing or exposing a(nother) child to rape at the hands of her father. The forensic nurse examiner's delivery of care required Keisha and Sierra to avert the potential future violation of birthing and raising children conceived in violence. In addition, the shame of the sexual assault victim is unfailingly associated with the desire for emergency contraceptives and disgust at the idea of potentially carrying a child fathered by a man with whom one did not consent to have sex. In both cases, perpetrators were identified as men with whom the women had no consensual sexual relationship.

Keisha readily rejected the possibility of pregnancy and assented to emergency contraception in a manner that could be interpreted as properly expressing revulsion and disgust. Sierra, on the other hand, separated the possibility of maternity from the conditions under which conception might have occurred. By refusing emergency contraception and telling the nurse that she had been thinking of having a child for some time now and therefore "wouldn't mind" getting pregnant, she did not adequately express disgust and refusal in a way that was, perhaps, recognizable to a hypothetical jury of her peers.[5] Her insistence that she might fulfill her maternal desire points to the potential of the continued force of the violence of rape through the person of the child born of rape.[6] Additionally, in her effort to connect with the forensic nurse examiner, who she also suspected was unsympathetic to her because of the lack of evidence in her case, Sierra pledged to do a better job of preserving evidence by not showering if ever she was raped again. This promise shows that, in addition to her unwillingness to preempt the violation of pregnancy, Sierra does not give any assurances that she will be able to avoid falling victim to the violence of rape in the future.

While pregnancy and paternity testing have provided evidence to prove or disprove sexual assault cases in instances where perpetrators insist that there was no sexual contact between them and the victim, resorting to a paternity test is uncommon. Given the average six- to twelve-month time span that a typical rape case takes to go to court in Baltimore, if it is indeed on that trajectory, a pregnancy resulting from the sexual assault could be prominently visible in the early period of the average time span. How would a court of law perceive a 24- or 36-week pregnant sexual assault victim? As prosecutorial evidence, the sign of her swollen body would at best be interpreted as the failure of contraceptive measures and the continued incursion of violence against her person. If, however, the victim refused to take emergency contraception, the prosecutor may fear that the victim's consent to pregnancy was, or could seem to the jury, inseparable from her consent to participate in the sexual act. Whether this narrative holds any truth is inconsequential, as a clever defense attorney can suggest such to the jury without any bearing on how closely such a narrative aligns with the victim's actual desires.

Victims as Parents and Children: Embedded Relationships

While forensic nurse examiners offer emergency contraception in order to prevent sexual assault victims from becoming parents to children conceived in violence, sexual assault victims do not seek to avert the same futures that forensic nurse examiners imagine. Rather, victims' strategies take into account already fragile relationships fraught with violence, separation, and privation. Just as therapeutic processes come to have juridical weight in the course of sexual assault intervention, victims regard their participation and cooperation in the sexual assault intervention in relation to their fragile family relations. For some, the legal aspects of the intervention offered vindication and guarantees of more secure living conditions for themselves, their parents, children, or loved ones. In other circumstances, pursuing legal action could easily place burdens on the family that threaten to create more fractures rather than mend rifts. Finally, for those victims who saw neither an advantage nor disadvantage in pursuing legal action, participation in the intervention brought attention to the past, present, and potential vulnerabilities of the victim's network of care.

One afternoon in early September, I arrived at the hospital, having been summoned in my capacity as rape crisis advocate. I searched the usual places—the family waiting room, the examination room—but could not find Astrid, the woman I had been called in to see. I returned to the main waiting area where I noticed a miniscule woman hunched over a box of donuts. At first glance, she appeared to be an adolescent girl, but her drawn and gaunt face betrayed her slight physique. I cautiously approached her and asked, "Excuse me, would you happen to be Astrid?" She nodded, barely looking up from her donuts.

Astrid's case is quite striking in relation to those of other victims in that she related a tale of spending many years in preparation for death—potentially half of her life. Her body bore the tale of years upon years of hard drug use and suffering. Layers of scar tissue speckled every inch of her exposed skin. I was overwhelmed by the frailty of her bird-like body. Her fragile form did not, however, elicit much compassion from the emergency room staff as her body bore all the signs of heroin use. Astrid's every act, utterance, and gesture suggested drug-seeking behavior to the trained medical professional. Overall, the hospital staff was miserly with their kindness, and treated her with unusual coldness, with the sole exception of the forensic nurse examiner.

The first thing Astrid told me was that she was in a lot of pain. She had a large abscess on her right shoulder that needed attention. Her entire arm was turning an angry red color, and no one had examined it. She was upset as she had been waiting for quite some time, and though she had been through triage, no one had bothered to help her with her pain. Her demands for pain medication fell easily under the rubric of drug-seeking behavior, and attendant with her identity as "victim," the medical personnel, doctors and nurses included, took one look at Astrid and labeled her as "addict." It was this label that seemed to drive their interaction with her. Her abscess, then, was immediately assumed to have resulted from shooting up heroin, which, she conceded, was its cause. Her veins had all but disappeared, and a long, deep, wide scar on her right forearm showed where doctors had once operated to reach a vein from which they could extract blood and feed an intravenous catheter. It was hard to find any spots on Astrid's exposed skin that did not bear some sort of mark or scar. As stated earlier, the emergency room staff easily read these physical signs as indications of addiction and failed recovery. I, unfamiliar with how to read the signs on bodies typically traversing emergency rooms, did not recognize Astrid's body as that of a drug addict, though I noticed the discomfort that attended the manner in which the emergency room staff treated her. As an addict, they tacitly blamed Astrid for her current state of affairs. If she was experiencing physical pain, they seemed to imply that perhaps she deserved the anguish, and maybe some measure of physical discomfort would drive her away from her addiction.

There in the hospital, where pain medication was available, Astrid was allowed to suffer the physical pain of her abscess. On the floor of the main emergency room, many nurses, orderlies, and residents asked her, "Are you a user?" in loud, abrasive tones. Gloved hands gingerly handled her, whether from repulsion over the ever-swelling pustule threatening to burst open, or out of concern over infection. I also found myself repelled by her morbid physicality. I was cautious with my touch until I was shamed by the arrival of the forensic nurse who came to take Astrid's blood. Leah, the forensic nurse, was the first person who treated Astrid with compassion. Taking her blood was a daunting task as her veins were decimated from the heavy drug use. Leah slipped on a pair of gloves and began to palpate Astrid's arms. After a few minutes without any success, she shrugged and said, "I can't feel anything through these gloves," threw the gloves aside, and proceeded to handle Astrid's arms directly, her fingertips pressing into Astrid's arm, feeling for a vein from which she could draw blood. The simple act of removing her gloves drew a clear response from Astrid. Her eyes no longer wandered about the room, nor did she stare down at the floor. For the first time, she looked Leah in the eyes and became interested in what she was doing. When Leah retreated to take the blood for laboratory processing, I offered Astrid my hand.

Signs of Astrid's past and present health deficiencies were numerous, some subtle and others more obvious: dark circles under her eyes, yellowed and mottled skin, a raspy voice, an obvious tracheotomy scar on her throat. Indeed, the slightness of her body, the way her rheumy skin clung tightly to her bones, gave her the appearance of a body wasting away from within. Astrid attributed the marked signs of her rapidly declining health to her HIV-positive status. "I have been positive since the age of 17," Astrid told me. Still reeling in disbelief at her present circumstances, Astrid wondered about the man who had raped her: her mother's boyfriend who happened to be her own boyfriend's brother. "Why would he do it knowing I was positive?" she queried in anguish. The question of Astrid's survival extended beyond the instance of rape in question. Many victims express disbelief of their survival of the attack, and crisis counselors are taught to reaffirm the fact of survival and reinforce that emergence from this "episode" of rape is the first sign that they will be able to go on with their lives.[7] Astrid moved me to think beyond this frame as her concerns about her own survival were neither past, nor imagined. They were real, they were looming, and they were not going to go away. Nor was the project of survival one that she limited to concern for her own failing body.

Over the course of hours that I attended Astrid, a more complete picture of her circumstances began to emerge—raped as a child by her stepfather, she turned to drug use when her mother did not believe her. She learned she had contracted HIV at the age of 17, and had grown sicker and sicker as the years passed. She had three children, lost her first husband, and had been with her current boyfriend for nine years. Her mother refused to believe that this rape was not seduction, and Astrid wept copiously as she argued with her mother on the phone. She had been in the hospital countless times, including two years ago when she had been in a coma for 45 days. Her left lung had collapsed in one of her many bouts with pneumonia, and she had been in many methadone treatment programs. She told me she was dying of AIDS, and the doctors who had treated her had expressed to her their disbelief over her continued survival.

Following the forensic examination, Astrid still had not had her abscess treated, and it eventually erupted, spilling copiously onto the bed and floor. "Whoa," she chirruped, caught off guard, her eyes full of tears. "I think it feels a little better." "You're whole body is crying, see," I told her, provoking a small laugh. With blood and pus pooling on the bed and floor beneath her, Astrid was still unable to catch a resident's attention. I intervened at this point, excusing myself and knocking on the door to the Forensic Nursing Office where Leah was preparing her evidentiary report. As I had interrupted her in the middle of her documentation, she was not very warm. "Astrid's abscess just opened up and it is a big mess," I explained. "No one seems able to help her; could you please take a look at it?" Leah immediately paused and followed me back to the emergency room. After taking a preliminary look at the abscess, she literally grabbed a passing resident and asked her to attend to Astrid's arm. The resident cleaned Astrid's arm and lightly bandaged it so it could continue to drain. When Astrid continued to insist she was still in pain and needed some medication, she was told that she would first have to get an X-ray, and then it would be determined whether to prescribe pain medication. Her pleas to acknowledge the pain of her life seemed to be ignored by the hospital staff. Her addiction and sorrow were read as deficiencies of character, not as a testament to the hardships with which she struggled. Even her recent trauma of rape was treated as a symptom of her addiction.

Astrid's history of rape intertwines with the tropes of incest and seduction. In the complex blending of drug use, HIV status, incest, rape, and seduction, we see how criminality is folded into kinship (Das, Ellen, and Leonard 2007: 11). As a member of her mother's household, she has not been protected from the unwanted attentions of her mother's boyfriends. In one case, she was only a child, and now, nearly 20 years later, she is again subjected to forced sex. Her mother does not react to either instance as a rape, accuses Astrid of betraying her by seducing both men. The fraternal relationship between Astrid's and her mother's boyfriends further blurs the line between seduction and rape. The order of intergenerational relationships is confounded by the lovers' status as brothers. Astrid's boyfriend, she told me, was absolutely infuriated with his brother, and had not been home per her requests. "He just wants to beat him up, and I don't want him to go to jail, so I just told him to stay away from the house."

The existence of her own daughter complicated Astrid's attitudes toward her tense and embroiled household. Astrid mentioned her daughter early on during our conversation. Whipping a photo out of her wallet, she showed me a lovely girl of 16. "She is not HIV-positive," she told me several times. Astrid had recently received custody of her daughter. When I asked her if her daughter was with her mother, Astrid looked at me incredulously and responded, "She's at a friend's place." It was clear that Astrid had no intention of introducing her daughter to her mother's household. She lived in fear of having her daughter removed from her custody, and/or placed with her mother. "She is so smart, and she's so good at school," Astrid the proud parent beamed. Astrid's concerns about her future revolved around surviving until her daughter was self-sufficient and could secure her own livelihood, while shielding her daughter from her mother's household. Thus, Astrid lived in her mother's house so that she could funnel what would have been her own rent money to her daughter. She forbade her boyfriend from returning to the house, also the crime scene, in the name of preserving the peace and keeping him from being imprisoned. She worried about the forensic examination preventing her from reporting to her methadone program—she had been doing very well keeping off of heroin for the past week and feared a relapse. It is plain that neither access to emergency contraception, nor an educational message about making "the right choices," can meet Astrid's concerns about her family and its reproductive future. Rape here is not a "rupture" in an otherwise orderly life; it signals yet another fraught encounter for a woman who navigates an already threatening and tumultuous daily life.

Sexual Assault Victims Learning the Law

As victims become aware of how their livelihoods and reproductive futures come to hang in the balance, they struggle as well with the role of law in these shifts. Sexual assault victims also draw on a range of legal experiences in making decisions about how to comport themselves throughout the course of sexual assault investigations and prosecutorial processes. As Patricia Ewick and Susan Silbey have established, individuals draw on a range of experiences, events, conflicts, and institutions in navigating law's common places (Ewick and Silbey 1998). These experiences can also inform the "feel" of particular legal encounters, underpinning the legal consciousness of rape victims as they navigate the system (Merry 1990). Thus, a rape victim need not have a previous understanding or encounter with the legal processes surrounding a sexual assault investigation in order to draw on other legal experiences to inform her sense of what may or may not happen in the course of her participation in the criminal justice process. Many of the experiences that comprise victims' legal repertoires in Baltimore, Maryland relate to their status as parents and children, wards of state, and subjects of social service intervention. Maryland's Department of Health and Human Services reported that 9,074 children were in foster care in January 2009. Nationally, 400,540 children were in foster-care placements as of September 30, 2011 (Child Welfare Information Gateway 2013). As commonplace as experiences with and in foster care may be, legal scholars have emphasized the intense preparation that police and state's attorneys put into coaching sexual assault victims for participation in the legal process without exploring broader contexts of victim legal subjectivity (Kerstetter 1990; Konradi 1997). In addition to being wards of state or having their children taken into foster care, many victims also recounted experiences of arrest or incarceration. In general, victims who had been arrested or incarcerated in the past asked questions more frequently and forcefully than victims who have had no similar experience of arrest or incarceration. On the other hand, victims who have been wards of state tended to view the legal apparatus with more trepidation, deferring to the forensic nurse examiner, police officer, or attorney. The experiences upon which sexual assault victims draw, consciously or unconsciously, not only reside in abstract memory, but are associated with particular spaces in which these encounters have taken place over the years (Ewick and Silbey 1998).

Looking into victims' legal histories troubles the assumed specificity of the status of sexual assault victims within sociological, anthropological, and socio-legal studies (Das 2002). I avoid the singular typification of sexual assault victims as an exceptional legal subject position unrelated to any prior legal experiences that a person has had. I also want to complicate the notion that sexual assault victims are solely motivated by their traumatized states in the aftermath of sexual assault and rape, particularly in their concerns about how to initiate a "recovery" from the violence they have suffered (Campbell 2001b; Cosgrove 2000; Des Rosiers, Feldthusen, and Hankivsky 1998; Winkler 1994). The future the victim imagines is based on a broad understanding of her reproductive possibilities, while being rooted in her complex legal subjectivity.

As stated earlier, sexual assault victims typically raised the topic of four categories of legal experience within the context of the forensic examination. Though often unprompted, they sometimes mentioned experiences as a response to an open-ended question from the forensic nurse examiner. The four categories are: (1) previous involvement in another sexual assault or rape case either as a victim, friend, or witness;[8] (2) arrest, prosecution, and incarceration for committing a crime;[9] (3) participation in the sale or consumption of illegal substances; and 4) playing a role in a child custody case either as parent, child, or guardian. I take two cases here, that of Dennis and Rachel, to illustrate the layers of meaning and experience they each pondered in order to navigate the criminal justice system and their current roles in the system as victims of sexual assault (Menon 2000). Rachel and Dennis are comparable in two ways. First, family members victimized them. Second, they acted with concern to preserve already fragile family relationships, and to secure their own livelihoods. Carcerality touches on both their lives, but unfolds differently in each case.

A Visit to the State's Attorney

Rachel called me one Friday morning and asked if I could give her a ride to the state's attorney's office. She had a 10:00 a.m. appointment, and since she had been staying with her best friend in a hard-to-reach suburb 20 minutes outside of Baltimore City, she would need transportation in order to make it to the meeting on time. Her grandmother had called her frantically the night before to tell Rachel she had just received a letter saying that if she did not get in contact with the state's attorney by Friday, her case would be dismissed and all charges against her uncle would be dropped. Rachel had reported being sexually assaulted by her uncle when she visited him in a halfway house:

> I hardly knew my Uncle George. But my father asked me to get to know him, so I did. Me and my cousin, Violet, we went over to see him once. I didn't really know him all that much, and one of my aunts told me he had messed with another one of my cousins, but I didn't pay her any mind before. He asked me if Violet and I needed anything, and I said, "Uncle George, get me a job. Any job. I can cook, type, work a cash register."

> And he said, "You and Violet should dance." And I didn't say anything because I didn't know him and I thought that was a weird thing to say to your niece. But I didn't say anything—I just started talking about something else. (Interview 8/22/2005)

Uncle George was a recent addition to Rachel's life, as he had previously been estranged from her father. Now that he had been released from prison, the family was making efforts to reconnect with him. In Rachel's description of her first meeting with her uncle, she asked him for assistance finding a job in response to his offers to perform a familial favor for her. When Uncle George suggested to Rachel that she and Violet might try to earn a living as strippers, Rachel changed the subject:

> Come to find out that sometimes he smokes. Well, I was trying to be careful after that stripper comment and the thing my aunt said, later, but I had run out of money so he invites me to his room to smoke and give me some money so I can buy my own stuff, and that's when things happened. And I just couldn't believe it because I kept thinking "That's my uncle!" (Interview 8/22/2005)

Rachel found that she and her uncle shared an interest in smoking marijuana. When her uncle invited her to his room to smoke with him, she had accepted the invitation. Once in the room, he had locked the door and undressed completely. Rachel had been very forthcoming about the role of marijuana in her case. She had voluntarily disclosed everything to the police and state's attorney.

When Rachel called to tell me about her appointment with the state's attorney, she sounded nervous and eager. "I just want to get it over with!" she blurted out emphatically when I asked her how she felt about the impending meeting, "I'm so nervous!" She paused, and I felt she was teetering on the verge of a question, so I asked her whether she wanted me to go with her to the state's attorney's office. "Please!" she answered quickly and loudly, "Would you go?"

The drive from Rachel's place to the city offices of the state's attorney was about 30 minutes. It took us an additional 10 minutes to find parking, and then another 5 minutes to walk up to the courthouse where the attorney's offices were located. As we approached the courthouse, the physical signs of Rachel's nervousness became more and more obvious. She grew quiet and tense, her lips jammed together in a thin, tight line. Her arms began to shake and she cast her eyes downward. She smiled briefly at the security guard when he gestured at the sign indicating we could not bring any firearms or other weapons into the courthouse and then had us empty our pockets before passing through the metal detector. As we entered the elevator, Rachel leaned against a wall for support. I became concerned that she would pass out or fall over, as she appeared to be wobbly.

"Did I tell you that courthouses make me really nervous?" she asked in the elevator, straightening out and tugging her t-shirt into place as she stood without the support of the wall. I asked her why she thought that might be. "I don't know. Last time I came to court it was cause I got caught stealing. May be that's why I don't like courts." We exited the elevator into a quiet and stagnant hallway lined with oil paintings of the city's venerated judges. A sign pointed us to the sex offense prosecution unit, and we made our way to a suite of corner offices. The office ceiling seemed low, and the window gave the appearance of being in a garret. We were eventually led down a long narrow hallway by an Assistant State's Attorney into one of the very small offices, where Rachel was interviewed.

During the meeting, the attorney very methodically probed Rachel's legal history, and then proceeded to widen his scrutiny from Rachel to her friends and relatives who he viewed as potential witnesses should the case go forward. About three quarters of an hour into his meeting with her, he segued from discussion of Rachel's allegations to what would happen if the case were to go forward. He emphasized that the final decision to prosecute would be his.

He began by asking Rachel if she had a record. "Yes sir. I am on probation for shoplifting." He asked her to recount the events leading to her arrest. Rachel explained how a few days following her eighteenth birthday, her cousin Lindsey had called and invited her to go get some clothes:

> We went to the mall and into this store and tried all these clothes on. When we knew what we wanted, I said, "Lindsey, how are we going to pay for all this," and she said we weren't going to. And I was like, "wha . . . ?!" (Interview 9/26/2005)

Nevertheless, Rachel went along with Lindsey, and they were caught while attempting to leave the store with all the merchandise. Rachel hadn't known that Lindsey had planned to steal the clothes until they were ready to "check out." The state's attorney asked whether Rachel had a juvenile record. "No, sir. Just the shoplifting."

He shook his head incredulously following Rachel's story. "You waited until after you turned 18 to get caught shoplifting?" Rachel's stupidity should be obvious to us all, according to the attorney's logic. The more sensible legal subject, he seemed to imply, would have committed the crime prior to turning 18. His incredulity at the timing of Rachel's shoplifting bespoke a practical frustration, as he believed it easier to present to the jury a victim with an unblemished criminal record.[10]

With only the one charge against her, the state's attorney continued to probe. One by one, he addressed each of the persons in whom Rachel had confided following the sexual assault, asking about whether her best friend and her mother had ever been convicted of any crimes. "Tell me about your friend, Eartha. Does she have a record?" Eartha was Rachel's best friend and ex-girlfriend with whom Rachel was staying. Eartha, Rachel told the attorney, also had a criminal record. She had been convicted on multiple counts of drug possession and dealing. The state's attorney seemed unsurprised though slightly disappointed. "What about your mother, what is her situation? Would she testify?" he asked while looking at the paperwork pertaining to Rachel's case, as if looking down a list. Rachel grew silent and seemed to be weighing out a few possibilities in her mind. A few uncomfortable seconds passed as the attorney awaited her response. Rachel suddenly took on a look of resignation. "Well, the thing about my mother is there is a warrant for her arrest for violating parole, so I don't know if she would or not." The attorney nodded and did not say much. He seemed to make a few calculations of his own. "We'll need both your mother and Eartha to testify. Can you tell me how to contact them?" Rachel gave Eartha's contact information to the attorney, but withheld her mother's, telling him that she would check with her mother, Tina, and call him back that day.

An hour and a half later, we emerged from the office. Rachel's eyes were red-rimmed and swollen from crying, though her body shook less than when we had first entered. We made our way back to the elevator to ride to the ground floor and exit the building. In the elevator lobby,

Rachel stepped out of the elevators, walked a few steps, and then turned and regarded the elevator from which we had exited with a newfound interest. She frowned as she explained her reaction:

> Actually, I think I remember the last time I came to this building. It was when they took us away from my mother and my grandmother got custody. It was when my brothers and I became wards of the state. It was this actual courthouse. (Field Note 9/17/2005)

She seemed resigned as she shook her head and turned to continue her departure.

Almost two months later, Rachel phoned me to see if we could meet and talk. We sat next to a lake in the nearby suburb where she had moved. She was working at a local fast food chain and had recently opened a bank account. The audio recording of our chat that afternoon is filled with the sound of wind and Rachel's frequent pauses to remark on the beauty of the day, the locale, and her perception of distance from Baltimore. As soon as we sat down on the dock, Rachel told me she had called the state's attorney the day before and told him she could not move forward with the case. "Are you disappointed?" she asked me. I assured her I was not disappointed and asked her to tell me what had brought her to the moment.

> Well, I talked to my dad and he was so sad about the whole thing and really wanted me to forgive my uncle. And things out here have just been going so well. I really love working and I love my job. I am saving a little money and it is so pretty out here. And my uncle just got out of prison, so this would mean breaking parole.

Rachel's withdrawal from the case guaranteed that her recently reunited family could continue to reconcile for the time being. Her ability to put in many long hours at her job was partly achieved through her ability to avoid traveling to Baltimore. Asking her boss for time off every time she had an appointment with the state's attorney was not possible. Though she did not say as much, discontinuing the legal case also spared her mother and her best friend from having to testify. Though both had been willing to testify, this would almost certainly have meant imprisonment for her mother. Her mother was currently the sole caretaker of Rachel's infant brother, only seven months old, and Rachel had often spoken fiercely of her love for her brother and mother. Rachel also included her job among those things she passionately adored.

> I love it. Love, love, love it. If I could work every day, I would. I don't know what I like about it. I just like putting on the uniform, going in, and being *busy*! There is nothing on my mind when I am at work. I am just at work. When I just sit around, have no place to go, nothing to do, that is when I get sad.

The possibility of a future without violence was linked to continued opportunities to make a living. In addition to the crassness of Uncle George's remark that Rachel might become a "dancer," Rachel's uncle betrayed the bond of kinship toward Rachel by denying her help in securing a livelihood. It seems that Rachel's stability and happiness, as well as her willingness to keep the peace by withdrawing from participation in the case against Uncle George, were contingent on her continued and regular access to gainful employment. A steady job both regularized her economic life and steadied her kinship relations, in addition to providing a comfortable rhythm to the day-to-day. It also presented a hurdle to moving her legal case forward.

Fleeing and Forming Family

"After I am done talking to you, I am going to call my lawyer and sue the police for brutality. They made the officer who did this to me take me to the hospital, and when he found out it was actually broken, he was all sorry. Still, I am going to sue him." The first time I met Dennis, he had called and asked me to pick him up from the hospital. His left arm was in a cast. He had just been discharged for a broken arm, an injury he told me he had sustained from rough handling by a police officer who arrested him for loitering the previous day.

Dennis explained to me the situation that he found himself in at the age of 11. He reported that this was the age at which he knew that he no longer wanted to live with his mother and stepfather.

> Well, it started when I was nine. It started when I was nine years old, and my mother met this guy. About six to eight months after she met him, he moved in. And right away, things started happening with me. Do you want to go into detail or—? When I was nine, my stepfather started playing these games with me. We used to wrestle around a lot, and he would play this game where we would cover each other in baby oil. And we were wrestling, and we'd wrestle each other to the ground, and the game was to see who could masturbate the other way into ejaculation. And that progressed into oral sex, and that progressed, when I was ten years old, to being forced to have anal sex. It was going on until I was eleven, when I left. Along with having sex with me, he was having sex with my sisters. He was making me have sex with my sisters and him.

Dennis's stepfather had subjected him and his older sisters to severe sexual abuse for several years. Frustrated with the escalating frequency and intensity of the sexual abuse at home and a lack of other options for relief, Dennis told me that he decided to run away from home and stay away until he was 18 years old. During the interview, I noted that Dennis quickly shifted from the intensities characterizing his experience of sexual victimization, to his imminent concerns about how to survive and make a living as a runaway.

Knowing he would likely have to live on the streets for a while, Dennis decided to move to Florida. He felt the warmer weather would make homelessness more bearable.

> I started studying a map for the best route to Florida. I started saving up my money. At first I was going to save up money and take a cab and get out of town, and hitchhike from there.

Upon reaching Miami, Florida, Dennis called his mother from a pay phone. When she answered he said, "Mom, it's Dennis. I'm alive and okay," and promptly hung up. Over the next few years, he made these calls every 6 to 8 months or sometimes less, just so his mother would know he was still alive.

To support himself, Dennis tried panhandling, petty theft, and then settled into the drug trade. His association with drug traffickers began only a few months after his arrival in Florida. Like many of the homeless children he knew, he worked as a delivery boy, and over the years, his role shifted until he was selling drugs himself. In the course of illicitly earning his livelihood in the drug trade, Dennis developed a drug addiction. He developed a caring relationship with Hank, the man he worked for, who suggested that a 16-year-old Dennis move to a small town in South Carolina.

> I stayed in Florida, on and off, until I was 16. The people I was working for—it's not a very lucrative lifestyle, he was a drug dealer, but he did care about us, and he put us up in a house and he gave us clothes and money. I had a brand new vehicle, I had a legitimate fake I.D., and he took care of us. And one of the other things he was giving us was a lot of drugs. So I was doing a lot of cocaine. When my boss found out, within two weeks, he had driven me to South Carolina, and gave me to some friends of his. Those people helped me get set up there, and introduced me to people around town, and set me up with an apartment. My boss kept tabs on me. I got cleaned up and stopped doing cocaine at the time. (Interview 6/20/2005)

Hank thought that Dennis could manage some of his local business interests while attending drug rehab. With Hank's support, Dennis was able to remain drug-free for over two years.

In the life story that Dennis relates, there are signals of his awareness of the law and his self-conscious relationship to it at various critical moments. In his telling, Dennis is attentive to the limited legal enfranchisement of himself as a child. The formulation of his plan returns him to the family only after reaching the age of 18, the age of legal adulthood. This dividing line is a potent and meaningful boundary for Dennis. It is the moment at which he can take responsibility for himself and resist the reign of adults, whether they have been inattentive to his suffering or perpetrated violence against him.

The fact of his restricted legal status as a child takes on meaning in his participation in the drug trade. Childhood is not simply marked by restricted rights, but also obligations, responsibilities, and capacities. For Dennis, childhood becomes a commodifiable asset he could use to seek gainful employment and secure a livelihood in a lucrative and illegal sector of the economy. While working as a deliverer of contraband, Dennis mentioned frequent run-ins with police officers. None of this would affect his permanent criminal record as he undertook this occupation prior to turning 18. Dennis was caught once and sent to a juvenile detention center to serve a sentence. Upon leaving the detention center, he later asked for his juvenile record to be expunged in order to give himself a "fresh start."

His awareness of the necessity of legal documents, such as an identification card, is expressed in his appreciation of the forgery with which Hank provides him. At the age of 18, Dennis did return to his mother in Maryland. In the course of his time away, his mother had separated from his stepfather, so Dennis did not feel the need to take further action. He had achieved the goal he had earlier set for himself, to shelter himself from his stepfather's abuse until he was an adult who was no longer under his mother and stepfather's guardianship. Having successfully stayed away, Dennis felt free to move on. It was not until a few years later that he and his sisters learned that his stepfather was in a relationship with a woman who had children. Upon learning this, Dennis convinced two of his sisters to tell their mother about the abuse. They went on to contact the police and filed a formal report against Dennis's stepfather (Mulla 2014).

Over the years, Dennis's mother had befriended the detective in charge of investigating Dennis's disappearance. Though the detective was no longer on the case when Dennis resurfaced after being away for seven years, Dennis's mother called him to share the news of Dennis's return. It was this detective who Dennis contacted to press charges against his stepfather. The detective had left the police force by this time, but still had friends and contacts with whom he quickly put Dennis in touch. When Dennis reported his stepfather to the police, things began to move very quickly. Within eight months, a trial date was set and the trial held over three days. Two of Dennis's sisters also testified about the sexual abuse, and their stepfather pled guilty before the trial had come to an end and was sentenced to seven years in prison. Shortly after the trial stopped, Dennis hired a lawyer who would help him get visitation rights to see his oldest child. The lawyer helped him to frame his request to his ex-girlfriend in a very compelling way. "She was in her 20s and I was 14 when we first started dating. The lawyer told her that if she tried to get sole custody and deny me visitation, he would raise the issue of statutory rape. I know it was an ugly tactic, but it worked, and without having to go to court."

Dennis always placed himself as a rights-bearing subject in relation to the law though variously a victim and an inmate. Even in his latest arrest, Dennis indignantly retaliated against the excessive use of force by the police officer who had taken him into custody. He did not voice any major objections to the grounds on which he had been arrested, except to briefly say that he felt the arrest had been based on arbitrary standards. It was his treatment by the police officers after he had been arrested that filled him with a sense of outrage.

His intention to file a suit against the police force, and the account of his custody battle with his eldest child's mother, revealed an orientation toward the law as a tool that could be used by him as readily as it could be used against him. Having been arrested and incarcerated a handful of times, Dennis was obviously aware of the moments when law had intervened into his life to hold him culpable for acts he had committed. In his telling, however, an awareness of the law and its potential uses seemed to be manifest from a very early age. Running away from home and only returning at the age of 18 pointed toward his sense of his limited legal enfranchisement as a child. At 18, he would have access to particular legal protections. Because the law defaults by recognizing a parent's right of custody of children, Dennis was vulnerable to his stepfather's abuses.

Dennis's characterization of the law was neither positive nor negative; it simply existed as a resource for him to access or resist, and was an institution with which he had much experience. When I asked him about the timing of his pressing charges against his stepfather, Dennis told me he had learned that his stepfather was living with young children, as I have already mentioned. Not wanting his stepfather to victimize any other children, Dennis filed a report and went through the process of giving a deposition and testifying in order to contribute toward his stepfather's conviction. Here we can see that, beyond the sense of law being wielded against or by Dennis, he also had an impression of law as wielded by the state for the benefit of the public good, and the protection of children, a protection he himself had not been afforded.

Dennis also cast figures embodying legal authority, such as police officers, within this understanding of law as a tool that could be put to work by him or against him (Temkin 1986).The police officer who had broken Dennis's arm, a menacing figure who had overstepped his legal authority in using excessive force when detaining Dennis, was at one end of the spectrum. On the other side was the police detective with whom Dennis's mother had forged a trusting relationship who later became an important resource in initiating the charges against Dennis's stepfather. Dennis displays a particular confidence in law and the boundaries that can be activated by invoking legal forms and negotiating family relationships through such legal formalities.

Preserving the Future of Fragile Relationships

The brief descriptions of the cases of Dennis and Rachel illustrate the dense web of social relations through which they are differently situated within the sexual assault intervention as sexual assault victims. These variables speak to how Dennis and Rachel will forge ahead in the future, as legal subjects and also in family relations. Though the period described follows the investigation stage of each case, at first glance, Dennis and Rachel's narratives feature three of the four typical legal experiences mentioned earlier in the chapter. Both of them have experienced arrest, and prosecution, though only Dennis discloses a period of incarceration. Both have in the past or present participated in the sale or consumption of illegal substances. Finally, both have played a part in custody cases, Dennis as a parent, and Rachel as a child.

These recollections have surfaced not simply as utterances, but also as attitudes and embodiments and practices. For example, Rachel's pronounced physical reaction to entering the courthouse may derive from her nervousness, but it must also be linked to her association of the courthouse with a moment in which she was separated from her mother as a child or as the subject of juvenile prosecution. Rachel's deferring to the state's attorney by answering all of his questions and politely listening to his explanation of the requirements to proceed are part of her characteristic deference to the law as a force which has always acted upon her, if sometimes on her behalf. In contrast, moments in which the law has played an important role punctuate Dennis's life, even when its force is against him. Even in custody, Dennis has retained a profound sense of his rights. For Dennis, attorneys, police officers, and the courts have served as resources to be wielded in a number of circumstances. The successful outcome of his case against his stepfather, his subsequent ability to maintain visitation and custody rights over his children, and his desire to sue the police officer for excessive use of force against him point to a continuous and creative engagement with legal processes.

Perhaps the difference in Rachel's and Dennis's dispositions toward legal institutions is clearest in their relationship and attitudes toward 18 years old being the age of majority.[11] For Dennis, it has stood as an important benchmark, one that kept him from being an enfranchised member of his mother's household as an abused child. Awareness of his curtailed legal rights and responsibilities as a child also served as a marketable resource in the drug trade. For Rachel, though 18 came and went, it did not stand in her mind as a significant landmark. Instead, she participated in her first criminal activity a few days following her birthday. The state's attorney seems to deride Rachel's timing, incredulously asking, "You waited until your eighteenth birthday . . . " While Rachel herself never explicitly marks her own life as legally framed, Dennis does so on many occasions.

Subjecting Sexual Violence to the Law

It is difficult to make definitive pronouncements "diagnosing" Dennis and Rachel's attitudes towards the law in general and their roles as sexual assault victims in particular. This chapter has demonstrated that they have drawn on a number of legal experiences in seeking to make sense of the process in which they are involved. The state's attorney, for the right or wrong reasons, was equally interested in particular aspects of their legal histories. For the state's attorney, the law necessarily holds a certain curiosity in a victim's potential status, past or current, as a perpetrator.[12] Victims may themselves draw from a wide array of experiences with the law, as perpetrators of crime, wards of state, or even just a sensation or feeling associated with a location (such as the courthouse) to navigate the present. While one always hopes that sexual assault is not a common or everyday occurrence, for Rachel and

Dennis, everyday violence and legal encounters do not cease to be relevant throughout the exceptional circumstances of sexual assault and its specific legal intervention.

In sexual assault interventions, participation in and compliance with legal processes are often subordinate to the future of one's family. Where emergency contraception offers to avert children conceived in violent encounters, violence appears as a commonplace rather than an exception in the lives of victims. Legal prosecution of sexual assault may further deepen fractures between family members, or deprive vulnerable individuals of their caretakers. While forensic nurse examiners and state's attorneys have a variable approach to heeding victims' desires in each case, dogged and insistent emphasis on prosecution may constitute reproductive violence in itself as it disrupts the ability of parents to care for children, and for victims to make a living.

Where sexual assault victims consider their reproductive futures in broader terms, forensic nurse examiners may approach the dangers to reproduction in relation to a narrowly defined parturition. Administering emergency contraception under the conditions of sexual assault intervention may further serve to satisfy the law in establishing the sexual assault victim's credibility as legal subject. As victims, patients must comply with regimes of emergency contraception to instantiate materially their willingness to avert the possibility of pregnancy and the generation of children born of violence. Such children bear the potential of fueling ongoing violence simply by expressing curiosity about the facts of their origin. Victims who demonstrate their desire to preempt future violence emphasize their non-consent to the sexual act by invoking the violence of forced reproduction. As legal subjects who draw upon a range of experiences with the law when navigating the sexual assault intervention, victims' credibility nests within a wide range of relationships both with the family and with law.

5

Facing Victims

Vision and Visage in the Forensic Exam

Precisely because the face is solely the location of truth, it is also and immediately the location of simulation and of an irreducible impropriety. This does not mean, however, that appearance dissimulates what it uncovers by making it look like what in reality it is not: rather, what human beings truly are is nothing other than this dissimulation and this disquietude within the appearance.
—Agamben, *Means without End*, 94,4

[T]he gynecological gaze can be theorized in both directions. Not only does the clinician look at the patient, but the patient can also look back at the clinician. [. . .] How can the patient-spectacle look back within the pelvic exam and how can we consider this look?
—Kapsalis, *Public Privates*, 26

While photographs do not recreate original subject matter, they do preserve a visible record of that moment in time.
—Crowley, *Sexual Assault*, 89

Examining Wounds the Forensic Way

This chapter considers a particular legal-medical artifact: the photos of wounds and injuries collected by forensic nurses who work with sexual assault victims. As we have seen in previous chapters, the use of medical expertise in legal procedures lends medicine's authority to law without necessarily adopting the therapeutic concerns of medical practice. In demonstrating how clinical practices hinge on potential courtroom proceedings, Mary-Jo DelVecchio Good has disaggregated "medicine's monolithic voices" (1995: 11) and traced the signs under which medical competence becomes a potent symbol in relation to malpractice. As chapter 3 demonstrates, while the forensic practitioner is also subject to allegations of malpractice, her competence is defined primarily as an expert witness and evidence collector in relation to the court of law. But in addition, the forensic nurse examiner is responsible for providing compassionate care for sexual assault victims (Plichta, Clements, and Houseman 2007). Forensic medicine is practiced under the sign of justice while producing its own practices of caregiving, an aspect of the intervention as yet unexamined in this book's focus on juridical technology and victims' experiences. While the previous chapter demonstrated the tensions between victims' experiences and understandings of reproductive violence in relation to the nurses' and legal actors' understandings, this chapter begins to examine the complicated emergence of caregiving in the forensic encounter. The chapter shows how forensic nurses produce a visual regime that draws on their training as nurses to perform the therapeutic aspects of sexual assault care while carrying out a juridical intervention. Here, we begin to see the resulting practices of caring for the victim of sexual assault as neither medical nor juridical, but rather expressed through a uniquely forensic visual modality.

In Baltimore, the face of the victim has always been photographed and entered in the body of legal evidence considered by a court of law. For a long time in its history, City Hospital's forensic nursing program produced photographs in which each injury photographed featured an inset of the victim's face on the upper right-hand corner of the photograph. The analysis in this chapter explains how the composition of this photograph comes into existence within a set of conventions of looking and being looked at that emerge within the forensic encounter. Focusing on forensic photography sheds light on interesting developments in medical culture. The techno-scientific possibilities that enable forensic encounters also align therapeutic techniques with legal directives in new and problematic ways. As in all other aspects of the forensic encounter, the forensic photograph is generated in anticipation of a courtroom encounter, and must serve as a medical artifact with probative value in a therapeutic environment. Thus, the photograph also becomes a technique for constituting forensic time, one of three temporal modalities discussed in chapter 2.

Visual Technology and the Forensic Gaze

Forensic nurses are trained in the use of several specialized technologies of evidence collection. These include, but are not limited to, various visual technologies used to check for and document injury. Deborah White and Janice Du Mont (2009) have highlighted various problems associated with increased reliance on visual evidence within Canadian sexual assault interventions. Among the effects they track in their study, conducted with a group of sexual assault nurse examiners, are the fragmentation and objectification of the sexual assault victim's body, and the fostering of a legal positivism that emphasizes findings of serious physical (in particular, genital) injury as the standard for non-consensual sex. Note that locating physical injury, particularly visible injury, has been shown to be relatively rare (Sommers 2007). Patricia Tjaden, in response to White and Du Mont, points out that "medical examinations of disease and injury have always depended on some degree of 'looking and seeing' and 'poking and prodding,'" further pointing to the possibility that "the perceived long-term benefits of invasive and embarrassing medical interventions tend to outweigh their short-term negatives, even among rape victims" (Tjaden 2009: 11). These observations, based on interviews with forensic nurses, invite scrutiny of forensic examination methods themselves, leading to questions about how and why such fragmenting of the victimized body occurs (Mulla 2008). What are the forms of poking, prodding, and posing that take place within the forensic examination regime, and what is at stake for those involved in the intervention?

While the ethnographic film has comprised a major focus of visual anthropology, the field has recently been reassessed to include visual technologies beyond film in constituting ways of seeing and being seen (Banks and Morphy 1997; Ginsburg, Abu-Lughod, and Larkin 2002; Poole 1997, 2005; Spitulnik 1993). Anthropology has addressed the question of photography's "other histories" by exploring the history and use of photographic technologies outside the "West" (e.g., Buckley 2000; Pinney 1997; Pinney and Peterson 2003). The idea of photography's other histories need not apply solely to "east-west" divides or questions of locality. Rather, photographic and visual technologies can be understood in relation to particular genealogies of profession. The possibility of exploring the practices of seeing and making images comprises the major strength of the anthropological method. Focusing on forensic visual technologies in this chapter leads to an analysis of the ways in which victims are faced and given faces. This ethnographic analysis is located in multiple genealogies of gynecological medicine and conventions around facial photography in gynecological and obstetric illustration. The visual artifact that emerges from the forensic encounter is indicative of the realigning of legal directives and therapeutic techniques in the course of sexual assault intervention.

Ways of seeing have shifted variously over time; the medical gaze, like any other scopic regime (Metz 1985), is trained through certain repertory practices, and also responds to innovation (Crary 1990, 2000; Foucault 1973; Kuriyama 1999). With appropriate training, it is possible for a medical practitioner to see a symptom that indicates a particular condition (Foucault 1973), to see "living structures" where, in fact, cell samples are dead (McGrath 2002), and to describe a wound as "beautiful." While Shonna Trinch (2003) has alluded to the ways institutions structure legal responses to sexual violence by examining language and narrative, this chapter builds on her analysis by casting photography not simply as a narrative form, but as an instantiation of legal training practices and a repository of institutional memory. A victim's narrative, however, aligns the forensic gaze in a particular way, informing the framing and composition of forensic photographs. The photograph is yet another form of address invoking testimonial memory by impressing a viewer or appealing to a community of citizens who can make up a jury (Campbell 2002: 204; Felman 1992). Within medicine, the visual scrutiny of women's bodies is animated by various concerns and conventions (Fisher 1995; Jordanova 1989; Lock 1993). Looking at the traditions in which female patients' faces are pictured in gynecological contexts, this chapter asks how the face is interpreted as a sign in multiple registers, ranging from the indexical to the affective. It also shows how forensic nurses adapt photographic techniques to capture the evidence required for the sexual assault investigation by manipulating time through images created to erase or demonstrate duration (Lakoff 1996). While visual imaging has a place in forensic practice, it must also account for the therapeutic needs of the victim. Thus, forensic nurses are obliged to shape their photographic techniques to an individual victim's comfort level. Through including the face as evidence of a juridical truth of suffering, nurses produce photographs that communicate this truth, perhaps through introducing a certain "disquietude" in viewers (Agamben 2000: 94,4).[1]

Each minute procedure within the sexual assault forensic examination bears much weight in assembling an evidentiary archive, the integrity of which is tested by the judicial system. A forensic nurse's methods involve several forms of visualization, some of which overlap with methods used by gynecologists on their patients. These include gross visualization of the victim's body, with special attention to her genital area. Another technique shared by forensic nurses and gynecologists is speculum examination, allowing inspection of the vaginal walls and the cervix. During the period in which this research was conducted, forensic nurses frequently opted to use a videographic technology sold under the brand name Medscope™. Later, the program, like many others across the United States, phased in digital photography.

As described earlier in this book, the sexual assault forensic exam begins with the forensic nurse taking the victim's statement, in addition to and independent of the statement taken by a police detective. The statement is elicited in narrative form, with further details gathered through a checklist of criteria. For example, asked by the nurse to describe the attack, one victim stated: "He grabbed me and then did what he wanted to." While this statement both captures the victim's emotional affect and establishes a fact pattern, duly noted by the forensic nurse in her report, it does little to indicate what an examiner may encounter on examination. Hence, the forensic nurse uses her checklist to get details to guide her in the examination. She begins by asking the victim what position (supine or prone) she had been in during the attack. This information, which may be difficult for the victim to share, specifies probable injury sites, giving the forensic nurse particular areas on which to concentrate her visual examination. Like any other medical practitioner, the question in contemporary forensic practice is "Where does it hurt?" or, in a sense, "What are your symptoms?"

Knowledge of the set of circumstances leading to the victim's injuries positions the forensic nurse's gaze. Indeed, physical affect and/or evidence may not appear significant, or appear at all, without the narrative of the victim. For example, victim's red eyes may appear to be irrelevant unless an examiner is faced with a victim who says she has been strangled, in which case the retinal hemorrhaging becomes evidence of strangulation. The forensic nurse may then go on to examine the neck more closely for signs of a chokehold, and so on.

Forensic nurses record their findings in two main formats: by noting them in writing on the appropriate forms belonging to the case, and by photographing all injury sites. Forms include spaces for written description of injuries and other physical evidence, and spaces for visual representation. While this chapter focuses on visual regimes, the written content and format of these documents is the topic of the next chapter. A drawn naked figure, frequently referred to as a body map, presented from several different perspectives, offers forensic nurses a space to diagram injuries, noting the type, size, and placement of the injury on the victim's body. After using gross visualization techniques to assay for injuries and other evidence, forensic nurses may employ other visual tools such as dyes to visualize cuts and abrasions too small to see with the naked eye. In interviews, however, prosecutors noted that micro-injuries are often less convincing as juridical evidence in that they may be interpreted as demonstrating relatively minor harm rather than seen as tangible evidence of the use of force.

The forensic nurse's search for evidence is structured and guided by two frameworks. The first is her bank of medical knowledge on types and likelihood of injury. The second framework is the narrative provided by the victim. While the forensic nurse scrutinizes the entire body of the victim with some care, she concentrates her gaze on the areas where she is most likely to find injury. The narrative she seeks to verify is the one provided to her by the victim. Her testimony will corroborate or contradict the victim's claims. The nurse photographs and records all injury sites in the narrative part of the paperwork. Both the photograph and the forms become a part of each case's file.

The introduction of both a written and a visual artifact into the body of legal evidence raises questions as to why both are necessary. The evidence stands as fact only in relation to the two frameworks within which the forensic nurse works. By interrogating why forensic nurses include the face of the victim as an inset of every photograph of her injuries, this chapter makes clear that the victim's face exceeds the simple purpose of supplying an identity marker within the photograph.

Photographic Pathways

To understand the purpose of and the implications of photographic pathways, it is important to consider the imagined audiences of this artifact. What trajectories and pathways characterize the circulation of forensic photographs? All forensic photographs are printed during examination and are stored on digital media. The printed set remains in the hospital with the victim's chart; the digital media remains under lock and key in the office of the forensic nurse program. The first ideal and commonly anticipated destination for the photographs is the court of law. The photographs are, after all, taken to serve as evidence for the judge or jury. They may be displayed and submitted as prosecutorial or defense exhibits. Where this happens, the attorney will call and request that a full set of the photos is printed from the digital media. A set of the printed photographs is then given to the attorney or a designated agent. The photos may also be further enlarged to detail a particular injury and increase their impact when and if displayed in the courtroom.

This trajectory, though routinely anticipated, rarely bears out, as most cases do not reach the stage of adjudication in a court of law. In some cases where prosecution did take place, prosecutors elected not to use the photographs as evidence because of the unpredictability of the jurors' reactions. As mentioned earlier, some prosecutors consider photos just as likely to diminish the significance of injuries as they are to emphasize it. Nor is it solely the jury or judge who can encounter the forensic photographs in the courtroom. In her study of prosecutorial preparation of rape victims, Konradi (1997) describes one victim who was shocked to see her own forensic photographs for the first time in the courtroom. Institutional desires to avoid the traumatizing impact of a trial on a victim contribute to the sense that it is not automatically a failure of justice when a trial does not result from an investigation. Most cases that are pursued are remedied through plea agreements. In these cases, it is often the mere existence and sheer materiality, rather than the content, of forensic photographs that figures heavily in negotiating plea agreements between prosecution and defense.

Among all of the aforementioned trajectories, the most likely fate of forensic photographs is that they end up where they are created: placed in storage until such time as they are needed, a potential source of futurity that rarely comes to fruition. Typically, they remain unneeded, so their journey ceases almost immediately following their creation. Thus, the circulation of the forensic photograph is largely imagined, and the moment of its greatest impact is in its creation while its future is potently ambiguous. In anticipating the space of the courtroom, however, the law comes to the emergency room as a modality through which images of suffering are captured. The anticipatory modality of the forensic photograph is a material artifact of forensic time, as discussed in chapter 2.

When forensic nurses were asked why faces were included as insets of all photos of wounds and injuries that are part of the case file, they consistently provided two main reasons. The first was to ensure that the photograph did not get misplaced or mistakenly placed in the wrong file. Having the inscription of the victim's face with her case number on each photo would minimize the danger of putting the wrong photo in the wrong file or, at least, ensure much recourse for correction should this occur. Second, in interviews, forensic nurses stated that trial dates were anywhere from six months to one year following the evidence collection proceedings, and that having the photo of the victim's face helped them to remember the circumstances of each case more precisely. In this explanation, the face is linked both to identity and, in relation to identity, memory. This response correlates the aesthetic of photographing the face, as it closely resembles a mug shot. Victims often comment on this as they hold the envelope with their case number under their faces, and are sometimes surprised that only a frontal shot is needed when they automatically turn and give the examiners their profiles after the frontal photo is snapped. Concerns about the use of the face to prevent the misplacement or misrecognition of file photographs exists despite the knowledge that Medscope™ technology is secured via digital time stamping by the computer that processes the image bank. In fact, Medscope™ promotional literature lauds this security as disposing of the need to photograph faces where there are no facial injuries, giving victims added privacy and confidentiality.

In addition to the narrative forensic nurses provided in interview setting, there is the sometimes contrasting evidence of observations of nurses working with photography. Observational data strongly suggest that identification is not the only reason to provide an image of the victim's face. Ludmilla Jordanova observes that with medical drawings and photographs, as with other visual genres, women's images often personify abstract qualities such that women can serve as "a ready substratum onto which shared values and collective commitments can be projected" (1989: 135). Victims' suffering is often depicted such that juries can project their own understanding of suffering sexual violence onto the victim's face. In the 44 cases of forensic examination observed during this study, a typical interaction between victim and nurse might go like this: Upon arrival, the victim's demeanor may be tearful and agitated, and the forensic nurse notes this on the appropriate form, where the field reads: "Victim demeanor: Calm, Agitated, Flat Affect, Tearful, Other (describe)." Given the victim's demeanor, perhaps the forensic nurse will try to build rapport with her. In fact, they may get to a point where the victim is still shaken, but beginning to feel more comfortable, confident, and safe. Laughter may erupt in the exam room as the forensic nurse and the victim share jokes. Sensitive questions are asked and answered. The victim may become relaxed enough to tolerate the pelvic examination with relatively little physical discomfort, which the forensic nurse will then conduct, carefully photographing all evidence of physical trauma. Finally, the forensic nurse hands the victim an envelope with her name and case number on it, and asks her to hold it up under her chin so that she can be photographed. The Medscope™ will create an inset of the photo of the victim's face and case number on every photo related to the case. The forensic nurse snaps the photo and prints it out. She glances at the printout, looks at the victim again, and says, "Honey, you smiled for this photo. We need to do it again." Responding to the forensic nurse's request, the victim will pose for the photograph a second time, this time composing her face to match the "tearful and agitated" demeanor that the forensic nurse has noted in her chart.

How can one interpret the negotiation between the examiner and the victim? First, it is an effort to record the body of evidence in the legal community's rubric of suffering. The forensic nurse who retakes a photo to capture the "correct" expression on a victim's face circles back in time, marking a moment already passed. Rather than snap the photo upon first seeing her patient, she gives her patient time to grow more comfortable with the process, and then takes the photograph that will document the victim's affect upon her arrival. Thus, she has included her patient in her effort to document evidence that may or may not come to bear in an actual trial.

The "correct" composition of the victim's face is, in some ways, a return to an earlier moment, in other words, the past in which the victim was more visibly emotionally shaken. Once again, as in chapter 2, the chronology of forensic investigation simultaneously points to both past and present, without intent of capturing the complexity of the present moment. The composition of the victim's face is a doubling: a moment in which the forensic nurse and victim work to mimic what a victim should look like. The elements of an ideal face for a victim are reinscribed by an actual victim who surrenders her own face for one which the jury may find more convincing. Once again, the victim's visage is composed with respect to an acceptable emotional spectrum, the composition the handiwork of the forensic nurse, an expert in emotional mastery, as discussed in chapter 3.

Concerns about confidentiality are overridden by the possible (juridical) consequences of excluding the victim's face from the photographs. In the minimal verbal exchange between nurse and victim surrounding the retaking of the photographs to erase the earlier versions in which the victim smiled, saying becomes inadequate given the choice of showing. For a potential judge, juror, or attorney examining such a photo, the inclusion of the face could indicate the following: (1) that the photo presented was correctly associated with the case in question; (2) that the injuries appearing in the photo were found on the body of the individual pictured in the photo; (3) that the individual in the photo appears upset and/or otherwise emotionally distressed; and (4) that the individual in the photo is the same individual appearing in the courtroom, and there is a marked difference or similarity in the appearance of her emotional affect in the photos and in her emotional affect in the courtroom.

If the face of the victim were excluded from the photographs of her injuries, these avenues of knowing would still be possible, but rather than being mediated via the visual intervention of a human visage, they would be presented solely through, rather than in addition to, the testimony and written reporting of a forensic nurse. As visual testimony, the photos capture the experience of the victim rather than providing a photographic image of a memory (Campbell 2002: 167). The effectiveness of this approach can be assessed by taking into account how words and images travel through time, and especially, the difference between the ways an image of a victim's face travels in time in comparison to the way the images of a victim's wounds travel in time.

Pelvis-Patient-Person

Thus far, this chapter has described the circumstances under which the face of a sexual assault victim is archived as evidence in relation to her wounds. The reader may weigh the significance of the inclusion of that face by considering its role as a means of identifying evidence, its comparative value, and its place in communicating the victim's emotional affect. Beyond these factors, one can also consider the images of these photographs in the genealogical context of visual conventions within gynecological traditions shedding light on the composition and juridical life of forensic photographs.

While sexual assault forensic examinations serve both medical and juridical agendas, the performance of the exam and particularly the regimes of vision within the exam room are modeled very closely on gynecological practice. The potential intimacy and awkwardness of performing a pelvic examination are mitigated by a process of objectification. That is, a distinction between the patient as person and as a pelvis are rigorously maintained in the way that gazes are mediated. In many traditions of gynecological practice, the ideal patient is one who can shed her personhood while on the exam table and succumb to the transformation into pelvis (see Henslin and Biggs 1971: 245; Kapsalis 1997: 15). Gynecological professionalism demands that during the examination, practitioners orient toward their patient solely as a pelvis. Thus, a gynecologist will encourage the use of a drape or robe that isolates the patient's genitals, and while the patient is in the lithotomy position, she will ignore face-to-face interactions and will rarely maintain eye contact with the patient, even when she is addressing the patient. The patient, in turn, does not subject the practitioner to her gaze. Rather, she directs her eyes to some fixed point on the ceiling and responds to the practitioner's queries as though the pelvis under scrutiny is not her own.

These relations are apparent within visual representations of gynecological subjects. Women who have served as subjects within traditions of gynecological illustration and/or photography are characteristically pictured without their faces. The illustrative techniques maintain the work of the drape separating the face from pelvis. Within traditions of nineteenth-century illustration, drawings of gynecological conditions are commonly modeled on actual cases (Matthews and Wexler 2000: 107–17). The frame of the drawing is limited in that it includes either parts of the body, in other words, the trunk, and/or the entire body cut off at the chin. Early twentieth-century illustration further idealizes the separation of pelvis from face by adopting the convention of appending an artistic and imagined rendering of a face to a "real" illustration. Such an occurrence within a textbook is indicative of the ability to generalize from the particular visual representation to a class of patients, all of whom may embody the malady or condition pictured in the illustration. With the advent of photographic technology, the practice of truncating or excluding patients' heads and faces from gynecological images was reinforced. Before taking a photo, practitioners would either drape the patient's head in a towel or piece of fabric or frame the photo so the face was excluded from the shot, ensuring that her identity would remain confidential and her status as pelvis, rather than person, would be uncontested (ibid.).

This separation of person from pelvis was modeled and advocated in James Henslin and Mae Biggs's 1971 analysis of the gynecological examination (Kapsalis 1997: 11). At the time this study was conducted, gynecology was dominated by male practitioners. Thus, for Henslin and Biggs, the problem was how a female patient would "expose her vagina in a nonsexual manner to a male" (1971: 244). While all but one of the forensic nurses at City Hospital were female, the use of gynecological techniques that presuppose a male practitioner examining a female patient are part of the gendered power relations between nurse and victim. In short, the nurse's "male" role as examiner and her wielding of the appropriately coded techniques become part of the power she wields as she works with the victim. Henslin and Biggs proposed a solution for diffusing the tension between patient and (male) examiner by suggesting a dramaturgical model in which the examination was staged in scenes, with the drape sheet serving as a sort of curtain separating the back stage of the patient's person from the front stage of the pelvis, allowing the examiner to proceed by focusing only on what lay before the curtain. This staging facilitated the transformation of person to pelvis, desexualizing the examination, so that "the individual is transformed from a full person into an object, into a 'person-possessing-a-pelvis' and even into a 'pelvis-that-incidentally-belongs-to-a-person" (Henslin and Biggs 1971: 251–52). The authors stress the importance of the drape sheet once more: "The drape sheet effectively hides [the patient's] pubic area from herself while exposing it to the doctor. With this, we have a beautiful example of a mechanism that effectively covers the pubic area for one actor while exposing it to the second" (258). It is this model of gynecological pelvic examination that is transported into the forensic practice. Because forensic practice is not a gynecological practice, the fit of the exam for the needs of forensic practice are uneasy at best. For one, while forensic examiners strive to maintain the separation of the drape during examination, the sexual assault victim is definitionally a sexualized body. Thus, the separation may desexualize the patient during the course of the exam, but this desexualization cannot be projected on to the evidence that is being collected.

In Henslin and Biggs's description, both the patient's face and gaze are constitutive of her person. As long as her face and the gaze are separated from the object of focus, the pelvis, the person of the patient is deemed to have withdrawn from the examination. Henslin and Biggs idealize the separation of person from pelvis, criticizing cases in which a patient insisted on asserting her personhood by complaining of discomfort or refusing to comply with some stage of the examination. For the authors, the compliance and separation of person from pelvis is the only way in which the pelvic examination can be carried out without embarrassment. The significance of patient compliance in the context of sexual assault intervention is treated at length in chapter 8.

As with many medical techniques and technologies innovated for use in one area of practice, it is often evident that the gynecological examination practices are adapted for forensic genital examination rather than designed to suit the precise needs of forensic nurses and sexual assault victims. While forensic nurses do not complain about the limitations of conducting a genital examination using gynecological examination techniques, the drape's unsuitability at particular moments during the exam is demonstrated by one common response of victims. In eight of the observed cases, the victim would continually push the drape aside during the genital examination. First, this would unobstruct her own view of the forensic examiner, allowing her to gauge the forensic examiner's facial expressions throughout the exam. Second, it would expose her body completely to the forensic gaze. Exposure might be understood as a commitment to a process of juridical truth-making. All of the forensic nurses, trained in the gynecological model of examination, routinely and unhesitatingly replaced the drape every time the victim removed it.

While the purpose of the sexual assault forensic examination is to collect forensic evidence, it is, as stated above, modeled on gynecological practice. One advantage to adapting a procedure from gynecological practice is that a victim is often able to comply with the examination procedure as it is not completely alien to her.[2] The sexual assault victim finds herself in the familiar lithotomy position on the same type of examination table she would find in a gynecologist's office. She is offered the same gowns and drapes that any patient would be offered prior to a gynecological exam. The forensic nurse carefully maintains the use of the drape at all times, and while examining some body parts, ensures that others remain covered.

The transformation of the victim to pelvis is further evidenced in the directionality of gazes within the exam room. During the pelvic examination, the forensic nurse is located between the victim's legs so that she can conduct her exam and position the camera. A drape or hospital gown separates her from viewing the victim's upper body. A monitor on which the forensic nurse and victim can fix their gazes was located in the exam room perpendicular to the examination table, in full view of both the nurse and the victim. While the forensic nurse conducts the exam, her gaze will remain fixed on two points, either directly on the patient's genitals, or to her left as she stares at the monitor for magnification purposes and to check the quality of the image she is about to print out. Similarly, the victim can fix her eyes in two different places, either on some point on the ceiling, as a gynecology patient might do, or on the monitor displaying her genitals.[3] In almost all of the cases observed, a gynecological videoscopic exam was conducted. The only exceptions were cases in which no genital touching or penetration was reported. Examinations are conducted as swiftly as possible for two paramount reasons: to limit the victim's discomfort, and to collect forensic evidence that has a limited life before it begins to deteriorate, as described in chapter 1. The positions of the forensic nurse and the victim remain fixed during the pelvic exam, and all communication between the two occurs without the direct intersection of their gazes. Their field of vision intersects only at the point of the monitor, if at all. They relate through the pelvis displayed on the monitor, a pelvis that is often unrecognizable to the victim as part of her own body.

The temporary division of the sexual assault victim into person and as pelvis is more acutely evident with the introduction of a third person, and subsequently, a third set of eyes into the exam room. The rape crisis advocate who sometimes accompanies the victim throughout her hospital stay has her part in maintaining the separation of person and pelvis, participating in a division of care in which the forensic nurse would manage the care of the pelvis while the advocate cares for the person. Photographing injuries, treating wounds, providing preemptive care for sexually transmitted infections, and emergency contraceptives were all within the domain of care extended by the forensic nurse. The advocate, on the other hand, was left to help the victim fortify herself emotionally, to answer questions about the forensic examination procedures, and provide information and support for therapeutic resources in both the long and short term. The advocate also plays a role in facilitating communication between nurse and patient.

These separate labors of the forensic nurse and the advocate were reflected in the side of the drape to which each individual was designated. The forensic nurse is stationed between the victim's legs; the advocate is most often at the victim's right shoulder. The advocate's gaze may also fall in one of three places. The primary place her gaze falls is on the face of the victim, and most conversation in the room is between the victim and the advocate. The advocate's eyes may also fall on the same monitor upon which the forensic nurse and the victim gaze, if invited to do so by the victim. This invitation may be explicit or implicit. For example, if the victim should become concerned about what she is seeing on the monitor, the advocate may soothe her and encourage the forensic nurse to explain the image. The third site/sight of the advocate's gaze is to catch the forensic nurse's eye. This may occur when the victim has a question that she will address to the advocate, which the advocate then addresses to the forensic nurse. The inclusion of a rape crisis advocate draws attention to the tensions between law and therapeutics within the forensic intervention—the rape crisis advocate must communicate pain and uncertainty when victims have questions because the nurse, focusing her attention on producing images, does not necessarily monitor the victim's reactions herself. This may simply be a function of technique, as the pursuit of image capture requires concentration on the part of the nurse. When the victim communicates pain, the forensic nurse may respond to it as either proof of injury, target for therapeutic healing, barrier to effective examination, or all three.

Imbuing Affect In/With the Photographic Object

While chapter 3 explored the complex ways through which nurses are trained to manage the emotional challenges of working with victims of violence by focusing on truth-seeking criteria, photographs are an instantiation of the forensic nurse using emotion, or a perception of emotion, to create a truth-making artifact. Forensic nurses and state's attorneys are aware of the potential of photos to provoke emotional response. The emotional responses the photos may evoke, however, are often unpredictable and problematic from the perspective of legal personnel. Forensic nurses take these possibilities into account as part of their strategy to collect photographic evidence. Furthermore, the photo as image of trauma not only carries the possibility to provoke, but is an object with its own force of relationship to the viewer (Bennett 2002: 342).

Lucinda, a City Hospital nurse examiner, was awarded the "Golden Speculum Award" two months consecutively. The forensic nurses invented this honor to recognize one another for excellence in documentation of evidence, particularly when forensic labors resulted in desirable legal outcomes. The "prize" included a hand-crafted certificate with a spray-painted clear plastic disposable speculum glued to its front, and Lucinda proudly displayed it in the office. To earn the prize, she had worked on two cases which both had ended in plea bargains prior to prosecution. In discussions about her award, Lucinda commented on the overwhelming evidence in both cases. One had involved strangulation and Lucinda had painstakingly photographed the resultant broken blood vessels in the victim's eyes, ears, throat, and vaginal wall, and the vivid hand-shaped bruises on her neck. There had been various cuts and scrapes on the victim's knees, elbows, and hands, each one photographed and correspondingly marked on a body map.

The resulting stack of photographs was quite tall, Lucinda said, and when faced with the tower of photographic evidence, the accused and his legal counsel immediately entered a guilty plea. The stack of photos itself elicited a forceful truth. "They did not even look through the pictures," she grinned, "they just caved as soon as they saw how much there was." In this example, the materiality of the photographs as one corpus of evidence, rather than as individual images of wounds, elicited the desired legal response.

As noted earlier, the trajectory of forensic photographs does not necessarily land them in a court of law, even when prosecution takes place. Photographic evidence cannot be counted on to move observers in a predictable fashion. When interviewed for this study, one Baltimore County prosecutor stated that he never used photos in a courtroom. "The jury never reacts well to photos," he reflected. "Injuries don't look like injuries and they don't like to look at photographs of genitals." He preferred to have diagrams or line drawings of the wounds rendered onto body maps. He would then call on forensic nurses to explain to the jury what they had seen on the day of the examination. The prosecutor in this case preferred the drawing of wounds, as the photographs of genitals provoked a response of discomfort from jury members. In addition, genital injury, he implied, takes an expert eye to recognize and identify. The jury, likely unversed in the appearance of genital organs in a normal state, may be unable to recognize the trauma to the area. It requires the forensic nurse's intervention to render the photographs into diagrams and then narrate them as the wounds that they represent. In this example, in contrast to the first, the visual content of the images overwhelms the veracity of what is pictured in them. In this prosecutor's experience, photographs of genital trauma provoked a reaction of repulsion—the act of showing had to replace the act of seeing in order to prevent the jurors' reactions of disgust.

How do prosecutors use visual representations of genitals without provoking the visceral response of repugnance from jurors? The challenge of translating female genitals from a three-dimensional organ to two-dimensional renderings is accomplished, in part, by flattening the space with time in a double sense. On the one hand, the passage of time requires that an image stand in for the actual body of the victim, and a forensic nurse's words must narrate what she witnessed when the victim presented in the emergency room. The second sense in which time is used to "flatten" the vagina is in the language used to locate trauma on the organ. The metaphor of the clock face is used to place wounds on the vagina and anus. A forensic nurse might testify that there was a two-millimeter abrasion located "at three o'clock" on the labia. Or she might use the clock face to denote the size and location of the trauma without referencing the metric system at all. For example, she could state that a vaginal tear ran "from three o'clock to six o'clock." Thus, a familiar two-dimensional referent, a clock, becomes the stand-in for an alien three-dimensional object, a vagina or an anus. These techniques reflect only some of the ways in which the forensic photograph is not offered as direct evidence, but rather is interpreted, illustrated, or explained by the forensic nurse for maximum impact. As U.S. culture becomes more immersed in digital methods of time-keeping, it is easy to imagine that the clock face may become an archaic metaphor for mapping the medicalized body, an artifact of time-keeping as it is taught to generations of school children over the years.

Presenting Person and Pelvis: Removing the Drape

Given the possible avenues and directions gazes fall within the examination room, and the paths and terms of communication that parallel these avenues of gazing, it is clear that the dramaturgical model of separating person from pelvis is adhered to within the parameters of the sexual assault forensic exam. This allows us the possibility of understanding how it is that the visual artifact produced during the course of the examination comes to be so unsettling, potent in its affective charge. The photograph is a space in which gazes intersect (Lutz and Collins 1991). It is not, however, simply the viewer's gaze that intersects with the victim's gaze as the photographic object. It is also the nurse's expert gaze that mediates the framing and content of the photograph. The nurse, as she works the visual technology in anticipation of a trial, doubles as the gaze of the courtroom.

In the forensic photograph, the careful division maintained by the drape sheet is violently removed, collapsing person, as face, and pelvis into the same space and the same visual field. This coincidence of face and pelvis is scrupulously avoided in the examination. With the coincidence of pelvis and face/person into the same visual field of the photograph, the work of the drape sheet is done away with in an instant, and one is left to acknowledge not only a "pelvis-that-incidentally-belongs-to-a-person," but the "person-possessing-a-pelvis," and then to further contemplate that the person is the one who possesses this pelvis in particular. While the main concern for Henslin and Biggs is the sexualization of the patient, this is not what perturbs a viewer in gazing upon the photographic artifact.

Introducing the face of a sexual assault victim into a photo of her wounds does not necessarily carry the threat of making the victim face her sexuality. Rather, the introduction of her face personifies her. No longer the sum of faceless parts and catalogued wounds, the sexual assault victim stares back, signaling the possibility of communicability. In the mode of forensic time, communication has effectively erased the temporal distance between the victim and the person who comes to gaze at her photo (Luhmann 1995: 154–55). She is immediate and present in a striking way. While the image without the face can be processed as carnage, the image with face suggests other paths. For Agamben:

> What the face exposes and reveals is not something that could be formulated as a signifying proposition of sorts, nor is it a secret doomed to remain forever incommunicable. The face's revelation is revelation of language itself. Such a revelation, therefore, does not have any real content and does not tell the truth about this or that state of the world: it is only opening, only communicability. To walk in the light of the face means to be this opening—and to suffer it, and to endure it. Thus, the face is, above all, the passion of revelation, the passion of language. (2000: 92, 2)

This opening and the possibility of communication characterize the image as evidence. The face of the victim is more than a mask. The "correct" composition of the victim's face forged in cooperation with the forensic examiner is part of the struggle to convey truth to the jury. As Agamben further states, "appearance becomes a problem for human beings: it becomes the location of a struggle for truth" (2000: 92,1). The inclusion of the victim's face in her photos, with the prospect of communicability it affords in the present and future, is also a calculated risk: a jury could look there and find something incredulous in their interpretation of her visage. The silent physical wound in the photograph is made legible to the court by the forensic nurse's interpretation. The person of the victim as recognized in her face, with her possible induction into the community of the jury, is not limited to existing solely in the past. Her face, with its attendant communicability, hints always at some present or future possibility of communication.

As mentioned earlier, however, the use of the photograph in a juridical context is the least likely trajectory within the prosecutorial reality of Baltimore City, and the visual artifacts and visual regimes have the most impact when the examinations are conducted and photographs taken, as they structure the interactions between the victim and the forensic examiner. In essence, two different visual regimes exist: the snapping of the facial photograph with all of the conventions and niceties that taking a photo may imply, and the clinical routines around which a pelvic examination and pelvic photography are conducted. Forensic nurses intersperse both modalities, at times retreating to the "traditional" gynecological positioning they rely on during the pelvic exam, and at other times, engaging in the rapport-building many nurses view as necessary to their compassionate care. Slipping back and forth between these registers often gives the forensic encounter an uneven quality—one moment, the victim is in easy conversation and cooperation with the forensic nurse; at another, she is a silent object of scrutiny. These modalities of engagement, in part constituted by the differing demands of the visual technologies put to work in forensic practice, are generative of not only forensic time, but a forensic affect. The forensic nurse's gaze anticipates and mirrors the legal gaze, producing evidentiary artifacts through protocols of clinical care that maintain the conventions of the sequestering gynecological gaze even as those conventions are deliberately and intentionally suspended in the production of the visual artifact itself.

Conclusion: Community, Care, and Justice

In his writing about the face, Agamben clearly distinguishes between face and visage, but also stresses the coincidence of the two. As he describes, to be human is to have a face, and in the idea of human is the possibility of shared language. By taking in the visage of a particular individual, a viewer is confronted by the intersection of the visage with the face, lifting the curtain and revealing the shared basis of language extending between beholder and beheld. This recognition and acknowledgment does not automatically occur between beholder and wound. The forensic nurse is not able to communicate the suffering inscribed in the wound without the addition of the face. The introduction of face as visage creates a nexus between wound, victim, and beholder that lends itself to any potential recognition by a trier of fact. The drape between pelvis and person has been deliberately removed. In this calculated risk, the forensic nurse and victim have collaborated to create a visual artifact that invites judgment within a particular temporal web, a web that can catch us in community with the victim who has a face.

The anticipated impact of forensic photographs indicates that while legal practitioners often emphasize the facticity of juridical truth, affect plays an important role—a judge or jury must be moved by what they apprehend. The coincidence of wound and face, composed appropriately, will create this intended effect. The composition of the face of the victim will be keyed to what the jury expects to see and hear from a sexual assault victim as opposed to reflecting the reality of a particular sexual assault victim. If a victim feels herself less encumbered by the difficulty of an earlier moment, she must return to that earlier moment and face, again, her travails. The visual artifacts do not challenge the accepted understandings of what a "real" sexual assault victim looks like. Instead, they calcify these ideas by giving them form in a photograph. The victim may never have her "day in court," but is witness to the creation of the form of suffering her experience must take in order to resonate with a judge or a jury.

Even as the forensic photograph effaces the singularity of a particular victim, replacing it with a representation of victimhood that mirrors popular imaginaries, the erasure is effaced and we are asked to accept the photograph as a juridical truth. The technique by which the artifact is created is also effaced from the artifact. While forensic nurses frequently work time so that they may circle back in order to capture moments that have passed, temporal elasticity is eliminated in the presentation of the juridical artifacts. The strict sequestering of the person and pelvis observed during the pelvic examination is also part of the hidden technique. Medicine lends its authority to these legal artifacts, producing a spectacle of victimhood that inculcates the victim into the process and flattens the intricacies and specificities of each individual case into a broader, more statistically normative image of the legal victim. This image does not do its work alone, but rather is contextualized by the conventional narratives of documentary inscription. It is to these documentary technologies that the following chapter turns.

6

Documentary Agency

Institutional Dispositions toward Gender and Rape Myths

Care and the Family in Forensic Documentation

This chapter analyzes the documents that serve as the vehicle for recording the findings of a sexual assault forensic examination as they provide insight into the competing imaginaries of kinship and care that arise from the intersection of legal protocols and medical techniques. Because documentation is such a central feature of sexual assault forensic examination, this chapter shows how a document might preserve and proliferate many problematic and damaging attitudes about sexual assault and sexual assault victims, despite the best intentions of practitioners who are relying on these documents. While the normative prevalence of acquaintance rape is a documented fixture in studies of sexual assault, rape myths—particularly that of the stranger rapist—continue to operate within the forensic intervention itself despite the best intentions of individual personnel who labor in the forensic setting. These myths persist in the recesses of institutional memory, perpetuated not because of the biases or intentions of individual actors, but because of the social lives of forensic documents, protocols, and legal instruments. Forensic nurses and police detectives work with sexual assault victims to structure their accounts so as to satisfy documentary requirements that reflect outmoded notions of sexual violence—ideas that the institutional actors themselves need not subscribe to in order to reproduce. While institutional actors may have the most up-to-date knowledge, institutional protocols may have been developed in the past without reflecting present-day research about rapists and their victims. This chapter examines how the documentary requirements of forensic examination reflect or erase the lived realities of sexual assault victims and their families while reproducing rape myths in the daily functions of the institutions themselves. As discussed throughout the book, in many of the cases included in this study, sexual assault victims were often victimized by intimates or relatives. The documents used in these cases, however, are set up so as to tease apart and establish the facts of the relevant set of events using the same logic as though the perpetrator were a stranger. Within the documents used to capture the legal truths of sexual assault investigation, these assumptions persist in a subtle form—as traces of imaginaries of the relationship between victims and perpetrators, rather than fully articulated stereotypes.

A glimpse into the conversations and concerns that take place within the emergency room suggests that the victims, their kin, and caregivers often have complicated affinities with the alleged perpetrators. Debates over responsibility for safeguarding the victim within the space of the domestic frequently spring up among friends and relatives accompanying the victim to the emergency room. As they are named in the documentary protocol, the alleged perpetrator is disarticulated from their role within the kinship network. They may appear in one place in the documentation as suspected perpetrator, while in other spaces they are called upon as parent or guardian. What's more, the reading practices and audit mechanisms by which the documents are handled reveal a larger set of imaginaries about gender, kinship, violence, and healing that are derived from various genealogies and practices. A tension arises between the victim's experience of sexual violence on the one hand, and the documents, auditing practices, and imaginaries of who or who may not be the most likely perpetrator of sexual violence on the other.

In order to understand the persistence of documentary imaginaries, this chapter will focus on the ways nurses complete the documents, the fields that are available for entering data, the instances in which audit mechanisms "trigger" an exception, the subsequent debates that unfolded as a result of an auditor's comment, and the reading practices by which personnel interact with the various documents with which they come into contact. The documents considered here were formulated in the late 1990s, primarily by the state crime lab, and were not revised until 2009. They were used in more than 2,500 sexual assault forensic interventions over this time period. In an average weekly review, the supervising physicians were typically silent and rarely offered feedback to nurses. Focusing on cases that merit an auditor's attention draws out the normative patterns that characterize the majority of cases that circulate through the medico-legal intervention and do not invite comment. The instances that trigger an auditor's scrutiny are indicative of standards that are applied to the documents—these standards are not directives that have been inscribed or written in a single location. Rather, they subsist as traces within the available modalities of documenting sexual assault in the forensic setting, and the standards that auditors apply to these documents. In identifying imaginaries as the focus of analysis, imaginaries are defined as the ideas, shared or individual, that persist as institutional rationalities that are enacted within daily institutional practices—what Richard Harper and others have labeled the institutional "facts of life" (2000).

One approach to analyzing the documentary protocols is from the perspective that they contribute to uniformity and standardization of forensic practice while serving as a repository of institutional memory and public oversight. The standardization effect is not simply to be found in the fields and organization of the documents, but in the modes of engagement they invite from the personnel who will produce and monitor them, and the victims whose narratives will form the subject matter to be documented. The victims' narratives, as mentioned above, frequently overflow the structures of the documents as the documents also reflect anticipation of a courtroom encounter—an anticipatory structure that has thus far been attributed to forensic nurses in this text. It is important to note that victims do not necessarily share this anticipatory disposition. In forensic documents, anticipatory structures are evident in the great attention afforded to specific rules of evidence in criminal cases. In their studies of informal courts, John Conley and William O'Barr (1997) have demonstrated the differences between legal accounts produced without evidentiary constraints in contrast with those that are. The novelty of telling a relatively unmediated and unedited tale as part of the legal process is not limited to a court of law. The constraints of evidence deeply inflect the unfolding of forensic examination during the course of investigating allegations of rape. As the book has argued thus far, the sexual assault intervention is not a simple legal intervention. Rather, it is compound, characterized as both legal and therapeutic, and the nurse examiner is charged with both collecting evidence from and caring for the victim of sexual violence. Thus, the evidentiary constraints apply both to the framing of the legal narrative as it is documented during the forensic examination, as well as to the unfolding of the care plan that takes place alongside evidence collection.

What, then, are the relevant documents and processes included in this analysis? There are numerous documents that play a part in sexual assault interventions in Baltimore, Maryland. As mentioned earlier, City Hospital serves as the sole provider of care and evidence collection for sexual assault cases in the city. A uniformed police officer or plain-clothes detective will escort the victim to the emergency room in order to establish and maintain chain of custody. Chain of custody remains a concern of the forensic nurse examiners as they complete their documentation and evidence collection. As explained early in the book, following the uniformed officer's initial contact with the victim, the detective, who the uniformed officer has called in, conducts his own interview lasting anywhere from 45 minutes to two or three hours. If this interview is conducted at the hospital, the victim is registered as an emergency room patient and triaged prior to any interviewing or forensic intervention.

The detective's report is added to the case file, along with the uniformed officer's report. Neither the detective nor the uniformed officer will consult with each other. Rather, they will ask similar or overlapping questions and independently compose their reports. In this way, they are establishing a particular time line (see chapter 2 for a detailed discussion of the twists and turns of determining the relevant time frame in a sexual assault intervention), as well as anticipating the compelling nature of corroborative evidence. Practices that produce corroborative narrative evidence are implemented despite law enforcement claims and legal reforms that the shift toward reliance on forensic evidence has deemed corroborative evidence moot (Bevacqua 2000). This effect is doubly evident in that the forensic nurse represents a third interviewer who also conducts an independent inquiry in which she has no knowledge of the contents of either police report.

In the hospital, the victim is further interpellated into three separate types of documentation, that of the forensic examination, hospital health records and discharge instructions, and the rape crisis advocacy records. While the three sets of documents are generated by different agencies, the crime laboratory, the hospital, and the rape crisis center correspondingly, the location of the intervention within the emergency room space makes these distinctions a bit blurry. As stated above, police detectives will frequently conduct their interviews in the emergency room before forensic nurses step in to commence the forensic examination. Forensic nurses simultaneously attend to hospital paperwork and forensic protocols so as not to hold the patient in the hospital for an unduly long period of examination. Rather than asking the victim direct questions, rape crisis advocates keeping records for the local rape crisis center may fill out their paperwork simply by overhearing the victim's conversations with other personnel during the course of the forensic intervention.

The general purpose of the rape kit documentation is to create a record of the victim's narrative as well as the evidence found during the examination. Photos and drawings, like those discussed in chapter 5, can be added to these records, or referenced for future use. In addition, the kit contains a consent form that gives the forensic nurse permission to conduct the examination. A second form in the kit is given to the victim to submit to the state's attorney in the event an arrest is made, and allows for HIV testing of any person subsequently charged with sexually assaulting or raping the victim in this case.

The second set of paperwork shaping the victim's experience is that of the hospital. Once the victim is registered, a formal City Hospital record is generated. The minimum participation in emergency room medical intervention, registration, and triage, are noted in the patient chart. During intake, victims sign another form that gives their consent for treatment by the hospital in order to stabilize their health. There are two more elements introduced in the hospital's documentary practices. One is a consent form offering emergency contraception to victims who wish to take a prophylactic treatment to reduce their chances of pregnancy. The second set of documents include the hospital's discharge instructions, containing information about the procedures the victim has experienced, the treatments that were given, and information about after-effects or "symptoms" to be aware of, as well as contact information for future reference and follow-up examination advice.

The third set of documents that plays a part in the sexual assault intervention are those generated by the rape crisis center in cases where a rape crisis advocate accompanies the sexual assault victim. These forms changed three times during the course of this research project. They began as a form on which demographic and case information could be recorded. They then expanded to two forms, one of which contained identifying information on how to contact those victims who requested follow-up from the rape crisis center, and a second form on which case information could be recorded with no link to the rape victim. This second form was once again revised, going from a more narrative format with a blank space in which rape crisis advocates could record a prose-heavy account of the victim's story to a set of fields with different criteria from which victim advocates could make selections without writing any subjective narrative. These changes were made out of concern for complying with health privacy laws, as well as a desire to de-identify rape crisis center data collection in order to ensure it was of as little legal interest as possible to either prosecutor or defense. Attention to health privacy policies and the potential subpoena of rape crisis center documents resulted from the voiced concerns of a newly appointed lead prosecutor in the sex offense prosecution unit of the state's attorney's office, as well as local conversations about the April 2003 compliance date of the Health Insurance Portability and Accountability Act of 1996.[1]

While on the surface these three sets of forms appear to serve a very different purpose and circulate via different trajectories, they are not as disparate as they appear both in content and in purpose. In addition, though they originate and pass through different institutional spaces along the way, they share overlapping trajectories. The narratives collected by the police officer, the police detective, and the forensic nurse examiner will be reunited in the files of the state's attorney if the case moves toward prosecution. The information collected by the rape crisis center shares many overlapping fields with the official paperwork included in the rape kit. The rape crisis center will serve as one repository for the information collected by the rape crisis advocates as they accompany rape victims in the emergency room, but the rape crisis center will additionally compile the information and forward it to the Department of Health and Human Services, who also collects similar or overlapping information from the forensic nurse examiner's program directly. The department does this as the main distributor and oversight agency of VOCA (Victims of Crime Act) and VAWA (Violence Against Women Act) funds. Both funding programs fall under the jurisdiction of the Department of Justice. The Department of Justice also serves as the clearinghouse for incidence data collected by the police department—thus the reports compiled by the police in response to the sexual assault and rape complaints are reported to the Department of Justice.

In addition to the overlapping trajectories and repositories for the information that is collected during the early moments of an unfolding sexual assault intervention and investigation, there is a heterogeneity in terms of how the paperwork is handled by those who complete it, as well as the ways in which the victim and her family are interpellated into the various documentary practices. Some personnel may honor the order in which fields are laid out on a document and follow it as if it were a script, while others conduct their data collection in a different order that suits their own style of practice and engagement. As a result of the many agencies collecting data and creating documentation, sexual assault victims find themselves repeating their narratives for different stakeholders. The questions appearing on the documents are generated by specific criteria laid out in legal statutes, or reporting requirements by government agencies and funders. Chapter 2 discusses how victims offer up the information required of them in the repeated questions of various stakeholders, while they learn and internalize the institutional perspective on which details matter and which are inconsequential. The content of the institutional perspective does not only indicate the formal legal criteria that must be tested during investigation and prosecution, but also the normative structures that guide social perceptions of sexual assault, who falls victim to it, and who perpetrates it.

The different measures in place to review and scrutinize the documents produced by the various institutions and personnel involved in the sexual assault intervention are focused on many aspects of the intervention. On a weekly basis, two different physicians review the reports produced by the forensic nurse examiners. One physician has oversight over the adult cases while the other reviews pediatric cases (victims from 13 to 18 years old in this case). Both physicians are specialists in emergency medicine and have focused on forensic intervention in their emergency medicine practices, though neither have formal training in forensic intervention as their involvement in these programs predates the advent of such specialized training. In addition, the supervisor of the rape crisis advocate program at the rape crisis center is responsible for monthly reviews of the documentation produced by the rape crisis advocates.

Interpreting the Trace

Given that much, if not most, violence occurs between intimates, how and in what capacity do the documents make record of the individual who may well be both perpetrator and relative? The forensic interview and examination transform the victim's speech and the material evidence gleaned from the process into legally actionable documents contributing to a potential case. Like the narratives that emerge from domestic violence complaints, "in order to gain authority, the text must undergo a series of changes. These changes inevitably lead the narrator right back to a position of danger" (Trinch 2003: 28, 151). The danger in the case of sexual assault victims, however, is not only the victim's susceptibility to suspicion as the words that fill the document are not precisely hers, but that the investigative and therapeutic functions are combined in the forensic intervention.

Emphasizing a document's potential to drive clinical interactions and experiences of narrating violence builds on the fact that sexual assault cases are unlikely to be prosecuted or to culminate in courtroom proceedings. With sexual assault frequently falling out of the criminal justice system after it is reported, one could argue that the practices through which the victim is imbricated into the world of the documentary protocols may form the paramount function of the legal documents (much like the photographs discussed in chapter 5). As of January 5, 2009, the Violence Against Women Act of 2005 (VAWA) requires states to give victims access to forensic examination without police detective or prosecutor approval—it remains to be seen whether this will impact reporting or prosecution rates in the long term, though it is apparent that the volume of forensic examinations seems to be on the rise. In November 2009, Baltimore forensic nurses reported that they felt a significant increase in the number of examinations requested since the compliance date for the VAWA legislation had passed. For the moment, it seems that more victims are undergoing forensic examination and thus, more men and women are encountering the protocols founded by the documents associated with forensic examination. As these forensic interventions are carried out with increased frequency, victims will increasingly find themselves interpellated into the forensic imagination of sexual assault through these documentation and examination procedures.

In drawing on the language of imagination, this analysis can excavate the normative structures that animate interactions between victims, forensic examiners, rape crisis advocates, and documents. Such an exercise involves engaging not only the language or schema that are presented in the documents themselves, but a reading of the evidence as a trace in the Derridean sense. In his work on writing, Jacques Derrida sets forth the idea of the trace as a signifier. To understand the significance of the trace within both systems and content of writing, one must account for how the trace is experienced by those who encounter it. To understand documents, the absent must be weighted as heavily as that which is present. Rather than regard language as transparent and immediate, the trace marks the non-presence of the present—to encounter the trace is to return to another past, present, or future. In the case of the forensic documents, the traces contained there form impartial pairings, suggested metonymies, and analogical structures that reside within typologies that are deemed irrelevant or outmoded among contemporary stakeholders of sexual assault intervention. These analogical structures form the scaffolding of rape mythology, reproducing these myths with a subtle persistence.

A cursory inspection of forensic documents reveals that the fields and blanks that populate the documents within the forensic examination appear similarly organized and phrased. Looking at the analogical resonances between categories that are drawn from very different genealogies (i.e., the collection of evidence that originates in gynecological examination technique versus the collection of evidence that originates in techniques of dental visualization), one sees how potentially disparate fields appear to become uniform, even when the standardization of the fields results in imperfect equivalencies or is itself brought about through uneven processes. That is, fields may seem to correspond to one another visually or through linguistic grammar, but this uniformity does not decree they are wholly sense-making. For example, Alan Hyde discusses a similarly drawn analogical resonance in a search warrant (1997). He describes a search warrant that is issued for the apartment and the vagina of a particular person. While the apartment and the vagina will both be searched for drugs, the ease with which the legal tool articulates both as searchable compartments does not match the practical concerns of the personnel who will conduct the searches of the apartment and the vagina. That is to say, though the warrant may name both the vagina and apartment in the same sentence, even casting them as the same part of speech in a grammatical sense, and call for their being subject to the same process, the disparities between the apartment and the vagina cannot be willed away by the force of the document's injunction, though one could argue that the warrant is at least partly successful in objectifying both targets of its search. This is one instance that demonstrates how linguistic grammar is not always equivalent to philosophical grammar; the possibility of the utterance is not necessarily tantamount to the possibility of the world described by the utterance. As this analysis shows, the analogical structures of forensic documentation work on a more subtle level than the vagina-apartment example. Where the analogy in the example relies on the parallel structure of a simile, in which a vagina is inferred to be like an apartment, forensic documentation hinges on more metonymic relations. The parallel structure that is implied is often a synecdoche, in which a part stands in for a whole. What's more, the synecdoche is only partially articulated because the equivalencies are entrenched within the fields of documentary paperwork rather than explicitly named. Returning to the example of the warrant, it would be as if the search of the vagina was called for without the additional instruction of the search of the apartment. The mere "searchability" of the vagina may suggest the metonymic relationship between an apartment and a vagina to someone accustomed to searching an apartment. In the forensic documentation and auditing mechanism under analysis, the underlying metonymic structures suggest that caregivers cannot be perpetrators, perpetrators cannot be female, and victims are always female.

While the rape victim's body may be treated as though it calls for a step-by-step approach to evidence collection at various sites and locations on the body itself, each step fits into the forensic examination with varying degrees of felicity or infelicity. That is, the descriptive narrative that emerges from within the documentary practices details a fraught and tentative world in which intimates are perpetrators, victims, and caregivers, yet the documentary practices are not configured to capture these realities. As previously stated, the diverse origins and investments in projects of healing and investigation that are brought to bear on forensic processes are revealed by analyzing the handling and completing of the documents that are tied to each stage of the investigation, as well as the modes of auditing these documents at various institutional sites along the way. These moments in which auditors voice their concerns and objections often reveal the ways in which relationships between intimates, perpetrators, victims, and caregivers are imagined and accounted for within forensic documentary protocols, materializing the trace in the encounter with the documents.

Sex, Audit, and Imaginary

This and the following sections discuss two different instances in which the reviewers of each realm of documentation, forensic examination and rape crisis advocacy, identified a potential problem. This analysis will demonstrate how the instances that triggered an audit "alarm" reveal very powerful imaginaries of rape, particularly with regard to issues of intimacy and danger. Exploring both the forensic auditing practice as well as that of the rape crisis center reveals the persistence of the mythical imaginary of rape perpetrators as men who are primarily strangers motivated by sexual desire within the institutional structures of rape intervention. The ethnographic examples considered here include a pediatric case that earned extra scrutiny from the reviewing physician, and a discussion at the rape crisis center concerning the link between domestic violence and sexual assault.

Over a weekend, I sat with Lola on her overnight shift. Lola was one of the few nurses who worked her shift in the hospital rather than on an on-call basis. For a few years, City Hospital had been able to secure funding to staff the program on the weekend as they had ample evidence that rape reports increased on the weekends. As Lola came in every week for the Friday to Saturday overnight shift, she would take care of paperwork and recordkeeping, and field any inquiries that had been left for her to handle during the week. As Lola did her work, she told me about an outraged call she had taken from the supervising pediatric physician earlier in the day.

The gist of the conversation, as I later recorded in my notes, was that the pediatric physician had been reviewing the week's cases when he saw a case involving a 13-year-old male victim. The pediatrician called the forensic nurse examiner's supervisor, outraged that an unnecessary procedure had been carried out: swabbing of the victim's penis. Lola was the forensic nurse examiner who had conducted the exam, and she was annoyed by the pediatrician's accusation that the penile swabs were unnecessary. While she did not tell me about the details of her conversation with the pediatrician, she did relate her perception of the misunderstanding with the physician. According to Lola, the physician had assumed that the victim had been attacked by a male perpetrator, and had jumped to the conclusion that the boy had been anally penetrated and would thus require an anal examination; within this same logic, penile swabs were excessive and illogical. The narrative Lola had written, however, clearly indicated that the boy had been walking home from school, and had been asked to come into a house by a woman in her mid-thirties, who then had sexual intercourse with the young boy without his consent. Lola recalled the young boy had appeared very demure and had stated he conceded to the perpetrator's request that he come into her house. He related that she had asked him to stop in two to three times before on his school route. Typically, she would ask him to conduct some chore, like taking out her trash or moving a heavy box. When she had asked him in this last time, he told Lola he felt a bit annoyed by her requests but felt it impolite to decline. While a female perpetrator may seem to be atypical, her behavior was quite typical for a sexual predator in that she incrementally pushed boundaries to see how much control she could exercise over her target. The forensic nurses had been taught that this type of a pattern is typically mapped onto the typology commonly known as "the gentleman rapist," in which the rapist uses politeness to connect with the victim, but introduces more and more tests to probe the victim's boundaries before carrying out the sexual attack, so-called grooming behaviors that are extremely typical in cases of child sexual victimization. Though the stereotypical gender roles in this attack may have been "reversed," the fact pattern was fairly typical.

While Lola's report indicated that the sexual contact between the male victim and the female perpetrator involved contact between his penis and her vagina, the physician had reviewed the examination report without really reading its content. The physician was so certain that a male victim would have been subjected to anal penetration by a default male perpetrator that he dubbed the swabs unnecessary. Here, it becomes clear that in the process of auditing the paperwork to maintain the procedural integrity of the forensic examination, the physician demonstrates how the imaginary of a necessarily male perpetrator overpowering a male victim overrides what is written in the documents themselves. Lola must reply to the allegations of the audit by recommending that the physician read the narrative once more.

The physician's imaginary of the perpetrator as male was evident by his outrage over what he imagined as an error in forensic practice. The arrangement of the paperwork and the location of narrative details in relation to procedural details enabled the physician to persist in his own error. The narrative statement, in which details about the perpetrator would be included, is in a wholly different section than the page that outlines the evidence collection that was carried out. This page, in which each step of the procedure is documented as either having been completed or omitted (with a justification if the step was omitted), is a completely separate page that opens up onto the inside of the evidence collection forms. Its facing page similarly omits any information about the perpetrator, though some of the fields present on these two pages also suggest a normatively male assailant, while others are oriented toward gender neutrality. For example, the field asking "Condom used during assault?" gives "yes" or "no" as the possible answers without specifying whether the victim or the assailant wore the condom during the assault. On the other hand, a few inches down the page, the forensic nurse examiner is asked to mark a response to the question "suspect ejaculated," to which there are six potential answers the forensic nurse may select from, as follows: (1) vaginally; (2) orally; (3) anally; (4) on body (specify); (5) no ejaculation; (6) unsure if ejaculation occurred. Putting aside for the moment whether ejaculation refers only to male seminal fluid, the form does not give the additional choice of noting the sex of the assailant in this area of the form as one reason why no ejaculate was present. The use of a condom, presumably by an assailant, and the presence of a suspect's ejaculate are suggestive of a male perpetrator; analogically, condoms and ejaculate are parts that indicate a gendered male whole.

In her interview with the sexual assault victim, the forensic nurse examiner will seek information about the sexual attack against the victim in order to determine which examination techniques to use. Thus, Lola determined that a penile swab was a necessary item to include in the victim's examination. She collected and air dried the swabs before packaging them in the "miscellaneous collection" envelope and noting what they were on the envelope as well as on the form. The envelopes are included with rape kit materials to hold evidence and also collect information about this evidence; forensic examiners can write explanations in the note fields on the envelopes. The envelopes, however, are not audited, as once they are used during the examination they must remain locked in a safe or in the possession of law enforcement in order to maintain the chain of custody. Thus, the physician is left to audit only the forms without the envelopes that accompany the narrative recorded within the form. The separation of the text of the forms and the text of the envelopes can give rise to confusion, forcing auditors to rely on their institutional imaginaries when filling in blanks.

Just as the individual fields on the first page of the physical examination paperwork are inconsistent in their gender neutrality, sometimes assuming a male perpetrator and sometimes leaving room for either a male or female perpetrator, the facing page contains similar slippages in terms of the sex of the victim. For example, at the bottom of the page the schematic drawing section includes both male and female genitals for noting injuries to either a male or female victim. At the top of the page, however, where evidence collection is referenced and logged, penile swabs must be noted by writing them under "miscellaneous collection." In the event that no miscellany is collected, the nurse may mark "no" to indicate that the collection was not done. Similarly, she has a choice between "yes" and "no" for the collection of pubic hair, head hair, fingernail scrapings, oral swabs, anal swabs, bitemark/licking swabs, blood samples, debris, and even whether a physical examination form was completed for the case. These fields all reflect evidence that can be collected for either male or female victims. The only field that is deemed obligatory is that marked "vaginal swabs" (see figure 6.1). The

VICTIM'S NAME

	SENT TO POLICE LABORATORY (CHECK)
Pubic Hair	Combings: Yes_____No_____Plucked: Yes_____No_____
Head Hair	Plucked: Yes_____No_____
Fingernail Scrapings	(If indicated) Yes_____No_____ Victim scratched assailant? Yes_____No_____
Saturated Vaginal Swabs (4 total)	From: Vulva_____Vaginal Pool_____Endo-Cervix_____Perineum_____
Saturated Oral Swabs	Collected: Yes_____No_____
Saturated Anal Swabs (Perineal/Anal)	(If indicated) Yes_____No_____
Bitemark/Licking Swabs	(If indicated) Yes_____No_____
Purple-top tube, Victim's Blood	Collected: Yes_____No_____ (LABEL TUBE WITH VICTIM'S NAME)
Victim's Underwear	Collected: Yes_____No_____
Debris Collected	(If indicated) Yes_____No_____
Miscellaneous Collection	Collected: Yes_____No_____
Copy Of Physical Examination Form	Included in kit? Yes _____ No _____

Figure 6.1. Vaginal swabs (fourth row down) are the only field for which the examiner may not mark uncollected.

obligatory inclusion of a vaginal swab demonstrates the metonymic structure in which the norm of a victim with a vagina indicates a female victim. Penile swabs, on the other hand, are miscellany that must be written in, not a standard field to be omitted in the case of a victim without a penis. All victims are presumed to have vaginas, on the other hand, and must have a vaginal swab. In the event that no vaginal swabs are collected, the forensic nurse examiner must make an awkward note to the side of the fields, indicating that this was the case. She is able to make a note, as above, on the envelope in which the swab is placed, but once again, these envelopes are not available to the auditors who review the procedures (see figure 6.2).

At present, male sexual assault victims are examined by the forensic nursing program at the rate of about one case per month, and the perpetrators in these cases are predominantly, though not exclusively, male. The configuration of the paperwork, however, only allows examiners to select from particular sets of choices that are far from sex- or gender-neutral. Though these sex and gender norms may be keyed to fit a particular normative fact pattern, one in which the victim is female and the assailant is male, in cases where this does not hold true, the paperwork is such that it does not necessarily allow the particulars of the case to emerge and establish their unique circumstances. Rather, the paperwork alternates between sex- and gender-neutral items, and then "non-neutral" items, such as a log for findings from vaginal examination as mentioned above. The physician's audit trigger in this case, the notion of an unnecessary procedure conducted on a young male victim, is a trigger only in the context in which the imaginary of a male perpetrator is firmly intact. That the

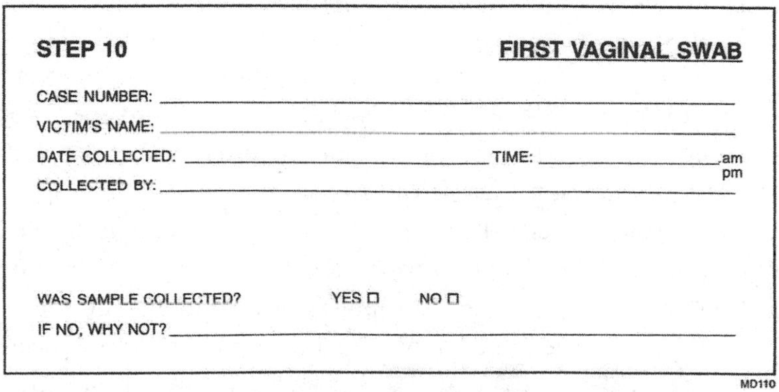

STEP 10 **FIRST VAGINAL SWAB**

CASE NUMBER: ______

VICTIM'S NAME: ______

DATE COLLECTED: ______ TIME: ______ am pm

COLLECTED BY: ______

WAS SAMPLE COLLECTED? YES ☐ NO ☐

IF NO, WHY NOT? ______

MD110

Figure 6.2. Evidence collection envelope includes space for notation.

perpetrator in this case used her femininity to leverage access to the boy is subsumed under the assumption that it is only men who victimize young boys. Note, also, that the physician's audit potentially stems from his concern for the young man undergoing the forensic examination—his objection may be embedded in an ethic of care. The imaginary of a male perpetrator, however, reproduces the notion that sexual violence is motivated by sexual desire rather than by power; the implication is that a female perpetrator cannot overpower a male victim.

With this imaginary intact, the physician is outraged and contacts the forensic nurse examiners to berate them. The forensic nurse examiners then refer him to the forms he is auditing in order to demonstrate that the male-male victim-perpetrator dyad that he expected to underlie the attack was, in fact, a male-female dyad. These imaginaries may fall in line with statistical patterns, but the fact is that they operate as much more. In a world in which only men harm while women proffer care, the realities of a female assailant are veiled. Women, in their "caring capacity," filter into the paperwork predominantly as victims or family/caregivers of victims.

Domesticity, Audit, and Imaginary

This section turns to a very different instance of auditing paperwork from the sexual assault intervention. In this case, the oversight was through the rape crisis advocate coordinator at the rape crisis center as she reviewed the advocates' documentation from the past month's emergency room calls. The advocates' documentation included some basic demographic and case information. Rape crisis advocates would record the victim's race, sex, age, number of assailants reported, and whether the victim had requested follow-up care. If the victim requested follow-up care, the advocate would specify the type of follow-up contact that the victim desired (phone call? mail?) and specify how to reach the victim. Advocates also distributed flyers and pamphlets in the emergency room so that victims would have information about the services offered through the rape crisis center. The rape crisis advocate coordinator encouraged advocates to add their own notes to the form, particularly under a heading that asked if the victim had any particular concerns to which the rape crisis advocate coordinator might provide follow-up. In one instance, a note about a sexual assault victim's request for shelter came to the coordinator's notice and sparked an interesting series of conversations and a subsequent policy change at the rape crisis center.

In the case in question, the victim requested assistance in seeking both emergency and long-term shelter placement. The victim felt she could not return to her home as the assailant was her boyfriend with whom she lived. The rape crisis advocate described how the victim feared for her own safety, and expressed her desire to be placed in some type of shelter so that he would not be able to find her. This request caught the coordinator's attention, not because it required additional resources in order to house the victim, but because emergency shelter was typically offered to domestic violence victims, not to rape victims. This rape victim was clearly also a victim of domestic violence, but seemed to fall outside the purview of those individuals to whom the crisis center typically offered emergency shelter.

This distinction makes sense in light of the following additional information about the rape crisis center and its services. The rape crisis center that provided victim accompaniment and a full range of services to sexual assault victims was a dual-service agency in that it also offered a similar set of services to domestic violence victims, including patient accompaniment during emergency room visits. While a single hospital in Baltimore carried out all of the sexual assault forensic investigation, many local hospitals saw victims of domestic violence. The crisis center provided emergency room accompaniment for domestic violence victims at several different hospitals. The same group of volunteer rape crisis advocates served the rape victims and the domestic violence victims. They underwent training to handle both types of cases.

Emergency shelter was routinely offered to domestic violence victims who could not secure entry to a domestic violence shelter. Furthermore, whenever rape crisis advocates saw domestic violence victims during an emergency room visit, they routinely screened for sexual assault. The opposite, however, was not true. Though an earlier version of the rape crisis advocate information sheet asked if the assailant was known to the sexual assault victim, later versions eliminated this question altogether. As noted earlier, the removal of particular data fields in the paperwork of the rape crisis center resulted from a desire to collect less information about sexual assault victims lest court officers seek discovery of the crisis center's records. The rape crisis center eventually determined that sexual assault victims should certainly have recourse to emergency shelter services. A certain level of incredulity, however, colored the discussions among the rape crisis advocates, and a general consensus of confusion about the oversight resulted.

First and foremost, the rape crisis advocates were upset by the idea that a stereotype of a stranger as assailant seemed to be animating the intervention protocols for victim accompaniment. If domestic violence victims were routinely screened for sexual assault, then why wasn't care taken in screening sexual assault victims for domestic violence? As one rape crisis advocate told me in an interview:

> When this came up, we were all like of course sexual assault victims should have shelter if they need it! Of course they might be DV [domestic violence] victims, too! But I was so used to going down the list—and it's there in the DV forms, but not the SA [sexual assault] forms.

Here, a rape crisis advocate's documentation serves as a script prompting her to offer one set of services to a domestic violence victim and another set of services to a sexual assault victim. The distinction suggests an imaginary of home as a site of safety and one's intimates as caretakers in the case of sexual violence. This distinction is also due to the legal structuring of the event of domestic violence and sexual assault. Sexual assault is defined in the uniform statutes by a set of very narrow criteria that also require a bounded metric of time (see chapter 2), whereas domestic violence is a chronic set of crimes in which a fact pattern is established over a longer period of time. Thus, domestic violence can contain within it the act of sexual violence. A sexual assault investigation, however, is more legally punctuated and therefore seems less likely to contain within it, for the purposes of building a legal case, the circumstances of domestic violence. The auditor's "catch" reveals the power of this imaginary within the rape crisis advocate's world.

Ethics of Reading

While the previous two sections have attended to recording and audit practices, this section of the chapter describes the ethic of reading that guides forensic nurses' interactions with and reliance on the documents that form the basis of the forensic intervention. As discussed in chapters 1 and 5, some nurses rely heavily on the forensic examination form to guide the victim examination and evidence collection. They take care to record the victim's narrative at the outset of the examination, and refer to this recorded narrative at several points during the examination. As they collect evidence and add notations to the documentation, they may even read directly from the form, asking victims to select from among the possible choices in the "multiple choice" fields. Other nurses will incorporate each separate question into a more conversational style, collecting information as it emerges, and not necessarily following the form as a script dictating the order in which they must carry out particular procedures. These different approaches exemplify two very different ethics toward interweaving the voice of the document with one's own voice.

In addition to victim examinations, the forensic nurse examiner staff at City Hospital conducts suspect evidence collection. This includes collections from suspects in cases beyond sexual assault. When police take a suspect into custody, they will accompany him or her to City Hospital for evidence collection if it is early on in the case, typically within three to five days of the initial incident being reported, as organic evidence will not survive beyond this time frame. The police detectives must produce warrants or court orders allowing suspect evidence collection to occur. These orders are multi-page documents. Forensic nurse examiners spoke to me about their experiences with suspect evidence collection and how their practices had shifted over the course of their career. Namely, early in their careers, they would read the entire warrant from front to back. This typically included a detailed description of the crimes with which the suspect was charged, and then instruction on what procedures the forensic nurses should conduct. Over time, many of the nurses remarked that they stopped reading the statement of charges and just skipped to the section detailing the procedures. Note that this reading ethic is quite different from the one in place during victim examinations, in which nurses frequently reference the victim's description of the crime because the details that emerge from the description suggest which procedures to carry out in accordance with their knowledge of where the most likely types of injury are found under particular circumstances. These two reading ethics reveal the janus-faced nature of the forensic nurses who gaze simultaneously at the victim and the state, with different reading practices deployed for each.

As with collection of evidence from victims, it would seem that knowing details about the case could help focus forensic scrutiny where it belongs when it comes to the suspects. Many nurses, however, commented that reading the charges quickly became irrelevant and unnecessary for two reasons. For one, the procedures that could be undertaken were court ordered, so the forensic nurse could not stray from the warrant. She simply had to carry out the instructions of the warrant as the warrant is, literally, the letter of the law. Like a summons, the warrant addresses its reader (the suspect in this case), compelling action (Yablon 1992). The nurse's judgment as to what procedures should be carried out is irrelevant, and her competence need only apply to the way in which she carries out the evidence collection that has been ordered.[2] According to the nurses, the second reason it is unnecessary to read the charges is because the nurses are less likely to have their objectivity compromised if they do not know the charges. "Most of the time," said one nurse,

> these guys come in and you don't know what they are arrested for and they just seem pretty clueless. And if you don't read the order, you don't know what they did, and most of the time you don't want to know.

Compare this ethic of reading to the earlier case of the pediatric physician who found fault in a list of procedures undertaken because he interpreted the list without knowledge of the relevant narrative. Although there may be practicalities associated with ignoring a forensic narrative while closely scrutinizing a log of forensic procedures, the invisibility of the victim's narrative contributes to the persistence of the imaginary of rape animating the physician's audit.

Inscribing Kinship and Care

The auditors' concerns and forensic nurses' reading ethic lay bare the fragmented nature of forensic documentation. Each painstakingly collected piece of evidence, whether testimonial or material, is a small part of a whole. This whole can be acted upon by the prosecution or the defense in order to make a legal case. Earlier in the book, I mentioned that during the period inclusive of this research project, fewer than three of every ten cases receiving a forensic examination resulted in a court trial. Thus, on some levels the significance of the forensic examination and its practices of documentation may resonate more strongly with the victim and his or her network of caregivers than with the legal system. Rather than serving purely as a legal tool, the documents also become a way in which the victim's narrative of his or her domestic world and relationship to kin, intimates, and network of care becomes articulated for purposes of making sense of the event of rape, as well as its aftermath and a return to the everyday.

On one level, through its documents, the forensic examination is interested in the domestic through narrowly defined parameters. For example, the chapter that follows will discuss the multiple ways in which home may be inscribed in the documentation and how this reveals the difficulty of accounting for home as the locus of risk rather than healing. Like the location of home as location of assault, the alleged perpetrator's name can be listed on Maryland forms without necessarily designating the role of the perpetrator in relation to the victim, although a note may be added to the narrative section of the forms. While this approach to accounting for the location of assault is directly reflected within the forms, traces of the imaginaries of sexual assault extend to more subtle inscriptions in the world of forensic examination.

Take, for example, references to "mother's lap." While reviewing several commonly used textbooks that serve as references for the Baltimore forensic nurse examiners with whom I worked, I noted the various models of forensic documentation in the appendices. Among the documents included in one of the most commonly assigned forensic textbooks, Crowley's *Sexual Assault: The Medical-Legal Examination*, were those used in Tennessee (1999: 172–73). In Memphis, the examination forms for both adult and child victims require a notation on the patient's position during the pelvic examination. A genital examination may be conducted in one of three positions: (1) supine, (2) knee chest, or (3) mother's lap. The inclusion of the "mother's lap" position conveys an exclusion of the mother from the role of perpetrator within the forensic imaginary. This notation erases, or ignores, the possibility of the mother as perpetrator of violence, therefore demonstrating the uneasy relations between medical and legal frameworks. Forensic forms, however, are quite diverse in their structures, fields, and composition. There are likely as many different types of forensic documentation as there are diverse state-by-state criminal statutes governing sex crimes, one of the many features that is characteristic of the intensely local character of sexual assault intervention referenced earlier. While the Maryland documentation contains no such notation or reference to mother's lap, the term and its inclusion in the other paperwork does form one of the models with which forensic nurse examiners are trained and oriented as they prepare to gain credentials as forensic nurse examiners and begin their nursing practices. Crowley's text is issued during training and certification programs and is one of a few texts on hand in the emergency room for consultation. Although the Maryland forms have not been generated with reference to the field, the Tennessee model suggests technical possibilities as well as language that can be included in the open notation if the need arises.

To what does "mother's lap" refer exactly? Any number of obstetric and gynecological textbooks usually include a diagram of the examination position, in which a child, typically female, is held facing forward and straddling the adult's lap in order to facilitate genital examination. Typically, the child is female and the adult is also female and purportedly a mother. Where this image, in the context of a medical textbook, appropriately references and demonstrates the positioning of a child straddling an adult's lap for the purposes of carrying out a pelvic examination, in the context of a forensic intervention, the image may well double as the image of victimization and not medical intervention. Encountered within the context of a forensic intervention, the caring female figure is called into being even as the female perpetrator is elided through the inheritance of gynecological and therapeutic traditions. Other fields and categories are derived from the fact patterns around victimization with which criminologists and legal scholars are most familiar, such as those describing the identity of perpetrators of violent crime as friends, family members, or acquaintances of the victim. Yet a third set of queries enter the form through the statutory criteria defining the commission of a crime. While the personnel who wield these documents may be familiar with the logic that requires the knitting together of such disparate fields, for the victim, the forms and the questions and procedures associated with them are often unfamiliar. The various origins and requirements are left unexplained as victims respond to the queries put to them. Recall, for example, Keisha in chapter 2, who was asked if she knew the perpetrator, and who incredulously responded, "Did I know him? He's my father!" While the sexual assault forensic examination creates an account of kinship, care, and connection that arises from the intersection of legal protocols and medical techniques and serves the purpose of being legally actionable, it is unlikely that the victims who participate in the creation of these accounts recognize as their own the geography of care and network of affinity as it comes to be described within forensic documents.

By understanding forensic documentation through the ways in which they are encountered, this chapter has sought to excavate not only the material realities of the documents, but the reference worlds that are called upon by the various stakeholders who work with the documents as they circulate through the forensic intervention. The imagination of sexual assault that arises from these reference worlds corresponds to an imagination of sexual violence as a crime committed by a stranger, most likely male, and outside of the familiar space of home. These imaginaries assert themselves regardless of the intent of the forensic nurse, physician, or rape crisis advocate who may identify with positions that favor victims' rights and acknowledge the fallacy of rape myths. Recognizing the traces inscribed into the document reveals the rape myths that persist within the institutional protocols that shape victims' narratives according to the conventions of legal culture, despite the best intentions of individual forensic examiners and healthcare providers to carry out an intervention that respects victims' particular circumstances. This chapter has argued that the work of forging gendered and kin relations between victims and perpetrators is located within institutional protocols themselves. It is the agency of forensic documentation rather than that of forensic practitioners that actively promotes and materializes the perseverance of imagined incursions of stranger rapists over the reality of the familial or familiar perpetrator. Overcoming the perseverance of these problematic imaginaries requires us to think seriously about the institutional protocols practitioners inherit and embody over time, and the traces of imagined relations that inhere within these protocols. These imaginaries have consequences in that they are not simply repositories of institutional memory and gendered imaginaries of sexual assault, and, as the next chapter shows, also double the home of the victim as a place of harm and healing, a phenomenon with potential repercussions for the victims who must return to the site of victimization upon leaving the emergency room.

7

There Is No Place Like Home

Home, Harm, and Healing

Building on the gendered norms that emerge from forensic documentary protocols in the previous chapter, this chapter examines the ways in which home and the sexually violated bodies within particular homes are configured and administratively rendered by the state. Violence between intimates, acquaintances, and "friends" is seen to be particularly destructive, and these distinctions carry over into the formalization of "stranger" and "acquaintance" categories by law enforcement personnel (Estrich 1988: 4–8).[1] A recent study of sex offenses in the United States determined that eight out of ten rapes were acquaintance rapes (Tjaden and Thoennes 2006: 21). The term "acquaintance" encompasses various types of relationships and degrees of intimacy. Crime scenes, too, can fall into categories of strange or familiar. While formal distinctions apply to the perpetrator of rape, there are no official distinctions for sites of sexual assaults.[2] Sexual assault victims, however, convey a sense of place in their disclosures of the event. "Home" is often the location in question.

In the hospital emergency room, victims pepper their disclosures of sexual violence with descriptions, stories, objects, or familiar/familial figures of and from home. This narrative, once again, structures the forensic nurse's orientation to the exam she will conduct. In this case, forensic scrutiny will uncover evidence that links the sexually violated body to the domestic crime scene. This chapter argues that in cases of sexual violence located in the victim's home, forensic techniques allow the shifting of the "scene of the crime" from the home to the body and create the conditions of possibility for the emergence of a domestic that has (at least) two different characters. The term "domestic" refers to a set of norms defining kinship, care, and intimacy, while "home" serves as the predominant form for expressing domestic norms in the locality in which this research was conducted.[3] The first face of the domestic is as the source of violence and vulnerability. This "dangerous" domestic unfolds alongside a second aspect, that of the domestic as the place in which one returns to everyday life (Das 2006a). The intervention imbues home with the capacity to heal; hospital discharge instructions name it the ideal site of return. Within a forensic scopic regime,[4] the contemporaneous features of the domestic are disarticulated from one another and enshrined within institutional protocols and documentary practices. It is within the forensic documentary archive that the dangerous and healing qualities of the domestic are constituted as related but discreet. As institutional protocols disarticulate the two domestics, personnel are able to meet both juridical and therapeutic ends, which they imagine as separate.

Statistical and Categorical Imaginaries of Crime in the Home

> The location of about a quarter of incidents of violent crime was at or near the victim's home. Among common locales for violent crimes were on streets other than those near the victim's home (19%), at school (12%), or at a commercial establishment (8%).
>
> For violent crime, about half occurred within a mile from home and 76% within five miles. Only 4% of victims of violent crime reported that the crime took place more than fifty miles from their home.
>
> About seven in ten female rape or sexual assault victims stated the offender was an intimate, other relative, a friend or an acquaintance. (U.S. Bureau of Justice Statistics 2005)

The existence of aggregated statistical data on crime and injury at or near home indicates a view of home as an object regarded by the state over a long period of time. Heeding these statistics as an accurate picture of the geography of harm in the United States would lead one to regard the home with trepidation and caution.[5] According to the Bureau of Justice Statistics, it is in or near home that an individual is most likely to be hurt, killed, or otherwise subject to violence. The most likely perpetrators, moreover, are relatives, friends, and acquaintances. These patterns of crime incidence may also apply to political violence. Many historical and anthropological studies reveal that in some cases, home is a common site of politically motivated killing, torture, and abduction (see, for just a few examples, Das 1996a; Das et al. 2001; or Roth and Salas 2001), although in these cases, the source of violence may likely come from outside the home.[6] While violence does befall many in unfamiliar places at the hands of unfamiliar people, anthropologists, historians, criminologists, and statisticians hold that these remain the least likely character of incidents of harm.

Although popular imaginaries regard and construct home as a location of intimacy and stability (e.g., McKeon 2005),[7] the indexing of a range of behaviors and events within continually evolving discourses of "home invasion" (Nielsen 2005) or "domestic violence" (Fineman and Mykitiuk 1994) demonstrate the institutionalization of statistical patterns of harm in or near the home. With regard to its incidence, sexual violence shares some features of these same patterns. Intimacy and cohabitation carry grave risks acknowledged through the invention or persistence of such classifications as incest (Porter and Teich 1994), domestic violence, and marital rape (Russell 1982).[8]

In their research on post-sexual assault examination practice in Canada, Deborah Parnis and Janice Du Mont found that, "while corroborating evidence may be gathered from a number of sources, including the scene of the offence, the suspect, and witnesses, great emphasis has been placed on that which is obtained from the body of the woman who has been assaulted" (2002: 847). Throughout the many classes, orientations, and presentations observed in the course of the research conducted for this book, Baltimore, Maryland forensic nurse examiners echoed the emphasis, often repeating the phrase, "the body is the scene of the crime." Once again, the conceptual frame of the "scene" connotes both a theatrical and temporal perspective. Ann Smock notes that "the word 'scene'" suggests something spectacular while lending itself "to evoking what 'happens' in the interim, in that at least it allows one not to speak as though of something taking place in time" (Smock 1986: xi).[9] "The body is the scene of the crime" is a phrase reiterated for the benefit of nurse examiners, police detectives, rape crisis advocates, state's attorneys, and grand juries.[10] Asking Emma, a forensic nurse introduced in earlier chapters, to unpack the meaning of this expression led to the following exchange:

EMMA: My job as a forensic nurse is to treat the victim and her clothing as a crime scene. My job is to collect any type of trace evidence, any type of bodily fluids, anything I can of the alleged perpetrator. I am the DNA collector.

ME: So you document the crime scene?

EMMA: Yes, which is her, and her clothing. So hopefully I will recover the perpetrator's DNA from her clothing or from the outside of her body or from the inside of her body. Of course years ago there was no such thing. DNA technology has absolutely exploded. And it amazes me what's going on now, and it's going to be truly amazing what's going to be in ten years. It's going to be very science fiction-like. It is.[11]

Emma responds to my query about the description of a rape victim's body as a crime scene by patiently telling me that the victim and her clothing hold and therefore can be searched for trace evidence, bodily fluid, and DNA. The effort to recover the perpetrator's DNA includes searching both the inside and outside of the victim's body. Emma's equation of the victim's body to the crime scene is quickly followed upon by a remark of appreciation and wonderment over the technological advances of forensic science. For her, the victim's body opens out onto a world of genetic sequencing and DNA fingerprinting that will soon approach the "science fiction-like." The role of forensic technology in constituting its own scopic regime begins to emerge through Emma's exclamation of pleasure and curiosity in potential techno-scientific developments.

As Christopher Forth and Ivan Crozier describe, disturbed domestic tranquility can be "rewritten" or displaced onto the body (2005: 1). If the body is the scene of the crime, what happens to the other (geographic) scene of the crime? What happens to the accounts of domestic violence, child abuse, and acquaintance rape frequently related by rape victims? It is not simply Emma's description that disassociates the body of the rape victim from a place or setting. Forensic intervention itself draws the nurse examiner into the minutiae of bodily examination while an investigator from the Maryland Crime Lab or the police department will attend to the crime scene. Though they are disaggregated at the point of forensic intervention, the evidence will potentially be reunited in the legal case. This division of labor leads nurse examiners to encounter the home in the two aforementioned domestic registers of risk and healing: the first as trace evidence on the body of the victim, and the second as the place to which victims are commended for follow-up care. Thus, victims are routinely discharged from the emergency room to their homes, even if the home is the reported site of the sexual violence currently under investigation. While forensic examination may require a somewhat narrow optic, its practice within the field of nursing raises questions as to how harm and healing are so closely connected within the domestic. To demonstrate that the harm of the domestic is not a distant and shadowy world that glides imperceptibly beneath narratives of sexual violence, this chapter returns to the cases of Keisha and Laura, and also introduces the case of Leda. All three women matter-of-factly refer to home as a place replete with potential for violence. In some instances, this characterization is conjoined with their expressions of longing for the domestic.

Keisha: Dangerous Fathers, and "Trustworthy" Mothers

Keisha's case is detailed in some depth in chapters 2 and 4. Keisha was a teenaged woman who had been raped by her father in the early hours of the morning. In the pre-examination interview, Kelly asked where the sexual assault had taken place. When Keisha indicated she had been raped in her home, Kelly followed up by asking Keisha to be more specific. The exchange followed along these lines.

KELLY: What room were you in?
KEISHA: My father took me down to the basement.
KELLY: Did anyone else notice you were gone?
KEISHA: There were a lot of people. It was a party.
KELLY: Did you shout? Did anyone hear you?
KEISHA: It was loud. No one heard. He left after he was done and went back to the party.

The party was in celebration of Keisha's father's return from prison and had continued from the previous evening into the morning. As best as Kelly could approximate, the attack had taken place at approximately 7:00 a.m. The forensic examination began about four hours later, at 11:00 a.m. It was the second exam of the day for the program, but the first during Kelly's shift. She felt that the chances of finding evidence during Keisha's examination were very promising since the attack was in the recent past. Underneath the glow of the alternate light source, Kelly's prediction proved true. Keisha had been standing during the attack. With the assistance of the light, we could see that both her legs were covered with rivulets of some substance that, to the nurse examiner's experienced eye, fluoresced in a manner characteristic of semen. The image of Keisha's fluorescing legs was both dramatic and impacting. Kelly spoke longingly of some way to show the jury what she was seeing. She experimented with a 35mm camera, the MedScope™ videographic camera, and different combinations of lighting for several minutes to see if she could create a photographic image of the legs covered in the ghostly glowing rivulets. She sketched the glowing areas onto a body map and then collected dry and wet swabs from five different regions of Keisha's legs. Afterwards, she expressed frustration with the technological limitations on her efforts to collect evidence. A clear image of Keisha's fluorescing legs could only be created using digital photography equipment currently unavailable at City Hospital (Vogeley, Pierce, and Bertocci 2002).

Soon after the exam ended, Keisha's mother was allowed into the examination room. Kelly recommended to her that both of them seek therapy, handing them several brochures and phone numbers for counseling services. She also explained that Keisha had elected to take a morning after contraceptive pill, norgestrel,[12] and that the first dose had been administered. A second dose should be administered in exactly 12 hours. Keisha's mother had mentioned her earlier misgivings about the effects of emergency contraception on her daughter's fertility. Kelly assured her that the pill would not have permanently damaging effects. She reasoned, "I mean, you don't want her to get pregnant now, right?" She then handed an envelope containing the pills to Keisha's mother—the time for the second dosage was written on the envelope in thick black marker. Kelly warned that Keisha may experience nausea and that she should eat something before the second dose: "If she throws up, you have to call us because then the pills won't work."

Keisha's assurance that her father had been arrested and immediately jailed on the grounds of parole violation did not allay the uneasiness of entrusting all of Keisha's care to her mother. Neither Kelly nor the police had made inquiries as to whether Keisha would be returned to a safe environment. As her guardian, Keisha's mother might be an especially suspect caretaker since she seemed unable to shield Keisha from her father's past and recent abuses. Nor was Kelly unaware of the aura of suspicion that Keisha's mother carried. In her conversation with Keisha's mother about the morning after pill, Kelly had been frustrated by concerns that the pill would render Keisha sterile. Afterwards, she shared with me how this had upset her: "Did she [the mother] actually want her [the daughter] to bear her father's child?" Yet the nurse had given the second dose of contraception, discharge instructions, and referral information to the mother alone. The intervention expressly excluded a systematic evaluation of whether the home the victim returned to was safe. If Keisha had opted not to undergo forensic examination and been tracked through the emergency room as a gynecological patient, her examination would have included screening for infections, and medication. Finally, the nursing care plan would have called for an assessment of the patient's home environment. This step is routinely omitted, or circumvented, in the forensic examination process. While the difference in emphasis is not explicitly articulated, the contrast that emerges seems to be between the victim who is tracked through the emergency room with the anticipation of going home and the victim who is tracked through the forensic examination program and will go to court. The victim who chooses a forensic examination is treated as though the moment of danger has passed.

Earlier in the book, Keisha's family is described as skeptical of her mother; one of her aunts made it a point to speak privately with me in my role as rape crisis advocate and make a note of all of the discharge instructions lest she had to step in and follow through on Keisha's future care. With their collective misgivings about the judgment of the mother and the unsafe home she was providing, Keisha's network of female kin seemed determined to protect her. The shakiness of Keisha's home and her mother's spotty past with regard to her ability to shield her daughter from sexual violence created a need for an extended and dispersed kinship network to mobilize itself.

Leda: The Fleeing Domestic Violence Victim as "Repeat Customer"

Leda was a "repeat customer." Maude, the forensic nurse examiner on shift, told me this under her breath when I reached the emergency room. During my time in the field, I had never met any of the repeat customers that nurses whispered and gossiped about. While rape crisis advocates were often requested immediately upon a victim's arrival in the emergency room, in this case I had been called after the forensic examination as per the victim's request. Leda was perched on a hospital bed only a few yards behind Maude, but the general tumult of the emergency room covered Maude's emphatic whisper. Perhaps Leda saw Maude jerk a thumb over her shoulder to gesture in Leda's direction. In the parlance of sexual assault forensic nursing, a "repeat customer" is an individual who frequently reports to the emergency room alleging sexual assault. The moniker is very common, and while problematic to the rape crisis advocate's ears, it is routinized within the talk of the forensic nurses of City Hospital.

In the emergency room, patients are also clients. Even rape crisis advocates have come to adopt this moniker, socialized to un–self-consciously refer to the victims they accompany as clients. "Customer" suggests the self-consciousness of the economics of healthcare, a field that has been addressed at length in the anthropological research on privatization of healthcare, managed care, and welfare reform (Lamphere 2005). Many interviews with forensic nurse examiners revealed that the myth of the false report of rape is often tied to the imaginary of destitute and/or uninsured women seeking healthcare. Specifically, women are thought to be using the system to access free emergency contraception following bad or unplanned sex. The presence of "customers" in the emergency room also draws on another type of financial exchange. I had been told, both by nurses and police officers, that repeat customers were mostly sex workers who would retroactively "cry rape" if they were refused payment. The language of the repeat customer institutionalizes the notion of those women that the law deems "rapeable" and those whom the law deems "unrapeable," squarely locating sex workers within the category of unrapeable. Within the context of the forensic intervention, the repeat customer is not only denied the resources of law enforcement and cast as a non-ideal legal subject, but also disqualified from accessing care. As Leda's case reveals, it is not simply sex workers who are vulnerable to being labeled as repeat customers.

In addition, women who regularly relied on hack drivers for transportation were included in the repeat customer category. As a rape crisis advocate, I was determined not to ask Maude to identify the circumstances that led her to label Leda a repeat customer, as I wanted to retain my ability to advocate for Leda's well-being as vigorously as possible. I felt confused when I turned toward Leda and took in her appearance. I immediately dismissed the possibility she could be a sex worker, and then mentally chided myself as I had been surprised by appearances before. Wearing tweed trousers, a button-down shirt, and stylish tortoiseshell spectacles, Leda's attire was that of a businesswoman. Though a few unruly strands hung in her face, her hair was exquisitely cut, colored, and styled. Her facial expression was blank; her red-rimmed eyes drifted from object to object, resting nowhere in particular as she stood leaning on her hospital bed. One eye was clearly showing signs of a contusion—it would turn black and blue by the end of our conversation. I noticed a profusion of red welts peeking out of the top of her blouse and on the side of her neck.

What Leda ultimately told me about her "path" to the emergency room was very unexpected given Maude's labeling of her as a repeat customer. Though I made an effort not to let Maude's introduction shape my expectations, I did not anticipate such a disparate gap between Leda's circumstances and the way Maude had referred to her. What first became evident was that Leda had not been admitted to the emergency room for a forensic examination at all—she had been referred for a forensic examination after being treated and stabilized following a suicide attempt. When she related how her journey to the hospital had begun, she was quiet and understated. In response to my query as to how she had been transported to the hospital, she said: "I tried to kill myself and they called an ambulance that brought me here." She rarely met my gaze when she spoke.

A month earlier, the police had brought Leda to the emergency room at City Hospital for a sexual assault forensic exam. Leda had recently fled from her husband after seven years of marriage. He was abusive and was becoming increasingly so. They had two children. She never spoke of their ages or whether they were boys or girls. She had called a local domestic violence hotline to find a shelter she could go to with her children. There was only one that had space for all three of them. It was, unfortunately, located in an inconvenient suburb to Baltimore, but Leda took the chance that she had been offered and took up residence in the shelter. She had a good job in the city, and every morning and evening, she would hack to and from work. There were no buses, taxicabs were much too expensive, and the shelter had not offered any transportation alternatives.

Three days after she began flagging down hacks to get herself to and from work, a driver pulled a gun on Leda and sexually assaulted her on the way home from work. Expelling her from the car in a remote area, he left her alive, scared, and humiliated. Leda had then flagged down a passerby who directed her to the nearest pay telephone where she had called the police. They brought her directly to the hospital where she had been treated, examined, and an investigation had been opened regarding the rape case. Social workers watched Leda's children during this (first) forensic examination.

Back at the shelter after her emergency room visit, the staff and social workers still provided no alternative suggestions for budget-conscious transportation to and from work. Leda resolved to move on with her life, pick her rides more carefully, and continue to hack to and from work. After all, her job was one of a few positive factors of her circumstances—it was what had allowed her to leave her husband, and if she was patient, she would soon be able to provide her own home for her family. Putting her safety first meant picking drivers who were women, had women passengers in their cars, or appeared older and more "respectable." It also meant not compromising her means to a livelihood and maintaining her reputation as a reliable and responsible employee.

Almost four weeks following the first attack by a hack driver, Leda was once again hacking back out to the shelter after work. An older gentleman pulled over in response to her signal and offered her a ride. "He seemed nice, didn't even want any money," she frowned. Halfway home, she realized that he had veered off course. She politely inquired about the detour, and he began to shout and curse at her. Pulling into an alley, he locked the car doors and demanded sex. Leda thought she might be able to talk her way out of danger, though she felt fearful. If she could draw out the conversation, surely someone would walk by and see she was in distress? When he refused to respond to her pleas, she desperately demanded to know whether he had a gun or knife. She momentarily breathed a sigh of relief when he indicated he had no weapons in the car. Her relief was cut short when he began viciously beating her with his fists. He repeatedly bludgeoned her face, neck, and chest. "He didn't need a gun," she reflected, "he didn't need a gun." Terrified and in pain, Leda had cooperated with his demands in order to stop the beating. "I just begged him not to kill me."

"He actually dropped me off near the shelter," she told me. Leda had all her rides drop her off a few blocks away from her destination. "The place is a secret, so I couldn't tell anyone the address." She walked the remaining distance to the shelter, entered, walked straight to the bathroom, and found herself looking under the sink. Among the cleaning products was a bottle of Pine-Sol. She proceeded to swallow most of the contents of the bottle. She did not disclose how and who discovered her attempt at self-poisoning and subsequently called the ambulance. "What do you want to do now?" I asked, concerned. "I need to see my kids. Get back to the shelter. There is a curfew and I want to get back there before . . . "

Forensic Examination: The Presence of Home on the Body

How can the cases described here lend insight into the great distance between the homes that are spoken of and the homes to which forensic nurse examiners prescribe the victim's return in discharge instructions? What are the mechanisms through which this "distance" is achieved? And what trajectory is the homeless victim subjected to following her release from the hospital? Rather than vilify Maude or Kelly, this analysis suggests that the problem is not the particular callousness and insensitivity of these nurse examiners. In fact, both women are exemplary in that they have impeccable reputations as professional and competent nurse examiners; other nurse examiners, rape crisis advocates, and victims have responded positively to their kindness and competence. Parnis and Du Mont have pointed toward nurse examiners' lack of uniform adherence to forensic examination protocol as infringing on the welfare of sexual assault victims (Du Mont and Parnis 2001: 70; Parnis and Du Mont 2002: 849, 851–52). Numerous training manuals, on the other hand, suggest that forensic nurse examiners develop their own style of examination practice, which may include modifying the order of procedures (Crowley 1999: 64).

Neither the personal attributes, nor biographies, nor exam styles of forensic nurse examiners, however, are the sole factors driving the consistent disarticulation of the harmful and healing aspects of the domestic within proffered remedies of sexual assault intervention. Equating the body as scene of the crime is more than an adage and a directive—it is a process constituted within the scopic regime of forensic science. Daily and weekly repetition and routinization of the procedures of forensic examination ensures that nurse examiners internalize the techniques of forensic intervention, thus deploying the scopic regime through which the domestic encompasses both the harmful and the healing. This is not to assert that the forensic examination is irrational in the sense that evidence is simply ignored and contradictory conclusions are drawn (Dawes 2001: 93). Nor does this analysis suggest that there is deliberate and intentional manipulation of a set of facts in order to maintain a blind spot where the domestic is concerned. This is not a case of what David Faigman terms "legal alchemy" in which the law misinterprets or misappropriates science (1999).

As mentioned earlier in the book, the Maryland State Police Victim Sexual Assault Evidence Collection Kit (henceforth "Evidence Kit") produces the routine through which nurse examiners develop their forensic sensibility. In chapter 1, the 17 possible steps to every forensic examination are laid out. "Step 1" is listed as the "Medical Examination and Report of Alleged Sexual Assault Form." Every forensic examination begins with an interview that is structured by the information that must be recorded on the report form.

In both Keisha's and Laura's cases, the nurse examiner is engaged in preexamination questioning. Many items on the examination form require very specific questioning. The opening questions typically include asking for basic information such as the victim's name, address, phone number, date of birth, sex, and race. The forensic examiner then moves to the more specific and "intimate" questions. These include the last date on which the victim engaged in consensual intercourse, and related questions in order to ascertain whether there is a possibility of finding semen or DNA from more than one individual during the examination. Scholars have pointed out that the sexual history that is standard to every sexual assault forensic examination is itself a challenge to the rape shield statutes that protect the privacy rights of victims throughout the process of adjudication (Spohn and Horney 1991).

Inquiring about a victim's recent sexual history also helps to establish the extent to which genital injuries might be caused by sexual activity taking place before or after the sexual assault. The next question asks whether a condom was used in the assault. The examiner has the option of selecting among the following three responses: (1) yes, (2) no, and (3) unknown. The forensic examination is interested in the domestic through narrowly defined parameters. The victim's home address provides a literal home address through which to locate and contact the victim. No single field provides a space for the location of the alleged assault, though the date and time of the assault, the date and time of police notification, and the date and time of the examination are noted at the outset. Another field requires the recording of the location of the examination. The location of the assault is pertinent to evidence collection in that findings on the body are often directly related to the site of assault, and indicative of features or traces that crime scene investigators might focus on or search for when inspecting the crime scene.

While most fields on the form require a single word response, or selecting from among a limited range of choices, not all of the items on the report form call for clearly defined short answer responses. When Kelly asks Keisha, "Did you know him?" she is probing for information that will allow her to complete a less-defined item on the report form. This question does not correspond to a particular blank space, but rather is asked under the heading of "Description of assault (as related to examiner)." An additional instruction directs the nurse examiner to use the enclosed Maryland State Police Note form, which provides an entire 8 ½" by 11" sheet for the recording of a narrative (see figure 7.1).

As part of her notes, the examiner commonly includes the location of the sexual assault on this form. In cases where the assault has

STEP 2

MSP Medical Narrative Notes

Victim's Name: ____________

Police Case Number: ____________

Examiner ____________ (Signature) Date: ________ Time: ________ am/pm

Page ____ of ____

White: Police   Canary: MSP Rape Kit   Pink: Hospital

Figure 7.1. The open format of the form allows the nurse to exercise her discretion, and her expertise, in recording a narrative.

transpired in the victim's home, the domestic appears within the records as both location of assault and home address. Within the description of the assault, the nurse would also record the identity of the assailant, potentially the name of a spouse, relative, or intimate, either current or former. This information appears nowhere else in the Evidence Kit. A further instruction on constructing the narrative advises nurse examiners to "Give description of pertinent details of the assault: oral, rectal, vaginal penetration; digital penetration or use of a foreign object; oral contact by assailant; oral contact by victim; ejaculation and location of such, if known by victim." While this instruction emphasizes the "pertinent details of the assault" by focusing on sexual acts and violent force, the domestic potentially appears once again within such details vis-à-vis the referenced "foreign object." Here, foreign objects are of forensic interest only if they have been used to penetrate the victim's body, putting a familiar or household object to menacing use. The significance of household objects in narratives of violence is often discussed in cases of torture; our attention is drawn to objects when they are implements of torture. In describing the structure of torture, Elaine Scarry links the act of torture to the making and unmaking of the victim's world. She does not locate suffering solely in the body, but connects it to the familiar environs in which the torture victim lives, is tortured, and "returns." In Scarry's description of torture, familiar people, objects, or locations are rendered unfamiliar through their participation in the act of torture (i.e., the chair or cup as weapons or restraints) (1985: 20, 38). The cases I observed differ in that they suggest that the home and the objects and rooms in which sexual violence often occurs remain familiar. Victims did not allude to the foreignness of objects used against them in a rape attack. Rooms and objects are often put to the same uses they are put to in daily life, and descriptions of being sexually assaulted within the home were full of familiar objects and locations. Tissues from boxes on bedside tables were used to wipe away evidence. When Laura, discussed in chapters 1 and 2, collects and "bags" all of the implements touched by her co-worker, they are the glasses and bottles from which he has drunk. The familiar world of the domestic is never unmade into a space of alien terror by transforming objects into other than what they are. The object contains within it the potential to terrorize or to comfort through its appropriate use. When a bed in the home becomes the site of rape, is this transforming the bed into something other than a bed, or transfiguring it from comforting or sensual in one instant to terrifying and menacing in the next?

Home and domestic life materialize in the rest of the examination as physical trace evidence. The location of sexual assault, either the home or any other place, may be substantiated in any of the following examination entries: (1) foreign substance recovered, (2) debris collected, (3) fingernail scrapings, or (4) miscellaneous collection. In these categories, evidence, such as carpet fibers or paint flakes, found on the victim locate the body in a particular space. Home can literally be scraped from underneath the fingernails, or tweezed off the clothing. Injuries constitute another category of examination through which the home can be present in the forensic documentation, for example through a scrape or cut caused by a specific abrasive surface. A common example would be carpet burns.

While the forms in the Maryland State Evidence Kit are fairly typical of forensic examination documentation, documents vary from state to state. Subtle variations in documentary fields can figure the home and the domestic within the forensic examination in very different ways. California, for example, explicitly includes the possibility of parental victimization of children at the outset (see figure 7.2). California Civil Code §34.9 is referenced in the form's header. These rules regard the examiner's obligation to notify parents or guardians in the case of an under-age victim. Parents must be contacted unless the examiner "reasonably believes the parent or guardian committed the sexual assault on the minor." In addition, the location of the assault is given its own field and labeled as: "Location and physical surroundings of assault (bed, field, car, rug, floor, etc.)" (again, see figure 7.2). In this version, the potential sites of a sexual assault include both familiar and unfamiliar spaces. These locations are intermixed without regard to whether they feature within domestic or non-domestic spaces. Compare this with the Maryland forms, which, as stated earlier, lack a designated field for recording the location of the sexual assault. The location "home" is buried within the narrative note, or materialized as trace evidence.

Returning to Leda's case, she is the only victim among those discussed here who has no home to which she can return. On the circuit of domestic violence advocacy, Leda's narrative may exemplify successful

Patients requesting examination and treatment only: Penal Code § 11160–11161 requires physicians and hospitals to notify a law enforcement agency by telephone and in writing if treatment is sought for injuries inflicted in violation of any state penal law. If the patient consents to treatment only, complete Part A # 1 and 2, Part B # 1, and Part E # 1–10 to the extent it is relevant to treatment, and mail this form to the local law enforcement agency.

Minors: Civil Code § 34.9 permits minors, 12 years of age or older, to consent to medical examination, treatment, and evidence collection related to a sexual assault without parental consent. Physicians are required, however, to attempt to contact the parent or legal guardian and note in the treatment record the date and time the attempted contact was made including whether the attempt was successful or unsuccessful. This provision is not applicable if the physician reasonably believes the parent or guardian committed the sexual assault on the minor. If applicable, check here ( ) and note the date and time the attempt to contact parents was made in the treatment record.

Liability and release of information: No civil or criminal liability attaches to filling out this form. Confidentiality is not breached by releasing it to law enforcement agencies.

A. GENERAL INFORMATION (print or type) Name of Hospital:

1. Name of patient Patient ID number

2. Address City County State Phone (W) (H)

3. Age	DOB	Sex	Race	Date/time of arrival	Date/time of exam	Date/time of discharge	Mode of transportation

4. Phone report mode to law enforcement agency: Name of officer Agency ID number Phone

5. Responding officer Agency ID number Phone

B. PATIENT CONSENT

1. I understand that hospitals and physicians are required by Penal Code § 11160–11161 to report to law enforcement authorities cases in which medical care is sought when injuries have been inflicted upon any person in violation of any state penal law. The report must state the name of the injured person, current whereabouts, and the type and extent of injuries.

Patient/Parent/Guardian (circle)

2. I understand that a separate medical examination for evidence of sexual assault at public expense can, with my consent, be conducted by a physician to discover and preserve evidence of the assault. If conducted, the report of the examination and any evidence obtained will be released to law enforcement authorities. I understand that the examination may include the collection of reference specimens at the time of the examination or at a later date. Knowing this, I consent to a medical examination for evidence of sexual assault. I understand that I may withdraw consent at any time for any portion of the evidential examination.

Patient/Parent/Guardian (circle)

3. I understand that collection of evidence may include photographing injuries and that these photographs may include the genital area. Knowing this, I consent to having photographs taken.

Patient/Parent/Guardian (circle)

4. I have been informed that victims of crime are eligible to submit crime victim compensation claims to the State Board of Control for out-of-pocket medical expenses, loss of wages, and job retraining and rehabilitation. I further understand that counseling is also a reimbursable expense.

Patient/Parent/Guardian (circle)

C. AUTHORIZATION FOR EVIDENTIAL EXAM

I request a medical examination and collection of evidence for suspected sexual assault of the patient at public expense.

Law Enforcement Officer

Agency ID Number Date

DISTRIBUTION OF OCJP 923 FOR EVIDENTIAL EXAMS ONLY

ORIGINAL TO LAW ENFORCEMENT;
PINK COPY TO CRIME LAB (SUBMIT WITH EVIDENCE);
YELLOW COPY TO HOSPITAL RECORDS

HOSPITAL IDENTIFICATION INFORMATION

OCJP 923 86 96690

Figure 7.2. The text on these California examination forms reads, "Civil Code §34.9 permits minors, 12 years of age or older, to consent to medical examination, treatment, and evidence collection related to a sexual assault without parental consent. Physicians are required, however, to attempt to contact the parent or legal guardian and note in the treatment record the date and time the attempted contact was made including whether the attempt was successful or unsuccessful. This provision is not applicable if the physician reasonably believes the parent or guardian committed the sexual assault on the minor."

escape. She has fled the site of perpetual victimization at the hands of her ex-husband while retaining custody of her children and access to gainful employment. When I encountered Leda, it was only following her forensic examination. Maude had already completed her interview and all steps of the examination. When Maude introduced Leda to me as a repeat customer, she saw Leda as someone who frequently elected to take risks. In chapter 8, the book will take up the implications of risky behavior in casting the sexual assault victim as a "good" patient. Leda's return to the emergency room within a month from her first visit contributed to this impression. Maude does not have access to Leda's earlier case file. Leda's name and earlier case number are recorded in the Forensic Program register, however, and her last admission to the hospital is recorded within the medical chart. The only potential trace evidence on Leda's body would correspond to the cars in which she had been assaulted—the physical traces of Leda's chaotic domestic world were non-existent. The significance of her travel to and from home gives way to the other patterns of her victimization; namely, that she commonly hacks and that hacking is a risky business. Like the instability and centrality of jobs and the need to make a living, transportation to and from work is a key site of liminal danger.

Living (and Writing) the Domestic

How does disarticulating two aspects of a domestic come to bear on the relationships of Keisha, Laura, and Leda to home? Or, if one were to consider, specifically, forensic documentary practices, "how does the broader speech/writing attitude structure the relationship of this specific type of legal text to the human relationship of the world?" (Messick 1989: 26).[13] One direct result of the inscription of two domestics within a set of paperwork is to preserve these domestics in enduring form as legal text (27). However, although it is a legal text, the documentation has potential therapeutic import.[14] By separating the risks of violence inherent within domestic intimacies from the healing aptitudes of the domestic, forensic nurses can issue prescriptions for victims to return home. Accordingly, Keisha and Laura are sent home. Moreover, being sent home reflects their desire to return home. It is I, as rape crisis advocate, who questions the safety of Keisha's home. When Keisha considers her safety in response to my query, she assesses her home as safe and dismisses its dangers. Her father, the perpetrator in this instance, has been taken back into custody. Her kinfolk, including her aunt, already suspicious of Keisha's parents, will be able to keep Keisha in their sights. Leda, who does not have a home to return to, as she is in the process of escaping from it, is dubbed a "repeat customer." My inquiry is perhaps based in the notion of an idealized, and non-existent, home in which the everyday is hermetically sealed off from acts of violence. This is not Keisha's experience of home, a space she has learned to manage by identifying elements of risk, such as her father's residency in the home, and navigating them. Keisha's vision of home as both the site of nurturance, even if only in the form of residential and economic stability, and harm is in line with statistical realities about violent crime and victimization. It is my own perspective that is encumbered by the powerful mythologies of home as "safe space."

Leda and Laura could be said to have a common history of flight from the domestic. But what distinguishes one from the other is the chronology of victimization and the enterprise of home-making. Laura's days of domestic violence are ten years behind her, and she has attained a home. Leda, who is haunted by the violence of the domestic life she shared with her husband in the recent past, is not yet able to find a way home. The scenic nature of the crime of sexual assault, as described by forensic nurses and in relationship to the victimized body, prevents Leda's body from being linked to a home, least of all her own home. Leda's body, the scene of two crimes, bears no traces of home—it is simply a parchment of her displacements (Cavell 1995: 87). Her displacements appear to continue into the future. As a person who has attempted suicide and is known to be a regular hacker, Leda is evaluated by the domestic violence shelter, calling into question whether she and her children would be offered continued residency there. Within the scopic regime of forensic intervention, the state, in the person of the forensic nurse, sees no home of return for Leda. Even as one victim is returned to a domestic arrangement in which she will have limited recourse for healing or restoration, it is the disarticulation of the healing and hurting qualities of the domestic that allows the state to avoid paralysis or inaction while acknowledging its own inability to affect a complete repair.

8

Patient and Victim Compliance

Drugs, AIDS, and Local Geographies of Care

This chapter begins by painting three ethnographic scenes in broad strokes: It is January 2002, and a rape crisis advocate-in-training shadows an experienced advocate to the local hospital to observe her accompany a sexual assault victim. The victim is in a special waiting room, still awaiting the arrival of the forensic nurse. She nods in and out of consciousness as the rape crisis advocate attempts to make contact with her. The advocate has a form she attempts to fill out to collect details about the case for the rape crisis center. The forms capture data required for reporting to the center's funders, a significant amount of which comes from state grants. The victim is not very responsive as her head bobs forward and her eyelids grow heavier, slipping closed. The advocate raises her voice louder and louder as she attempts to make the victim answer her questions. Finally, she barks in frustration, "Do you want this to happen to someone else?!" She is met with no response and hence, says loudly, "OK, I am leaving—and I am leaving a pamphlet here for you." On her way out of the emergency room, she says to the advocate-in-training, "Next time, you'll see a *real victim*, especially if you go up to [the other] hospital we service. That's where the *real victims* come."

In April 2003, a sexual assault victim, nodding in and out during a forensic examination, falls into what appears to be a deep sleep on the gurney. The rape crisis advocate in attendance suggests to the forensic nurse that she should perhaps wait for the victim to awaken before proceeding with the examination. The nurse shrugs and says that in some ways, it is easier for her to proceed with the exam and evidence collection while the victim is unconscious. She proceeds with the pubic hair pluck (a procedure that is now considered unnecessary in many jurisdictions in the United States and is no longer routinely practiced in Maryland). The victim suddenly awakens screaming in pain and demands that the nurse stop hurting her. The forensic nurse angrily asks if the victim wants her to stop the forensic examination. The victim indicates she does not want to be hurt. The nurse tells her she will then have to stop the examination because there is no way to proceed without pain. When the nurse leaves the room, the victim asks the advocate why the nurse is mistreating her.

In May 2005, there is the case of Astrid, which is detailed in chapter 4. The victim has already been examined by the forensic nurse, but because she has a large abscess on her arm, she is sent to the emergency room for further observation. The rape crisis advocate attempts to flag down a nurse because the victim keeps complaining that she is in a lot of pain. After her attempts to get any assistance for the victim are largely unsuccessful, the advocate is finally able to speak to a nurse, who informs the advocate that the patient is clearly an intravenous drug user who is exhibiting drug-seeking behavior. Thus, none of the nurses are keen to respond to her. The advocate must not be naive, the nurse implies. The victim is ignored until the abscess ruptures and she requires immediate medical attention. The forensic nurse steps in to ask the emergency room staff to treat the ruptured abscess. A resident orders a blood test and an X-ray, concerned about septicemia, as there is a telltale red creep spreading from the abscess down the victim's arm through her vein. When a nurse comes to take her blood, the victim discloses she is HIV-positive. The nurse declares she cannot draw the victim's blood because her "veins are in ruins" and calls upon the forensic nurse examiner to come and take the blood sample, as she had successfully done so during the forensic examination. The forensic nurse examiner, out of the victim's earshot, tells the advocate that the victim, though deserving the resources of a full investigation, will not be taken seriously because of her drug use. "The HIV-positive status doesn't help," she adds.

Thinking through the relationship between the medical and legal elements of sexual assault intervention, as this book has done in a diverse number of ways thus far, it is still tempting to dissect the institutional matrix into its discreet medical and legal units. This, however, is a misleading tactic as it is the intersection of the medical and legal that gives rise to the emergent forensic mode. Regarding the three cases with which this chapter begins, I, of course, was the trainee in the first case, and the advocate in the last two cases. These three cases are selected from among the 44 included within the research study, because they present exemplary instances of a drug using sexual assault victim. As a rape crisis advocate, I would come to recognize the telltale "nod" of the drug user in the six years I lived in Baltimore City—the use of alcohol and narcotics, particularly heroin and crack cocaine, was common among the population of patients frequenting the emergency room. The forensic examiner program in Baltimore conducted an internal study in the late 1990s which showed that about 60% of all sexual assault victims were intoxicated at the time of their sexual assault examination. Alcohol and cocaine were the two most commonly used intoxicants, with heroin the third most common. The study also found that among female patients, the older the victim, the more likely they were to test positive for intoxicants. These patterns among sexual assault victims matched the overall levels of intoxication in the general emergency room patient population, according to City Hospital's self-study.

Such trends make sense in a broad landscape of vulnerability. Youth, intoxication, and other forms of marginalization may facilitate conditions of vulnerability that sexual aggressors seek in victims. This is the type of rationalization that was commonplace in discussions among rape crisis advocates as we sought to account for the high rates of drug and alcohol use among our "client" population. But as is clear from the first example in this chapter, some of the more seasoned, and in some cases jaded, advocates among us considered these victims "not real." As the three ethnographic cases suggest, the forensic nurse examiners and medical staff also seemed to react to these victims with some degree of frustration if not outright hostility. They were considered neither ideal participants in the forensic examination nor deserving recipients of medical intervention.

Study after study has demonstrated the extreme bias in legal processes when it comes to victims who do not conform to particular stereotypes. Scholars have covered the range of criteria that law enforcement and prosecutors deem "ideal" in a sexual assault victim (Corrigan 2013a; Konradi 2007; Larcombe 2002; McMillan and Thomas 2009), inspiring investigators with greater confidence in successful resolution of the case. Clearly, victims who are drug users fall outside the scope of the ideal victim. In this final chapter, the book turns attention to the sensibilities with which forensic nurses react to drug using, and in Astrid's case, HIV-positive, sexual assault victims. Long before a case is deemed worthy of prosecution or is actively investigated, rape crisis advocates, medical staff, and forensic nurse examiners deploy notions of patient-victim compliance. These assessments inflect the face-to-face interactions between patient-victims and personnel. I use the term patient-victim in this chapter because the medicalized concept of patient compliance attaches to victim within this institutional setting, producing the patient-victim.[1]

Forensic nurse examiner programs like the one in Baltimore, Maryland, are frequently housed within emergency departments and staffed by registered nurses who come primarily from critical care and emergency medicine backgrounds. Labor and delivery is the other nursing specialty common among the nurses I worked with in Baltimore. Forensic nurses take on shift work in addition to their regular practice. Thus, a forensic nurse examiner is likely also primarily working shifts as a critical care or emergency room nurse. The 27 nurses that staffed the forensic examination program at the time this research was conducted ranged in experience from just out of nursing school to 32 years as nurses. The majority of the forensic nurse examiners had practiced locally as nurses for seven or more years.

Many of the forensic nurse examiners, emergency room nurses, and rape crisis advocates who had accrued substantial experience in the emergency room at City Hospital had become very familiar with the signs of drug use—track marks, scars, abscesses at injection sites, and the rapid falling into and out of unconsciousness that marked coming down off of a high. Often, victims made no secret of their drug use and were forthcoming in making disclosures to the service providers with whom they worked. As stated earlier, one of the prevailing narratives among rape crisis advocates was that drug users were especially vulnerable, and therefore likely to attract the aggression of sexual predators seeking compromised victims. This was not, however, the prevailing narrative that emerged in the interactive data—rather, the reactions of frustration and anger, or disinterest and dismissal, indicate a different operating sensibility, one that is likely informed not only by work with sexual assault victims specifically, but as a Baltimore-based medical practitioner generally. This chapter argues that the practice of dismissing drug using individuals as problematic patients (their pain is not real—it is a feigned symptom as they seek to manipulate staff for access to narcotics) and uncooperative victims (they are not fully committed to the forensic examination and therefore will make poor witnesses, not to mention their drug use will constitute a credibility problem) is contingent upon operationalizing and ordering localized notions of patient-victim compliance.

HIV/AIDS prevalence is also very high in Maryland (the third highest in the United States in 2009), and from the late 1990s to the mid-2000s, a steep spike in African American women's infection racialized the face of the disease in healthcare practice (O'Daniel 2008; Pounds 1993). Medical anthropology, medical sociology, and public health literature are already rife with research that ponders solutions for the problem of patient compliance within African American patient populations, arguing that mistrust of the medical system, lack of education, and socioeconomic factors keep African Americans from complying with healthcare regimes dispensed to them by their doctors. More recent work has problematized this approach by arguing that it overemphasizes health as an individual good and ignores the structural features that create the conditions of possibility for ill health of particular marginalized groups.

Exploring the origins of patient compliance historically and discursively, scholarship has demonstrated that patient-victim compliance is about much more than the idea that the compliant subject is cooperative and follows directions. Medical historian Jerome Greene has tracked the ways and moments in which the concept of patient compliance is deployed, first emerging in the 1950s, demonstrating that patient compliance is engaged in cases where medical treatments are ineffective and no other explanation for therapeutic failure exists (2004). For Greene, patient compliance stands in for therapeutic uncertainty. The work of patient-victim compliance, or, following Greene, the therapeutic uncertainty surrounding patient-victims, here in the guise of the "bad victim" trope, is to account for the poor juridical outcomes or lack of knowledge of outcomes that commonly result even after all of the resources, including care, evidence gathering, and investigation, have been brought to bear on the case. What's more, because the patient-victim is encountered as a compounded subject of intervention, that is, one who is both a participant in a therapeutic and a juridical procedure, the compliant victim must also be a compliant patient. They are held to a standard in which observant institutional actors make note of whether they embrace all of the therapeutic technologies offered to them, while projecting on to them the expectation that they must possess a demonstrated potential for healing. Remember, for example, the nurse's reaction to Sierra when she refuses to take emergency contraception (see chapter 3 and 4). By comparison, the HIV-positive victim is the non-compliant patient-victim par excellence as she has already been infected with a highly contagious and incurable illness, one that is often associated with intravenous drug use, promiscuity, and sexual activity while stigmatizing the victim's body (Weeks et al. 1993).

When HIV-positive status and drug use intersect, medical practitioners often interpret them as indicators of participation in "risky behavior." At the same time, the practitioners employ therapeutic strategies of risk and harm reduction to address the realities of a life of addiction while reinforcing the sense that addicted individuals are participating in highly risky behaviors. Drug addiction is frequently associated with prostitution, and many defense lawyers will argue that a rape allegation against their client is simply a lie to cover up transactional sex in which the victim traded sex acts for drugs, particularly if the victim is unmarried (Dunkle et al. 2010). Victims who come to the hospital exhibiting signs of drug addiction are often assumed to be prostitutes by the sexual assault forensic examiners and police who work with them, particularly if they bear the markers of poverty and general ill health (and even, as in Leda's case in the previous chapter, when they do not). The ease with which the category of sex worker is attached to a whole class of victims without regard to their disclosures demonstrates the willingness of forensic nurse examiners, police, and rape crisis advocates to stigmatize raped women and cast doubt on the veracity of their claims.[2]

As concerns with the uncertain outcomes of sexual assault cases permeate the institutional nexus within which sexual assault interventions are carried out, an expectation of patient-victim compliance surrounds forensic nurse examiners' interactions with sexual assault patient-victims. These interactions are further nuanced by local geographies of health and illness. Thus, in Baltimore, where there exists a high HIV/AIDS prevalence rate, and substance abuse and addiction are common, patient-victims who present with either one or both of these conditions are more likely to be cast as non-compliant and therefore less likely, I argue, to have their cases end in prosecution, while at the same time experiencing more judgment and diminished access to care and compassion during their hospital stay.

As with the DNA in chapter 1, the agency of non-human actants, in this case a virus and pharmaceutical substances, transforms the interaction between nurse and patient-victim. The presence of the HIV virus, pharmaceuticals, narcotics, or other intoxicants in the victim's body signifies non-compliance to the forensic nurses. In the two cases detailed below, the specter of non-compliance surfaces without regard to whether the victims voluntarily or involuntarily become pharmaceutical persons. To the police and forensic nurse, the patient who must take pharmaceuticals as part of mental healthcare is as problematic as the heroin user who admits her drug-seeking. Non-compliance is the placeholder for uncertainty within an adversarial legal system in which the compelling signs of violent force and abuse on the victims' bodies cannot guarantee a guilty plea or verdict.

Narcotic Persons: Hera and Heroine

Hera was an African American[3] woman who sat in her chair with back ram-rod straight, her head floating atop a long neck between two sharp shoulders. Her short, dark hair curled across her forehead, and her left eye was dramatically blackened, its hue deepening by the minute. She was dressed in a very new-looking, clean sweatshirt and unmatched sweatpants under a black trench-style windbreaker. A few white-grey curls peppered her hair, and I thought to myself, when I first walked in, that she reminded me of someone I knew. I could not quite place who. A former teacher or professor, perhaps? No doubt her elegant carriage prodded some memory of a respected middle-aged woman in my life. Her hands were clean, with short, shaped finger nails and long, tapered fingers. She wore a wedding ring on her left hand. A uniformed officer was still in the family room chatting with Hera when I arrived. Though he was the one in uniform, when she stood up I noticed that he was about a head shorter than Hera and a great deal younger. It was clear who was in control of the exchange. Multiple frown lines creased his forehead as he asked Hera question after question, sometimes muttering to himself while flipping through a small worn notebook as he pieced together the facts for his report. "So you didn't know these guys? And you just walked up to the van? And he didn't say anything? He just punched you? And no one heard you?" His questions seemed to cycle through many variations of the same theme, hammering out the details of the scenario in which two men in a white passenger van had abducted and attacked Hera. She responded calmly, succinctly, without leaning forward, maintaining her straight posture as his questions went on and on.

Hera was accompanied by her sister and a friend who later identified herself as her sponsor. When I arrived and introduced myself as rape crisis advocate and anthropologist, Hera seemed to take quite a shine to me. "May I speak to her alone please?" she eyed the police officer, expelling him from the room while conspicuously allowing her sister and sponsor to stay. She had something of an imperious manner, so the young officer gave us the room, catching my gaze and nodding as he left. "I'll be right outside." When he left, Hera turned to me and told me, without hesitation, that she was withholding information from the uniformed officer.

"He's not happy with me," she started by gesturing to the door through which the police officer had recently departed, "because I didn't tell him how I ended up in a van with two men raping me." At the first mention of a van, my ears had pricked with curiosity and concern, as several rape crisis advocates had recently reported cases involving a white passenger van with two or three men attacking women. After much discussion, our consensus at the rape crisis center was that there was one van, but a varying group of attackers using it. The places in which the van had appeared were fairly localized to two or three neighborhoods in the city. All of these neighborhoods were very poor and largely residential, marked by very few commercial establishments, while containing large publicly subsidized housing complexes occupied by mostly African American residents, as well as blocks full of abandoned and boarded up brownstones—an image that had come to be almost iconic of Baltimore (Goodfellow and Mulla 2008). These areas were also heavily associated with narcotic use and trafficking. Public access to online crime-mapping websites gives this landscape additional texture in the minds of local residents, who could generate maps and reports on recent crime in their neighborhoods on websites like crimebaltimore.com or baltimorepolice.org/your-community/crime-map (Bhrigenti 2012; Wallace 2009). It was always with interest that one might learn of a recent assault or mugging of an acquaintance and check the crime maps to see whether the attack had run the official institutional routes that resulted in it becoming a point on the crime map. In the rape crisis advocates' experiences, many reported sexual assaults never made it on to the crime maps. Just as crime-mapping is one hallmark of contemporary governance, public health professionals also seek to deploy mapping technologies on their understanding of morbidity and mortality (Meliker and Sloane 2011). Baltimore's landscape is assigned geographic meaning along axes of both crime and health. Hera's case was located on this "map."

Hera continued talking about the police officer: "He can tell I got a beating," and she raised the eyebrow, somewhat gingerly, over her dramatically blackened eye, "but I didn't tell him that I walked up to the van because I thought they were going to sell me heroin." Hera had been struggling with drug addiction for many years, she said. She did not offer any more specifics. She simply mentioned that she had been in and out of rehab through many cycles of drug use and sobriety. Her last period of sobriety had lasted three weeks, but this morning she had left the house, not precisely with the intention of scoring some heroin, but, as she put it, without the intention of avoiding a score. When two men had pulled up in a white passenger van and called to her, she thought they were dealers. "I was not expecting the guy to just pop me in the eye and drag me into the van, but that is exactly what happened when I walked over there. And trust me, if they find him, he doesn't look good either. I got in a few licks before the both of them were on me. I cursed him out, too. He must have been shocked to hear the words pouring out of my mouth—I know I was. But I was not going to go down into that van like some quiet bitch. He was going to have to listen to me curse him out if he was going to rape me." She then demonstrated the colorful invective that she had shouted at her attacker. The precise words never made it into my field notes, but a stream of "fucks," "shits," "bitches" and other words were among the less creative vocabulary in the mix. She seemed surprised that she had produced such a flood of obscenities, and actually held her hand to her mouth, a startled round "O," at the end of her description.

My training as a rape crisis counselor required me to "reflect" the content the victim I was working with had shared with me, and after years of doing this type of work, I responded automatically to Hera, "It sounds like it is really important to you that you were able to fight back against the men who attacked you, verbally and physically." This prompted a nod of agreement from Hera, who laughed as she commented that while those men raped her, they got an earful about it. Hera continued that she knew that it was not her fault that she had been raped, even if she was about to do something illegal. She did not, however, want to tell the uniformed officer what she had been up to when she approached the van since he seemed judgmental and suspicious. It mattered to her that his suspicion seemed to be a condition from the very beginning of their encounter, even before she told him her story. "I mean, I am sitting here, obviously hurting, having been through some shit, and this guy is not even sorry. He is immediately like, 'what aren't you telling me?' And I'm like, you don't know me like that to know whether I am lying to you or not. I mean, what does it matter, why I walked up to that van? I did not walk up to that van to be raped."

While this particular uniformed officer was suspicious of Hera and suggested her withholding of information was problematic, this attitude should not necessarily be generalized to all police officers. When two members of the Sex Offense Unit had conducted a training class for the rape crisis advocates, we had asked them how they dealt with sexual assault victims who were intoxicated or high. They promptly informed us that the law was very clear on this point, as intoxication could clearly indicate a lack of capacity to consent. Like the nurses in chapter 3, the police are mobilizing the same criterial reasoning. "We don't blame the victims for drugs or whatever. We only ask that they are upfront about what is happening. We won't press charges against them; we just want to catch the bad guy and we have a short window to do it in, so we just want them to be honest."[4] The young officer pressing Hera to give details was likely to be laboring under an impression that Hera' non-cooperation was jeopardizing his chances of getting to the bottom of the case. That he could treat Hera with more respect and understanding, even as a tactic for increasing her likelihood of cooperating with him, did not occur to him as an available strategy.

While Hera had ejected the officer from the room, she continued to speak with me, and our conversation eventually turned to the anticipated forensic examination. Hera sent me to find out whether the forensic nurse examiner had been paged and how long she could expect to wait. As I left the family waiting room, the uniformed officer stopped me and asked to speak with me. I followed him around the corner, and he immediately asked me what Hera had told me. "She says she just walked over to the van. Does that sound right to you?" I shrugged in response and explained that the circumstances of the assault did not impact my role as an advocate. I added that I was not authorized to repeat any of the things Hera had told me, and could not respond to his question. "Crisis center policy, sorry!" This joinder to the explanation I stated in a tone of contrition, as if I would have helped him if I could, because as a rape crisis advocate, I knew it made my job easier not to antagonize the police. Like the forensic nurses in chapter 3, we rape crisis advocates were also masters of particular forms of emotional labor, in particular, an institutional apologetics in which we placated the interests of the forensic nurses and police alike so that we would be able to accompany and advocate for the sexual assault victim navigating through the procedure. In fact, one might argue that rape crisis advocates also had to operate within a role of institutional compliance. We knew to navigate this line because rape crisis advocates had been asked to leave the hospital in the past, particularly after confronting forensic nurses or police officers in assertive ways. We also depended on the hospital to page us on the victim's behalf in the first place, and feared that if our advocacy appeared too assertive or contrarian, we would not be included in the intervention at all.

This exchange with the police officer took no more than a minute, so I was quickly buzzed through the secured doors and at the administrative office of the forensic nursing program. As it happened, the sexual assault forensic exam was not yet authorized as Emma, in the office carrying out her duties as program administrator, was still waiting for a detective to issue a complaint number. The detective was on his way, she told me, and since she was actually covering the calendar, she would not have to page a nurse to come in and do the exam. As long as the detective authorized the examination, Hera would not have long to wait. I shuttled back to Hera with this information. She thought about how to she would tell her story to the detective who was coming in. "I have to tell him everything again?" she asked me. I answered honestly that I thought this was the case, but having sat in on very few interviews, I could not be sure. "Maybe that is a good thing," she reflected, "that I have to start over. I think I'll tell him everything and see how he reacts."

When the detective walked into the room a short time later, he had stopped and been briefed by the uniformed officer. He walked into the waiting room with a serious look on his face, and Hera immediately disarmed him by cocking her head to the side with equal seriousness and saying, "Now I know you don't think you are going to give me a hard time? I mean, I have been through enough and I will tell you everything, but just don't be mean about it." She then joked about the detective's appearance, saying someone who looked as nice and fashionable as he did could not possibly have any interest in being mean to a rape victim. His demeanor changed instantly, and he asked all of us who we were, then asked Hera if she would mind if he spoke to her alone to take his official report. Hera decided that she would be alright on her own with the detective, so I left the room with her sister and sponsor. As I departed, I asked the detective whether or not to tell Emma he had arrived and to ask her to set up for an exam. He told me he would be back to give her the complaint number himself before beginning his full interview.

The Geography of Illegal Drug Users as Non-Compliant

Associated with a particular neighborhood infamous for its poverty and its heroin trafficking, and obviously omitting information from her first report, Hera represents a non-compliant sexual assault victim to the police officer. Note that Hera is met with suspicion and distrust by the police officer before she discloses that she approached the men who attacked her with the intention of participating in an illegal transaction. The slippery slope of illegality that haunts the story allows the uniformed officer to assume the worst. Namely, his assumption is that because she is withholding information and because she was attacked in a particular location, she must have been transacting for drugs. In all likelihood, he probably further supposes that she may have participated in transactional sex in order to acquire the drugs. Like the elaborate myth of the prostitute who made an accusation of rape when her customer did not provide payment, the "repeat customer" in chapter 7, the drugs-for-sex exchanges that went bad were part of the local police folklore. Drug users cried rape when men promising drugs did not deliver, they said. When speaking to forensic nurses about whether they worked with sex workers or individuals involved in transactional sex, they responded that this was exceptionally rare. It was a powerful trope among the police, however, leading to the conditions under which Hera, simply by locating herself within a drug-steeped geography, became a magnet for suspicion. Illegal drugs transformed her from a potential crime victim to a criminal herself. That her appearance, age, posture, and carriage might appeal to some, like me, as indicative of a certain gentrified respectability, was negated by the pharmaceutical geography of the urban landscape on which she appeared.

The perception of Baltimore's African American community as overtaken by heroin addiction in the late 1960s is heavily anchored in the experiences of the Narcotic Unit of the Baltimore Police Department, as they tracked and maintained files on local known drug users (Agar and Reisinger 2002). Such institutional practices and the visible transformation of Baltimore's streets sustain the local knowledge that heroin use has been an "epidemic" facing the city. While the epidemic of heroin use was not limited to African American city residents, public health consensus holds that African Americans are overrepresented in the heroin-using population (Nurco et al. 1980; Robins and Murphy 1967; Wilson and Fisher 1969) and numerous theories have explored why this may be the case (Agar and Reisinger 2002). The density of this debate and the sustaining discourses of public health, policing, and popular culture saturate Baltimore as a landscape deeply etched with illegal drug use and drug sales (Meyers 2013). As the landscape and particular neighborhoods come to bear these markers, the bodies that inhabit and traverse these landscapes come to be marked as participating in the drug economy, with or without confirmation.

For law enforcement, there are multiple narratives about the use of illegal drugs. On the one hand, they make drug users more vulnerable to the threat of sexual assault. On the other hand, drugs mark their users as criminals, and a crime victim who is also a criminal potentially lacks credibility. With investigations and trial outcomes so hard to anticipate, these developments introduce yet one more variable by which a case may end without an arrest, charges, or a guilty plea or verdict. Meanwhile, the therapeutic perspective is no less problematic in that "conventional paradigms of drug treatment present addicts as liars" (Ning 2005: 350). If we were to think of a drug addict as the intersection of a human and an object resulting in the instantiation of a pharmaceutical person (Goodfellow 2008), the institutional perspective holds that the pharmaceutical person is intrinsically unreliable and manipulative. While this may, indeed, be found to be true in some cases (Carr 2010), a health interventionist could, once again, frame the addict's personal characteristics as markers of vulnerability rather than signs of noncompliance. While these stigmas mark those who are touched by illegal drugs and their attendant geographies, how do law enforcement and the forensic nurses interact with those pharmaceutical persons who avail themselves of the use of prescription medication? The next section explores the case of Pandora, a woman undergoing treatment for a mental health condition.

Pharmaceutical Persons: Pandora's Personalities

Pandora, her name affectionately shortened by her friends, so Dory for my purposes, presented a very unique case for the sexual assault forensic intervention program. She called 911 immediately after her ex-husband forced his way into her home and sexually assaulted her. She also called two close friends (one from work and one from church) when she learned she was coming to City Hospital for a forensic examination. As Dory explained, she suffered from multiple personality disorder, and she needed the support of her friends in order to navigate the ordeal of reporting to the police, facing the exam, and dealing with the subsequent investigation. Multiple personality disorder is an identity disorder typified by a single individual developing multiple personalities or alters. According to the psychological literature on the disorder, these personalities emerge in response to trauma. It is a distinctively U.S. phenomenon, with more cases diagnosed in the United States than anywhere else in the world (Coons et al. 1991). Later, this chapter will consider the complications of multiple personality disorder as a diagnostic category and how this concern enters the emergency room, but for now, let us focus on Dory's understanding of her mental health condition and its impact on her experience of victimization and sexual assault intervention.[5]

The specter of a patient with significant mental health or cognitive delay issues is not altogether unheard of in the context of forensic intervention, where a notable number of complainants come to the forensic program through sites such as group homes or assisted living facilities in which caretakers are frequently accused of abusing their charges (Crossmaker 1991). Unlike individuals with disorders that render them severely incapacitated, Dory was very independent and managed quite well. While she had successfully managed her disorder for many years now, Dory told me and the police officer who brought her to the hospital that the crisis had triggered an acute episode of her disorder. When the attack began, she had begun to rapidly switch alters, and this cycling had continued for a few hours following the attack. As Dory was unsure of which alter (or alters) had been present during the attack, she did not know who would be able to talk to the police and give them the information they sought. Her friends were there to help her sort through this issue and keep track of which alters were in the know.

In the psychiatric community, multiple personality disorder is considered an outdated diagnosis, and the symptoms associated with this condition now fall within the DSM-IV[6] category of dissociative identity disorder (henceforth DID) (Gillig 2009).[7] DID has been and continues to be a deeply controversial disorder, and while some psychiatrists accept and treat the diagnosis, others consider it a disorder that is purely iatrogenic, reflecting a clinical misunderstanding of another dissociative disorder rather than the actual existence of a single individual with multiple alters (Fahy 1988; Gillig 2009; Merskey 1992). It is also a deeply gendered diagnosis, with a much higher incidence among women, and most theories identify the etiology of DID as related to sexual victimization and trauma as a child (Sinason 2002: 3–5). It is certainly beyond the scope of this work to account for the heavily gendered nature of the DID diagnosis and its prevalence among women. Some theories hold that boys are socialized to be more expressive and act out their trauma, thus externalizing their suffering. In contrast, within this theoretical frame, girls internalize their suffering, developing dissociative identities in order to survive (Sinason 2002). The individual is further unable to integrate the traumatic experiences into the principal personality and her alters become independent. This independence is largely characterized by the fact that alters do not have knowledge of the experiences of other alters, and thus the individual experiences the shifts in personality as blackouts or dissociative episodes.

While psychiatrists have moved on to the nomenclature of DID, multiple personality disorder is alive and well in the public imagination, frequently confused or conflated with schizophrenia and dramatically depicted on television. The persistence of multiple personality disorder in popular culture raises the question of whether those who make use of the older moniker, instead of DID, are more vulnerable to being doubted by health professionals. In my encounter with Dory in the emergency room, the reality of the disorder was much less remarkable than I expected. Dory did not adopt dramatically different postures, facial expressions, or tones of voice. Her shifting alters were barely discernible from one another in terms of demeanor, at least by one, like me, who did not know her well. Her friends would calmly explain, "It's not Dory now. This is Helen," or "This is Cassandra," as Dory seemed to lose track of her words and pause or trail off mid-sentence, expectantly waiting to be engaged. This happened every two or three minutes, but Dory's friends assured her that it was happening more slowly than it had been when they had first met her at home. After listening to the ways the different alters responded to the uniformed officer's questions, they concluded that it was Cassandra who seemed to have the most to say about Dory's ex-husband attacking her. Dory's friends were able to tell her this. "Cassandra knows what happened, Dory," they said. Dory wished aloud that Cassandra would be there to speak to the police detective when he arrived.

As it turns out, Cassandra was obliging and promptly appeared to answer the detective's questions. He seemed to accept the basis of the diagnosis as it was presented by Dory and her friends almost immediately. He interviewed Cassandra for around 45 minutes, producing the detailed description of the rape attack he would need for investigation. Cassandra remained calm throughout her interview. She had a very steady demeanor, barely showing reactions or changes in her facial expressions as she spoke, with only one exception. Her most marked shift in expression occurred during pauses, when she searched her memory in response to the detective's questions. After responding, her eyebrows would knit together gently, and she'd bite the end of her tongue while letting it protrude slightly from her mouth. This lasted for only a split second, and then she might add one or two more details. If she had nothing further to add, she would ask the detective, "Is that all you need to know?" He would nod in response, indicating assent with a deep affirmative, "hmmm." Leaving aside the details of her responses, what Cassandra described amounted to a minute-by-minute account of the assault.

After 45 minutes, Dory reemerged and was able to explain that she had answered the door when her ex-husband had first arrived, and could confirm that he had forced his way into the house and immediately wrestled her to the floor. She experienced the duration of the attack as a blackout, but she could definitely identify the assailant. The detective took a detailed description of the assailant, Dory's ex-husband, as well as taking his address, and went out to radio his colleagues to see if they could make contact and potentially pick him up as a suspect for questioning.

Abigail was the forensic nurse on duty that day. She was relatively less experienced in the forensic practice compared to other nurses in the program, but she was also much more recently trained and was working on a doctoral degree in nursing. Most of the nurses who staffed City's forensic intervention program had two-year associate degrees or a four-year BSN (Bachelor's of Science in Nursing) degrees, while Abigail had already completed her BSN as well as a master's before moving on to doctoral work. One of Abigail's graduate instructors was a psychologist, and had directed Abigail toward scholarship on psychology, mental health, and trauma since she had expressed an interest in a forensic nursing career. Abigail flipped through Dory's chart before she began her forensic interview, glancing at the health history taken by the triage nurse upon Dory's arrival in the emergency room. The history includes a question about any current medications, as healthcare providers are obligated to introduce checks and safety measures to prevent potentially harmful drug interactions. Dory took a prescription medication for her disorder, she had told the triage nurse, and had given the name of an anti-anxiety drug she was currently prescribed. Abigail frowned when she saw the anti-anxiety medication on the chart.

Presently, psychiatric consensus for treatment of DID promotes behavioral therapies, with ocular treatments and hypnosis often used to work with the individual toward integrating all alters into the original personality (Gillig 2009). This consensus was generally well-established by the mid-1990s, with some disagreement about the use of anti-anxiety medications as they were rarely effective unless paired with other behavioral therapies. Anti-anxiety medications were essentially viewed as adjunct treatments appropriate for accompanying psychotherapy (Putnam 1989). Some psychiatrists warned that anti-anxiety medications might prevent or impede behavioral treatments by maintaining the patient's feelings of being out of control (Barkin, Braun, and Kluft 1986: 114). When Abigail saw the prescription for anti-anxiety medications in Dory's chart, she asked her why she was taking the medication. "For my multiple personality disorder," she responded. Dory's use of the term "multiple personality disorder" was already out of fashion among psychologists, who had adopted the term "dissociative identity disorder" a decade earlier. As she moved with a flurry of energy, charts flipping open and closed, forms rifling, Abigail muttered, "but you can't treat DID with anti-anxiety meds . . . " clearly not addressing Dory as the comment was not loud enough to be heard by anyone but me and Abigail herself.

Through the rest of her interactions with Dory, Abigail was brisk, pointed, and thorough. I accompanied Dory to the exam room and sat with her throughout the forensic interview, leaving just before the physical examination as Dory preferred to be alone with Abigail. Abigail did not engage in any of her usual banter during the forensic interview. Usually, Abigail would ask patients about their hobbies or favorite television shows to distract them from the discomfort of the invasive questions she asked. She was unusually on-task with her verbal interactions when questioning Dory, limiting her verbal interactions almost completely to the questions required in the forensic documentation. Before she gave Dory a dose of contraceptive pills, she asked her to list her current medications. Dory again mentioned the anti-anxiety pills. Abigail asked her, a second time, what the anti-anxiety pills were for and was told, once again, that they treated Dory's multiple personality disorder. When Abigail briefly left the room to grab a form she needed, Dory commented that Abigail was not exactly "warm and fuzzy."

Diagnostic Uncertainty and Pharmaceutical Compliance

A week later, I had occasion to speak with Abigail as she was arriving at the hospital while I was leaving. We had already met for a formal interview a few months back, were about the same age, shared the experience of being doctoral students, and had a friendly relationship. I asked Abigail if she had a few minutes to talk to me about Dory's case, and she agreed enthusiastically.[8] "That was a one-of-a-kind thing, huh?" she began. Before I could ask any questions, Abigail launched into a discussion of how interesting she thought the case was. She had never met anyone with a DID diagnosis, and she was sure that Dory had been holding back. Her certainty on this point was linked to her concern that anxiety meds were not indicated for treatment of DID. Abigail wanted to make sure she recorded this in the medical chart in case something "came up" as the case proceeded through the criminal justice system.

I asked Abigail about her unusually business-like interactions with Dory during the forensic interview, admitting that this had surprised me. I mentioned a few memorable conversations she'd had with patients about television, telling her I usually found her more informal and chattier. Abigail nodded in agreement, saying she had in fact behaved differently. Since the case was so complicated by the mental health issue, she felt it was important to "play it by the book." When I asked her what she meant by "complicated," she further explained that there were so many unknowns in this case. Did Dory really have "multiple personality disorder"? She herself indicated the use of quotes around multiple personality disorder, her fingers bobbing expressively at her face. Was there some other reason the patient was medicated? Had Dory told her everything? In the case that the self-reported diagnosis was correct, what if the patient was being treated incorrectly? And how was Abigail supposed to interact with Dory and her alters? What if they had different preferences? Better, Abigail thought, to "stick to the script and document, document, document" so that some other authorities would have the best chance of getting to the bottom of the case.

In Abigail's response, one can see multiple dimensions of uncertainty animating her choices. There is the uncertainty around the diagnosis of multiple personality disorder/DID that arises, in part, from Abigail's professional opinion of the pharmaceutical regime Dory identifies as her treatment for the disorder. There is the uncertainty surrounding how one interacts with a patient who has this complex diagnosis. Given the nature of these uncertainties and their potential to compound uncertainty in the evolving case against Dory's ex-husband, Abigail did her best to stick to a forensic script that would not unwittingly compromise the case.

Abigail's concerns, we see, are neither purely about the legal case nor the medical concerns. She is concerned about misdiagnosis, erroneous treatment, and patient compliance. She concedes that the patient may be correctly diagnosed but incorrectly medicated, but also balances this possibility with the possibility that the patient is lying or omitting information. Not being forthcoming with a medical provider is non-compliant, as only with a full disclosure can proper diagnosis and treatment occur. Because Abigail does not know what is true, she retreats to her official role as forensic nurse examiner with the charge to "document, document, document" so that others may decide the facts. She is also aware that Dory is likely to have a hard time of it as a sexual assault complainant with such an exotic mental health condition, all the more reason for the case to lose momentum and not end in a conviction.

The result of Abigail's professional choices aimed to mitigate both therapeutic and juridical uncertainty was that Dory finds her less than "warm and fuzzy." Abigail's role as a forensic nurse examiner did not mesh with Dory's vision of her as a nurse. A nurse, for Dory, should be "warm and fuzzy," but in Abigail's behavior, left unexplained to Dory, there was none of the kindness Dory associated with nursing care. What's more, Abigail's concerns that a complicated case did not comply with the ideal standards for investigating and prosecuting a rape case, was tied to the specter of the non-compliant patient who is either lying about her diagnosis or withholding her complete diagnosis.

Patient-Victim Compliance

In many ways, Dory and Hera represent two strikingly different types of patients, and the details of their cases contrast greatly. Dory is attacked by an assailant who is known to her, where Hera is ambushed by strangers. Dory appears emotionally shaken but physically unwounded, while Hera, her eye visibly swelling and black, shares the fact of her verbal aggression against the attackers. Hera is an admitted heroin user, while Dory suffers from a serious identity disorder and takes prescription medication. As much as these details differ, where Dory and Hera overlap is in the ability of the nurses to interpret their behavior as non-compliant. Whether she admits her heroin use or is simply suspected of it because of the neighborhood with which she is associated, Hera's status as a drug user immediately suggests non-compliance as a patient. Her drug use may be seen as compromising her health, increasing her risk of violence and morbidity, even as she seeks legal recourse after being assaulted. For Dory, it is her use of prescription medications that casts doubt on her compliance.

In both cases, there is a great deal of uncertainty around the possibility of successful investigation and prosecution of the assailants Hera and Dory accuse. If anything, the difference in the circumstances of both the cases and the ways in which they stray from the favored mythological archetype of the virginal victim accosted by a nefarious stranger, suggest that the prosecutor could find it challenging to build each case. In Hera's case, her drug use could contribute to the perception that she is responsible for her victimization. For Dory, her identity disorder may contribute to the perception that she is an unreliable witness. Left unexplored is the challenge of Dory's identification of her ex-husband as the assailant in a culture in which the criminality of marital rape is not universally accepted (Hasday 2000).[9]

Just as Greene has argued that patient compliance arose to account for uncertainty when therapeutic regimes fail and no reason can account for these failures, patient compliance also arises in the context of the sexual assault forensic intervention to account for uncertainties around both therapeutic and legal outcomes. Because forensic nurses at City Hospital are rarely informed about the legal outcomes of the cases in which they participate, these are uncertainties that are rarely resolved over the course of their professional lives. Thus, Abigail's question about how Dory's diagnosis will play out in the legal context is never answered. In fact, neither she nor I know whether Dory's ex-husband was prosecuted at all. Likewise, neither Emma nor I know what the significance of Hera's drug use may be, or even whether the men in the white van will be located or arrested.

While very experienced forensic nurses may have the opportunity to observe, over time, that they are very rarely subpoenaed, and even more rarely called to testify, even this experience can be interpreted in multiple ways. For some nurses, it is an indicator that few cases escalate to trial, and therefore refocuses them on the therapeutic aspects of their interactions with patient-victims. For others, it indicates that while their presence is not needed at trial, their documentation may have an active juridical life they will never come to know. In fact, this may even be considered ideal. With few possibilities and resources to address the many uncertainties built into the forensic practice, forensic nurses will continue to operate within the space of uncertainty.

For the victims who come seeking care or justice or both, the professional choices that nurses make to mitigate the uncertainties of the task before them have many repercussions. As patients, victims may find themselves treated in a manner they do not identify as caring, and as victims, patients may find that nurses' sense of them as non-compliant extends from their patient status to their status as victims. In this way, the model of medical competence and nursing professionalism in which forensic nursing is embedded marks the emergence of a legal status: that of patient-victim. This indubitably impacts the individual's therapeutic and juridical journey. Like the forensic nurse, the rub is that the anthropologist and her readers may be blinded by the present and feel no more well-equipped to overcome the uncertainty, peer ahead into the future, and see for themselves how forensic intervention comes to bear on the patient-victim's therapeutic and juridical experiences.

Conclusion

"We're Not There for the Victim"

The Violence of Forensic Care

From the outset, this book has argued that the particular form of care that emerges from the interaction of legal and therapeutic practices imposes a particular violence on victims of sexual assault. This violence is born not from the intentions of individual forensic nurses who consciously set out to alienate the victim-patient with whom they are working, but rather from the particular institutional, professional, and historical location of forensic sexual assault intervention. The characteristics typical to the institutional location described throughout this text arise from the training regimes, professional mores, temporal practices, technological tools, documentary styles, and ethical orientations of both legal and medical origins colliding to produce a mode that is not an obvious admixture of legal and therapeutic components, but rather that is uniquely forensic.

The dozens of precise forensic nursing techniques that have been highlighted within this book are characterized by the routine violences that found and re-found a particular political and administrative order. Also at stake within the forensic intervention are competent, efficacious, and intelligent investigations of sexual assault cases, the care and recovery of sexual assault victims, the professional lives of the nurses who conduct these examinations, and the expertise and resources provided by the state in each case. Without insight into the institutional and cultural underpinnings of forensic intervention, victims are left to puzzle out the institutional mode with which their suffering is received, a mode that at times magnifies their suffering. Victims, and anthropologists, can frequently interpret the meaning and motives of sexual assault intervention through consideration of how the nurse interviews the patient, interacts with the patient and her family, collects and preserves evidence, manages her own and her patient's emotions, dispenses medication, reads or writes legal and medical documents, draws and photographs injuries, marks the passage of time, and charts a path forward for the victim and for the investigation. Indeed, the stakes within sexual assault forensic examination are high, for the very act of examination under the auspices of nursing care re-founds the existence of the state in the guise of its criminal justice system. The state is re-founded here through the ongoing collection of evidence from many American women and men, subjected to and participating in the founding and re-founding of a technocratic administrative order. This book has demonstrated that the technocratic order is not race-blind. Nor is it gender-neutral. Rather, this mode of governance is deeply gendered, and is embodied through the acts of both the nurses and the victims with whom they work. The victim's body is no longer simply a parchment of her own displacements, but rather, the displacement of her singular narrative by the foundational narrative of the state. How forensic nurses articulate their role in this foundational violence and gestures toward the displacement of the victim is perhaps best encapsulated by the frequent utterance of the sentiment: "We're not there for the victim."

"We're Not There for the Victim": Articulating Institutional Relationships and Priorities

When asked to define their roles as forensic nurse examiners, forensic nurses have responded with a definition that encapsulates some obvious unifying themes. Chief among their responses are various riffs on the role of an "objective evidence collector." The work that objectivity does in this self-definition may index a number of possibilities. First, it suggests that the nurse is aware of the ongoing nature of investigation that has not come to a close from a formal legal sense, in some ways voicing her alliance with the founding order of the state. Hence, the nurse is objective in terms of her assessments of guilt or innocence of the named perpetrator in the case. She further signals that in collecting evidence, she may be called by either the prosecution or the defense within the process of the trial. While it is more commonly prosecution who will call the nurse as state's witness, the possibility that she may be called by defense exists, and therefore the nurse may not "choose sides" in our adversarial legal model. Finally, she is objective in that she is object-oriented. She objectifies her patient by mobilizing narratives and techniques that transmute a patient into a victim. When the nurse finds that she feels overwhelmed, upset, disgusted, or saddened, she may even objectify herself, diverting her affective response by substituting criterial logic to sustain herself through the case. Where does the presence of this objective evidence collector in the sexual assault intervention leave the women and men alleging rape, and testifying to a range of other vulnerabilities that structure their daily lives? The emotional logic of actors participating in the intervention itself manifests in the demeanor of the forensic nurse, which may be confused as a withdrawal of care by many victims. An "objective evidence collector" conducts herself in a particular way, relying on the cool, clinical demeanor described at several junctures within this book. This conduct is both perceived and felt by the patient, who does not have the luxury of disaggregating her own victim and patient identity from one another and dismissing or qualifying the mode of care she experiences during her hospital stay. The nurse's demeanor may further be interpreted not simply as withdrawal of care, but as disbelief, contributing to the dynamic of re-victimization. The bereft patient-victim is left to struggle on her own, or perhaps with attendance of a rape crisis advocate, as the nurse performs her tasks in allegiance to some other force.

The Forensic Nurse as Figure of Care

If the forensic nurse is in danger of being perceived as withdrawing her care, what, in fact, is she caring for throughout her participation in the case? If she is not there for the victim, then who is she there for? Here, we can explore a number of possibilities, some abstract and others very material. For example, the nurse may see herself as serving the prosecutor, the defense attorneys, law enforcement, and the court itself. Her work, she imagines, makes it possible for these actors to investigate, charge, and build cases for their clients, the state, and the defendant respectively, as it is the state that is the plaintiff in criminal trials, and not the victim herself. From a perspective oriented more toward the general good, it may be society, or even justice itself, that the nurse imagines that she serves. In the early moments of the sexual assault intervention, we see that justice may take many forms. It is both the conventional and institutionally located process of the criminal justice system, as well as the informal avenues, that make sense to the victim herself as she wrestles with the events and the circumstances marking the intrusion of violence in her daily life. Justice may be the healing that is initiated in the moments of the sexual assault intervention, an indubitably unpredictable process with its own distinct time line into the future. Justice is also, perhaps, procedural or administrative justice, as the examination represents the greater part of the resources and attention that the victim will be afforded since her case's sojourn in the criminal justice system is most likely to come to a close without an arrest or a trial ending in a conviction. The examination itself, the expertise and attentions of the forensic nurse examiner, and the intimacy and concentration of the nurse's energies on the victim's voice and person, come to stand in as the most resourced stage of the investigation in the victim's experience. These resources are measured in technologies, expertise, personnel, and time. For some of the victims I spoke with over the six months following their exams, the memory of the forensic nurse became more idealized and positive as time passed. With the knowledge that a court trial would never take place, and that their cases had run their course through the criminal justice system, the care afforded by the forensic nurse examiner became more and more significant. The nurse herself, in two cases, became an almost fictive or mythic figure. "She's the only one who listened to me," said one victim.

Victims revisited their memories of the forensic examination several times over the six months following the exam itself. The subject was one they raised, partly because they knew I had an interest in it, but it also seemed to genuinely occupy a space in their imaginations. All the men and women I worked with over the six-month period were extremely vulnerable from an economic perspective. They made no pretenses about agreeing to participate in my research project both because they wanted to contribute to the welfare of other sexual assault victims[1] but also because they needed the meager $35 honorarium I offered at each meeting, which they collected every two weeks. It was a small sum compared to the rates advertised by other studies taking place in

Baltimore at the time. Every week, a two-page spread in the local *City Paper* contained up to 12 advertisements for studies currently enrolling subjects, but these often required particular demographic characteristics, or sizable time commitments, or even calculated risk. In addition, I provided companionship and travel assistance, and often sprang for coffee or a sandwich. It was not unusual for me to spend a day with one of the four men and women I worked with, simply driving them from appointment to appointment, many of which involved visits with social workers or trips to free clinics. For my research participants who navigated the precarious world of free healthcare, the three- or four-hour visit to the emergency room and the care and attention of the forensic nurse began to seem like a larger boon as it vanished into an increasingly distant past.

It is tempting to end the analysis here, ruminating that the business-like demeanor of the forensic nurse does, in the end, no harm, as the victims still come to have an overwhelmingly positive association with them, at least according to the very small group of victims with whom I worked. I am unable to make this generalization for victims as a population in general.[2] Returning once more to the importance of the forensic encounter in the experiences of sexual assault victims, I must first point out that the criminal justice system does not, often, deliver to victims anything that they remotely recognize as justice in a meaningful or personal way. This should be abundantly evidenced by the ways in which victims and nurses voice the struggle over narratives of suffering in the various ethnographic cases referenced throughout the book. Rather than leave the victim in a posture of experiencing justice, the encounter with law enforcement is frustrating, leaving them with feelings of being disregarded or even disbelieved. These feelings of being disbelieved, the reader must recall, are independent of the intentions as voiced by the actors engaging with the victims. That is, it does not matter whether the forensic nurse believes or disbelieves the victim because the institutional location and practices in which she participates leave the victim with the firm impression that she is disbelieved.

This is not to say unilaterally that no victim experiences justice as a result of his or her participation in a criminal investigation that is inclusive of a sexual assault forensic examination. If, however, women and men experience justice after being sexually assaulted, it is often because they mark out a path to justice for themselves. This may mean an investment in healing, self-growth, and the securing of a livelihood that also incorporates acceptance of the low probability of any formal criminal justice outcome. Thus, one key finding of this book is that if the forensic nurse examiners feel themselves committed to justice, a reasonable commitment to espouse in the role of forensic nurse, they might do better to emphasize their expertise as nurses and seek to provide care rather than to align themselves with agents of the criminal justice system. Indeed, the primary professional association that trains, guides, and develops best practice standards for sexual assault forensic nursing interventions has firmly encouraged nurses to be led by their training and professional nursing identity rather than succumbing to the desire to assimilate a law enforcement identity.[3] It argues that framing the forensic nursing profession within the framework of "objective evidence collector" reduces the forensic nursing role to mere technician and in fact annuls the nursing expertise and experience of each individual nurse, potentially eroding her credibility not only with her patients, but also as a witness testifying on the stand. The evidence of the study upon which this book is based provides an ethnographic basis for emphasizing the value of forensic nurse examiners as caregivers, suggesting that they make a meaningful impact as healthcare providers as many if not most cases still do not advance to an adjudicative stage. And, as we have seen, even at adjudication, many studies thus far suggest that forensic evidence bears no impact on outcomes in either plea agreements or jury trials.

The Cost of Anticipating the Trial

As has been noted many times, for nurses the reality of testifying in a trial is largely imagined. Most of the nurses I worked with testified fewer than five times, even in careers spanning two decades. The low likelihood of a case escalating to the trial stage perhaps lends greater importance to the reliability of the nurse's testimony if she is to testify at all. If so few cases reach the court, institutional logic perhaps dictates the importance of all of the stakeholders involved doing everything within their power to ensure that cases are optimally disposed. The reality of the unlikely arrival of the case in the court also draws attention to the greater likelihood of achieving a justice forged outside of or despite the realities of the criminal justice system, one that is perhaps as delicate and vulnerable and as worthy of careful shepherding.

It also bears examining, at this point, the intensity and seriousness with which policy responses to sexual assault have emphasized forensic intervention and forensic evidence. Forensic science is itself still a budding science, with much basic research still to be established and many juridical truisms called into question (National Research Council 2009). In short, apart from DNA identification, many other forensic techniques—such as fingerprint analysis, voice recognition analysis, and facial recognition software—still suffer from a dearth of scientific confirmation of validity, yet they are still admissible in most U.S. jurisdictions (Edmond et al. 2012). Policy solutions that emphasize forensic intervention also sustain stereotypical rape imaginaries by emphasizing injuries and positive DNA findings when examinations are likely to yield neither in a sexual assault intervention. And in cases where positive findings are recovered, the impact of forensic evidence on legal outcomes is often unclear, with a majority of studies showing that forensic evidence is of little or no consequence in sexual assault prosecutions (Johnson et al. 2012; Sommers and Baskin 2011; Du Mont and White 2007), and in prosecution of all violent crime generally (Peterson et al. 2010).[4] Wound analysis is another vexed expertise, as studies on genital injury have indicated the difficulty of identifying the differences in injuries caused by consensual and non-consensual sex (Anderson, McLean, and Riviello 2006; McLean et al. 2011), while many other studies continue to support the commonality of lack of genital injury to victims in cases of sexual assault (Riggs et al. 2000; Slaughter et al. 1997). The most recent studies that span multiple jurisdictions and multiple states seem to suggest that forensic evidence plays a very negligible, perhaps nonexistent, role in the legal outcomes of sexual assault cases, while also showing that those cases that do reach trial stage and are successfully prosecuted are highly dependent on basic police investigation. A study of one county in England even found that police detectives were more likely to under-investigate a case if they knew that a forensic examination was conducted, neglecting to track down and interview witnesses or even return to the crime scene and recover evidence (McMillan 2010). While this may change in the future, at present, it means that much of what transpires in the forensic intervention is based on imagined efficacies of forensic technology that have yet to bear out in reality. As seen, DNA evidence is of little relevance in most sexual assault cases as there is no need to make an identification of the accused perpetrator when the parties are known to one another, which is the normative pattern of rape victimization in the United States and many other jurisdictions.

Locating the Victim: Re-victimization or Victim-Centered Care?

Let us return, again, to the original question of where this leaves the patient-victim. If, despite the urging by their professional association to assert their expertise based on their identity as nurses, I can characterize many nurses' primary allegiance as being to the criminal justice system,[5] then this leaves the victim's personal journey toward justice as a secondary priority for the forensic nurse. The victim's own priorities and narrative may not coincide with that of the forensic nurse's, or may sometimes intersect with the institutional priorities and sometimes run a separate course. The victim's experience may reflect the difficulty of this non-synchronous positioning, as well as her blindness to the structural and legal conditions driving her encounter with the forensic nurse and the criminal justice system. She is dependent on the forensic nurse, and sometimes the rape crisis advocate, to inform her about the structural conditions under which she is undergoing examination; whether these explanations are offered or not is at the discretion of the individual nurses and advocates.

Thus far, this analysis has remained at the level of the individual patient-victims who are interpellated into the forensic regimes described in great detail in this book. Yet the stakes of these institutional arrangements, as argued earlier, span beyond the level of the individual and have wider repercussions. These institutional configurations are justified by policy makers and practitioners because of their sense that the problem of rape is not an individual problem such that if a few individual men and women must bear the burden of "re-victimization" by the criminal justice system, it is worthwhile in pursuit of mitigating the effect of rapists for the purpose of the social good. Here, it is important to tread carefully lest we scale up the problem of sexual assault in justifying our intervention and scale down its costs for individual sexual assault victims in minimizing the burdens that the intervention places on individuals. To reiterate one way in which this justification is made, what is a little poking and prodding to get results? (Tjaden 2009).

When one is an observer in the context of a sexual assault intervention, it is abundantly clear that sexual assault victims take the interventions very seriously. That is, they do not distinguish between the formal and informal aspects of professional practice as they experience it. The intervention itself clearly represents an official function to the victims: it is a moment in which they feel themselves in the presence of and subjects of the state. That the forensic nurse who conducts their examination in this case is employed through a private institution and is not an official agent of the state is not a meaningful distinction. The instrument that she uses, the forensic examination, is generated by the state and once again doubles the nurse not only as a private functionary, but in fact as a state functionary. As a state functionary, the nurse's care thus re-forges the social contract with the patient-victim. In this case, we might argue that it is in fact a materialization of Pateman's sexual contract between the feminized sexual assault victim and the patriarchal state (1988). With diminished chances of arresting, charging, or prosecuting the accused, the victim, not the perpetrator, is both object of care, and object of discipline.

The private hospital, as a designated agent of the state, exemplifies the increasing number of public-private partnerships that characterize contemporary forms of governance following the neoliberal turn (Bumiller 2008). In addition to privatization, neoliberal reform has also hyper-individualized social problems, which Melanie Beres, Barbara Crow, and Lise Gottell argue serve to both de-gender and de-politicize the problem of sexual violence (2009). While it certainly holds true that an emphasis on forensic intervention as the primary entry point into both the criminal justice and healthcare systems turns public sentiment away from larger issues like the patriarchal underpinnings of rape culture (Buchwald, Fletcher, and Roth 1993) and the structural inequalities that make women and children vulnerable to violence (James et al. 2003), the intervention itself, one might argue, is both intensely political and intensely gendered.

Tracking the forensic intervention as a configuration of time and space in which power is ceded and negotiated and alliances are forged, we see the forensic nurse depending on a strong alliance with law enforcement that might include the sexual assault victim, but more often than not, excludes the sexual assault victim. The victim may ally herself with the rape crisis advocate, who is present only at the whim of the forensic nurse who may or may not have paged her. The rape crisis advocate, unlike the forensic nurse, is a volunteer and not a paid expert, thus giving her a lower professional status and less powerful institutional affiliation. The rape crisis advocate herself tends to limit her advocacy either by keeping silent lest the forensic nurse and police officers ask her to leave the hospital, or by aligning her desires with those of law enforcement. Some rape crisis advocates find themselves differentiating between "real" victims and those who are not genuine based on their perceptions of victims as sober, cooperative, and worthy of care.

These dynamics are intensely gendered, with the forensic nurse and law enforcement taking on a paternal and masculine role, one that requires the forensic nurse to distance herself from the feminized nature of the nursing profession in part by adopting a cool affect, and also by prioritizing the needs of the forensic examination over the nursing care she will dispense. The forensic nurse is also able to attain a more-or-less independent practice, working with little to no supervision from the medical staff that has official oversight, so the role of forensic nurse is viewed by many nurses as a rise up the professional nursing ladder. The sexual assault victim is the most feminized figure within the institutional nexus, abject, possessing little expertise or knowledge about the process that she will undergo, and with the volunteer rape crisis advocate as a potential ally. The overall effect is one that reinscribes the victim's subject position by demanding cooperation and compliance (Corrigan et al. 2013). This cooperation and compliance are embedded within both medical and legal regimes, with few resources invested in nurturing and protecting the integrity of the nursing care intervention that simultaneously unfolds alongside the sexual assault intervention.

With the nursing care intervention often subsumed by the forensic evidentiary examination, nurses lose out on an important opportunity to reframe sexual violence as a gendered health-related issue. That is, relying on the approach of nursing assessments could result in regarding sexual assault not as an acute health condition, but rather more along the lines of a state of co-morbidity particularly exacerbated by structural vulnerabilities. The state is itself able to see such patterns through statistical scrutiny, for example, finding that particular populations, such as female college students or Native American women, are more likely to suffer from sexual assault than women in the general population (Fisher, Cullen, and Turner 2000; Tjaden and Thoennes 2000). Individual forensic nurses, however, see only the patient-victim before them, and in the program where I conducted my research, they see her almost exclusively in the context of the legal case that they anticipate will take place in the imagined future.[6]

Subsuming Care, Founding a State

The violence of the sexual assault intervention itself, with both the physical and psychological torment that victims often experience, regardless of the forensic nurse's best intentions, confounds the care that victims expect to receive in the hands of the state. The cool affect of the forensic nurses who attempted to maintain the demeanor of an "objective evidence collector" frequently provoked a response of confusion on the part of victims who did not know what to make of their treatment at the nurse's hands. The state's violence in the form of the forensic intervention is also justified (or, following Max Weber, its use legitimated) by its service to the state. The state's violence is not simply corrective, but foundational, as it re-founds the state's order, drawing the actors back into its structures and underwriting the social contract by which they abide (Benjamin 1979). The state that is re-founded by the ongoing collection of evidence from the persons of scores of American women and men asserts a technocratic administrative order. It bears pointing out that this technocratic order in which justice is largely administrative in form is not race-blind—it integrates medical and legal genealogies that cast African American women and men as less idealized candidates for victimhood. Race is not explicitly engaged as a category fraught with risk, but rather treated as a risk factor in morbidity, for example HIV/AIDS or drug use, and also criminalized by its elision through geography. One becomes the neighborhoods in which one lives and works.

If these neighborhoods constitute a risk to the lives and well-being of these individuals, the institutional perspective simply conflates the individual at-risk with the individual as risk.

These dynamics seem to be reproduced over time by the perpetuation of the same technologies across many territories, and the institution of particular professional standards that set up new programs following old structures. It is as if our policy makers, be they legislators, hospital administrators, or nurses, live in a world in which an epistemological barrier has been erected between themselves and sexual assault victims. That is to say, we live in a world in which we frequently imagine that legislators, hospital administrators, and nurses are not victims, and we fail to imagine or to prioritize how an intervention may be experienced by a victim. Overcoming this epistemological divide means expanding our imagination, or even acknowledging the victims and survivors among us, and legislating, administering, and nursing with compassion. It means embracing the uncertainty of sexual assault prosecution, and perhaps demoting the importance of the trial. It means laying claim to a professional expertise grounded in what one does know and has done, rather than on the imagined and as of yet untested and undocumented efficacies of many forensic technologies. Once again, the professional leadership guiding forensic nurses typically frames things in this very way, urging nurses to treat sexual assault victims as patients and to frame their experiences this way on the stand, as they have likely treated thousands of patients, but only a handful of sexual assault victims. To be an expert must mean to be a nurse, and not simply an "objective evidence collector." While I never asked any forensic nurses if they were also victims or survivors of sexual assault, many nurses volunteered this information during our interviews. With interest, I observed that only one nurse disclosed her status as a survivor of sexual assault, while the others either kept silent or, overwhelmingly, stated that they were not victims of sexual assault.

Overcoming the epistemological divide between victims and nurses also means sharing information and knowledge about the basic institutional logic behind the forensic exam itself. The victim should not be unaware of the formal and informal rules and regulations that are in effect. If she is to give her consent to participate in the process, then how can we make claims that this consent is informed given that it is secured when the victim is unaware of the standards by which she is judged? Sharing institutional knowledge and bridging the epistemological divide between victims and nurses is not a simple task. In order to do this, it means that nurses, and the teachers among them, must reflect on the institutional logics in which they operate. Reflection is a process that must be supported and facilitated, particularly if one works with the pressures of being under-staffed and under-funded, where time itself is a fleeting and potent resource. Many nurses have called for this type of reflection and institutional reform, but the question remains whether such calls will be heeded and supported.

As nurses struggle to negotiate the relationship between their investment in law and their investment in medicine and nursing practice, they must recognize that the forensic modality that defines their work is greater than their own intentions and efforts. This modality is powerfully located within institutional protocols and techniques themselves, spanning examination methods, statistical imaginaries, documentation regimes, and visual technologies. The resulting vision and practice of care is one that is confounded by its location within forensic institutions. It is barely recognized as care by many victims, and when it is, this recognition is fleeting or is achieved as the event of the forensic examination itself fades into the past. The care of the forensic intervention also brings the force of its own violence; this foundational violence produces a structure in which it is victims who bear all of the costs of sexual assault.

NOTES

NOTES TO THE INTRODUCTION

1. According to the 2000 U.S. Census, the most recent census to the period in which I conducted this study, there were just over 650,000 city residents, of whom 46.64% were male and 53.36% female. Census figures report the city residents were 64.34% African American and 31.63% white.
2. See “Rape Cases Dismissed by Baltimore Police Later Found Valid,” July 25, 2010, *Baltimore Sun*, and “Half of Discarded Rape Cases Reclassified,” December 1, 2010, *Baltimore Sun*.
3. The term “actant” is drawn from actor-network theory and references non-human agents.
4. Nancy Venable Raine’s *After Silence* (1998), or Robin Warshaw’s *I Never Called It Rape* (1988), are books I consider typical of the rape narrative genre. Cathy Winkler’s autobiographical ethnography *One Night: Realities of Rape* (2002) also includes some of these narrative features, though her analysis encompasses a broader range of community responses and institutional venues.
5. This, like all individual names, is a pseudonym.
6. While it is tempting to argue the merits of advanced education for credentialing forensic nurses, such changes would likely contribute to the staffing challenges of forensic nursing programs. This is particularly true of smaller programs located in less populous parts of the country, where access to medical and nursing professionals is already limited.
7. These collaborators have also published in the past as Parnis and Du Mont.
8. I admire and respect Winkler and Di Leonardo’s willingness to share their experiences as sexual assault survivors (or, as Winkler calls herself, a victim-survivor-witness) in such a public and open fashion. As one rape crisis advocate told me, “when a survivor tells her story, it should be treated as a gift.”
9. Winkler was denied tenure and subsequently left the academy. She attributes her failed bid for tenure to a lack of understanding on the part of her colleagues and an institutional culture that was unwilling to make allowances for life-changing traumas. Once a member of an anthropology faculty, she became an activist and a high school math teacher.
10. The project was reviewed under the name “Legal and Medical Sexual Assault Interventions in Baltimore” under HIRB no. 2004077. HIRB approval for

continued data collection was maintained from 2002 and expired in February 2009. Data storage protocols for the closed study are maintained under oversight of the Marquette University's Office of Research Compliance.

11. Precedence can be found in ultrasound as it posits fetal bodies as distinct and separate from the mother such that a future relationship with this fetus can be imagined and anticipated (Matthews and Wexler 2000; McGrath 2002; Strathern 1992).
12. In some jurisdictions, nurses are paid for their court appearances. At the time of my study, in Baltimore and many other localities, they were not paid for court appearances.
13. When presenting this work, I have frequently been asked about my own emotional responses to working with and on gendered violence. Research on sexual assault certainly comes with a particular challenge (Campbell 2001a). While there is room to engage this topic in the reflexive tradition of anthropology, I will simply say that all ethnographic research is potentially emotionally draining. When one works on sexual assault, one simply expects to be emotionally taxed. I, thus, made effort to nurture myself, while also noting that while the circumstances that bring victims to the emergency room may be dour, the emergency room is not necessarily a dour place itself. Rape crisis advocacy itself can be very rewarding and satisfying work in which one offers to listen and gives another person the opportunity to be heard and supported. What was far more disturbing to me was the idea of victims undergoing sexual assault interventions without rape crisis advocacy or accompaniment.

NOTES TO CHAPTER 1

1. For more information on The Innocence Project, one can visit www.theinnocenceproject.org, which states that the Project is "a national litigation and public policy organization dedicated to exonerating wrongfully convicted individuals through DNA testing."
2. In 2005, the state's attorney's office estimated 30% of cases reach different stages of trial, with an even smaller percentage of these 30% resulting in time served.
3. The other two models for forensic nursing programs are (1) to locate the program within a criminal justice facility and (2) to have an independent community-based center (Corrigan 2013b).
4. Following January 2009, VAWA now requires all sexual assault complainants to have access to a medico-legal examination without any police involvement; the decision is no longer to be in the police officer's hands. Some evidence suggests that there are still gate-keeping mechanisms by which victims are still kept from access to sexual assault exams, often by police officers who refuse to take victims to the hospital, or to alert them that they may request an evidence collection exam (Corrigan et al. 2013).

5. Alfredo's behavior of continued and escalating demands (for a place to stay, food from an inconveniently located restaurant, for an alcoholic beverage, and even his call to Laura directing her to come upstairs) is considered common casing or grooming behavior in incidents of acquaintance rape. The escalation of demands is meant to assay the victim's boundaries. The more she accedes to the would-be rapist's demands, the more he views her as a vulnerable target of sexual assault (McCabe and Wauchope 2005).
6. Laura's detailed description of the events leading to the attack contrasts with her quick gloss of the details of the attack. This pattern is common among the sexual assault victims with whom I spoke, who volunteered many details about events leading to a rape attack. In the victim's first report, the rape itself is often narrated in a very spare and quick way, using non-specific terms, or focusing on one specific act as opposed to providing details about the whole attack. The narrative gathers more specificity with each subsequent round of interviews, first by a uniformed police officer, then a sex crimes detective, and then a forensic nurse. Following these interviews, which draw on the characteristics that must be in place in order to determine whether a crime has taken place, and which crime exactly has been perpetrated, victims often internalize the details of narration imparted through the interrogations they have faced. Following the interview processes, victims' narratives tend to take on a more uniform quality in which they include details that speak to the legal criteria guiding the questions they were asked to answer. This process is discussed at length in chapter 2.
7. In fact, given the infrequency of DNA evidence used at trial (e.g., Sommers and Baskin 2011), it seems that this is more of a detectives' fiction about repeat offenders than a reality.
8. Patient compliance impacts the production of victimhood in the forensic intervention, and I detail the processes through which compliance emerges in chapter 8.

NOTES TO CHAPTER 2

1. The anticipatory structure of rape crisis intervention itself is another framework operating here. An experiential description of the rape crisis advocates' anticipatory structure can perhaps be characterized as the discipline of expecting anything, everything, and nothing.
2. See Mattingly (1994, 1998) for a description of emplotment as the co-production of a clinical narrative by patient and clinician. The normative chart-oriented forms of talk and the informal and storied discourse patients produce in the context of the interaction of patient and clinician both have a place in the clinical interaction, Mattingly argues. In Laura's tale, we can see the struggle between the clinical forensic plot that the nurse must tell, and the story that Laura tells that overflows the registers of criminal and forensic time.
3. A hack is the term used locally for an unauthorized taxi driver.

NOTES TO CHAPTER 3

1. Within the anthropology of law, there is a long-standing tradition of emotion as proof or tactic of witness credibility (Bailey 1983: 24; Just 1991: 290).
2. This is despite the fact that the prosecutorial outcomes are largely imagined.
3. The first chapter of Hyde's *Bodies of Law* discusses the use of the *Hawkins v. McGee* case as the first case used in many law school curricula. He argues that law students are shocked into adopting legal criteria by being forced to equate a hand with a machine. This constitutes the initiation of students into legal thinking (Hyde 1997: 19). (Interestingly, the case also suggests the intersection of the medical and legal imaginaries as the parties to the case were Hawkins and his doctor, McGee, who was sued over his inability to restore Hawkins's injured hand to its former function and appearance.) Similarly, medical anthropologists often note the use of dissection early on in medical school. In addition to familiarizing medical students with anatomy and physiology, they must also learn to distance themselves from the act of dissection and gain (or sustain) their emotional mastery (Carter 1997: 105; Segal 1988: 17). This analysis is similar to the case of forensic training I discuss in this chapter.
4. In fact, the field of crisis intervention and the prolific rate with which the volumes on crisis intervention model are published suggests a large industry attending precisely to the question of managing emotions in crisis situations, as well as many theories and strategies for training crisis interventionists in the most efficacious techniques. As I go on to discuss, in Baltimore, this preparation does not centrally figure in forensic nurse examiner training.
5. Douglas writes, "In a more exalted spirit, St. Catherine of Siena, when she felt revulsion from the wounds she was tending, is said to have bitterly reproached herself. Sound hygiene was incompatible with charity, so she deliberately drank off a bowl of pus" (1966: 7).
6. Abjection, as Kristeva defines it, is attributable to those things that are neither subject nor object—it is that which is cast off and we recognize as formerly part of ourselves.
7. Kristeva's discussions of the abject seem to pertain to this discussion in two more ways: first, the abject is ostensive—it makes itself known vis-à-vis showing, not saying, per se. Second, Kristeva elides relegating the abject to either the unconscious or conscious mind. Thus, it lends itself to an analysis of the ostensive pedagogical techniques that structure forensic nurse examiners' encounters with disgust.
8. In one case more fully discussed in chapter 4, a sexual assault victim who had just undergone forensic examination was held in the emergency room for observation. Residents read her chart and quickly noted her HIV-positive status as well as her history as a heroin user. The telltale abscess on her right arm sealed her identity as an intravenous drug user, and her complaints of pain were ignored as classic drug-seeking behavior to access painkillers.

9. Note that while I thought it was a choke mark, this was not medically confirmed, and so the nurse described it as a welt.
10. Before leaving the hospital, rape crisis advocates must notify the forensic nurse examiner and have her sign off on the advocate's call sheet.
11. In some states, though not in Maryland at the time of this research, offering emergency contraception to sexual assault victims is a legal requirement.
12. This chapter leaves aside the complex transformation of Sierra from suffering rape victim to autonomous potential mother. These assertions cast the victim in a non-compliant role, an issue I take up in detail in chapter 8.
13. "Suppose we ask: 'When a child learns the name of something (e.g. 'cat', 'star', 'pumpkin'), obviously he doesn't learn merely that this (particular) sound goes with that (particular) object; so what does he learn?" (Cavell 1979: 169).
14. Time cannot be underemphasized as one of the most important aspects of the work of forensic examiners. It shapes several features of the forensic intervention, and also comprises a central subject of scrutiny itself. Establishing a time line, working against the ravages of time in preserving evidence, and noting the precise moments at which evidence is collected comprise essential features of forensic labor. I discuss and analyze the place of time in forensic labor and its anticipation of the courtroom in the previous chapter.
15. Forensic nurses speak of high burnout rates in their ranks. Coping skills must be part of the expert's arsenal. Bad feelings and stress cannot be allowed to percolate and fester. As Peter Just writes of the context of Dou Donggo dispute settlements, "there is a sense here in which too much restraint seems to be socially dangerous, that hidden emotions are perilous" (1991: 295).
16. In fact, perhaps it is not a coincidence that the police and the forensic nurse examiner take a statement (and not a narrative, a story, a report, or a set of sentences) from the victim. If we think of J. L. Austin's apt criterial distinction between a sentence and a statement, a statement can be true or false. A sentence cannot be evaluated with these criteria (Austin 1962: Lecture 1).
17. As each state has its own Nurse Practice Act and Board of Nursing governing the profession, the same levels of accreditation are not common from state to state. In Wisconsin, for example, where I currently conduct research, there is no requirement that forensic nurses have any formal credentials beyond the RN.
18. According to the nurses, these distinctions are partly physiological and partly based on the likely identity of the assailant in child sexual assault cases. Namely, the expectation is that the child is most likely to accuse a caretaker and this requires some separation and protection from the assailant in the forensic setting.
19. Forensic examinations are very unlikely in child sexual assault cases as children are typically delayed reporters, and very few disclose abuse in an acute situation in which evidence is likely to be found.
20. This comment also evokes the deep-seated tendency to over-sexualize African American men and women in U.S. culture (Collins 2004).

21. Withdrawal of consent was challenged in Maryland case law, but was finally upheld (*Washington Post*, November 2, 2006; *Frontline*, Winter 2007; *State of Maryland v. Maouloud Baby*, May 9, 2007).
22. It is not uncommon for developmentally disabled individuals to be victimized, often by caretakers or, in group housing situations, other residents (Bowers and Veronen 1993; Mansell and Sobsy 2001). Of the 44 cases I observed, two involved such individuals. The scholarly literature argues that developmental disability itself constitutes vulnerability, and that sexual aggressors and predators target vulnerable individuals (Lee 2000). I also saw four cases of elderly victims, one of whom could not speak because she had previously suffered a stroke. She told her daughter she had been victimized by a hospital orderly. A second elderly woman came to the emergency room complaining that she had been raped by the physical therapist making home visits to assist her in her rehabilitation from hip replacement surgery. These instances of attacks against elderly women fit into the broader pattern of victimization of the vulnerable.
23. See Das (2000) for this formulation.

NOTES TO CHAPTER 4

1. I am citing only a few landmark studies. There is a deep literature that addresses mass rape and pregnancy in sociological, psychological, legal, and anthropological literatures.
2. Whether or not it results in pregnancy, studies of mass rape demonstrate how the phenomenon can produce shifts in intergenerational relationships and in criteria of marriageability, masculinity, and the ability to make a living (e.g., Das 1995, 1996b; Hayden 2000: 28). These are only some of the ways in which so-called peacetime rape shares continuities with mass rape (Olujic 1998: 31).
3. Comments such as those by Representative Todd Akin in 2012 (see "Senate Candidate Provokes Ire with 'Legitimate Rape' Comment," *New York Times*, August 19, 2012), who surmised that "legitimate rape" rarely led to pregnancy because a woman's body could "shut down" such unwanted pregnancies, suggest that popular knowledge about sexual assault and conception might still resemble sixteenth- and seventeeth-century standards.
4. The mechanism by which Plan B works is identical to regular birth control pills. Though it is post-coitally administered, it is not an abortifacient and cannot terminate an existing pregnancy. Rather, it prevents ovulation. It is unclear whether it even prevents the implantation of fertilized ova in the uterine lining (Wynn and Trussell 2006: 300).
5. Note that, like the nurses described in chapter 3, victims are also expected to fall within a predictable emotional spectrum.
6. There is another set of concerns emerging here about the role of single motherhood in low-resource communities of color, and women's suspicion of male partners and long-term heterosexual relationships (Edin 2000). As this was not

the focus of my research, I am not able to offer much more analysis, but want to index that Sierra's case is emblematic of a deeper issue.

7. The eventedness and singularity of incidents of rape in the crisis counselor's imagination is further emphasized by the experience of comparing sexual assault interventions with domestic violence interventions. Many rape crisis advocates found the domestic violence interventions much more emotionally exhausting and challenging, as domestic violence victims were likely to return to the situation in which the violence was ongoing. On the other hand, sexual assaults were considered "over" so the violence was seen as receding into the past. Thus, sexual assault interventions could be performed with something like greater hope for "success."
8. During the sexual assault intervention, some forensic nurses ask victims if they have previously been sexually assaulted. This often prompts a response about one's prior experience or one's involvement in a sexual assault case with a different victim.
9. During the facial photograph, protocol used to require that victims hold a placard displaying their case numbers just below their chins. Many victims would turn to the side following the frontal facial shot, as with booking photography upon incarceration. This would cause some victims to joke about prior incarceration, or mention that they were being made to feel like a criminal. The practice of photographing a victim's face while she holds the case number within the frame has been suspended in Baltimore since 2004.
10. Here is another instance of the failure of rape shield laws to guard Rachel's privacy. The state's attorney is operating under the assumption that the defense has a way of introducing Rachel's criminal history and must anticipate this move.
11. The success of the legal case against Dennis's stepfather may have stemmed from Dennis and his sisters' status as children. As minors, there was never a question of consent as they lacked the legal capacity and right to consent. Perhaps this imbued the distinction between child and legal adult with even greater meaning for Dennis. In Rachel's case, the state's attorney implied that the defense was alleging that she had consented to have sex with her uncle in exchange for drugs.
12. The Combined DNA Index System, or CODIS, demonstrates this curiosity or association. At the state level, the database includes DNA samples from all felons, unidentified DNA samples recovered from sexual assault victims, and DNA samples from male homicide victims.

NOTES TO CHAPTER 5

1. Note that Agamben's pagination in *Means Without Ends* (i.e., 94,4; 94,5; 94,6, etc.) follows this form.
2. As mentioned at other points throughout this book, this is at least true in cases where victims have recourse to gynecological healthcare, which presupposes a particular class status.

3. As many programs adopt the use of a digital camera, monitors are frequently absent from the exam room. Victims are increasingly unable to see what nurses see or to seek explanation during the examination unless the nurse makes it a point to show her the digital images.

NOTES TO CHAPTER 6

1. This law is commonly referred to as HIPAA by healthcare providers and is essentially a health privacy law governing the transmission of written information from health records.
2. From the perspective of the state Nurse Practice Act, because it is not the nurse but the suspect who is ordered to provide the evidence, the nurse is ethically obligated to seek the suspect's consent and the evidence is a type of limited practice of nursing care. Each hospital deals with this requirement in a different way: in some jurisdictions, the hospital has the suspect sign a consent form, while in other jurisdictions it is the police that have the suspect sign a consent form.

NOTES TO CHAPTER 7

1. The categories of "stranger" or "simple" versus "acquaintance" rape are further subdivided in the profiling of perpetrators. See for example Holmes and Holmes (2002: 139–56).
2. Location figures only as a generic site: a space where one returns to find material evidence, or to locate potential witnesses. It is also, as discussed later, an indicator of what material traces are likely to be found on the body of the sexual assault victim if her account is truthful.
3. In this chapter, I sometimes use the terms domestic and home interchangeably. In doing so, I am not suggesting that they are always the same thing. It is simply that at times they are mutually inclusive.
4. The concept of a scopic regime, as discussed in Martin Jay's "Scopic Regimes of Modernity," and elaborated by many others, including W.J.T. Mitchell and Christian Metz, typically refers to culturally and/or historically specific ways of seeing. It is neither solely characterized by social constructionism nor technological determinism. Rather, the social and technological are both constitutive of a particular scopic regime. The concept also suggests that contemporary modes of perception can vary from one another. Thus, in the case under discussion, the scopic regime of the forensic and the anthropological may overlap in some respects. Ultimately, however, each sexual assault victim comes to be "seen" quite differently as an ethnographic versus examination subject. It is the conditions of possibility for this scopic regime that I describe in chapter 6.
5. Applying a calculative statistical assessment to the sense of "home" is not a practice that should be applied uncritically (Poovey 1998; Porter 1995), nor can it be assumed that statistics or data about the home are easily collected and interpreted (Nations and Amaral 1991).

6. For this insight I thank Valeria Procupez, who first brought this to my attention in relation to the case of Argentina, and then reminded me of the many other circumstances in which one was vulnerable to political violence in the home, in particular with regard to abduction and "disappearance," as home was the place one was most likely to be found.
7. The aggressive insistence on domestic bliss in the United States is most often associated with post–World War II modernist architectural movements. The postwar home was forcefully "happy." Home was not simply a "backdrop" against which life was lived, but a way of living. The space of the home associated with everyday life was deliberately folded into a particular domestic (Colomina 2007: 5–20).
8. The significance and import of incest and marital rape are not fixed but informed by the particular historical and social framing of each instance.
9. Smock is referring to Blanchot's comments on the primal scene (Blanchot 1986: 72). For further structural features of the scenic in relation to the domestic, see Weber (1999).
10. The "body as the scene of the crime" orientation is not limited to Baltimore. I found numerous references to it in training curriculums, though the phrase is conspicuously absent from many mainstream forensic nursing textbooks. It also appears in police training manuals and law enforcement journals. See, for example, Larry Jetmore's 2006 column in which he writes, "in a rape there are two crime scenes: the location where the rape took place and the rape victim's physical person, including the clothing worn by the victim and the perpetrator." This is the only direct reference I have found to the perpetrator's body being included in the locus of "crime scene." As for Jetmore's inclusion of the perpetrator's clothing as an extension of the "rape victim's physical person," this association seems unintentional. However, it is suggestive in that the perpetrator is erased except as a force acting on and constituting the victim's body, or as the atomized traces of a perpetrating body for which the nurse searches in chapter 1.
11. Interview on September 10, 2004.
12. This is often circulated under the brand name "Ovral." Other pharmaceutical options, such as Plan B, exist, but the City Hospital program used Ovral until more recently.
13. See also Navaro-Yashin (2007) for how documents effect, retain, and carry affect (2007). This question need not be posed simply in relation to bureaucratic forms, but all representative modes that are legally recognized as annotation. For example, Povinelli considers the place of family trees in Australian aboriginal land claims, and how "their social relevance was in fact democratized and dispersed into the life-world of ordinary people" (Povinelli 2002: 218).
14. In the intimate-domestic domain, Berlant states, "jurisprudence has also taken on a therapeutic function . . . notably as it radically recasts interpretations of responsibility in cases of marital and child abuse" (2000: 1). In fact, Nolan argues that the increase of therapeutic intervention in adjudicating criminality is a recent reorientation of the juridical function of the U.S. state.

NOTES TO CHAPTER 8

1. For example, because all emergency room intakes require a mandatory blood screening to identify any intoxicants in the blood stream, sexual assault complainants also receive this treatment and have it entered on their medical charts. Forensic nurse examiners therefore carry out their work with this knowledge. Indeed, the purpose, if not the effect, of such testing is not to stigmatize or mark complainants as non-conforming to the "ideals" of victimhood, but rather to ensure that they can be safely treated by forensic nurse examiners.
2. It also demonstrates the dismissiveness with which reports of sexual assault made by sex workers are handled by the institutional matrix that in practice takes a stance that sex workers are always already sexually available and therefore unrapeable.
3. While I do not typically mention patients' race, it is relevant in this case because race is often interpreted by health professionals as indicating particular diagnostic likelihoods, for example, in the case of diabetes or HIV/AIDS.
4. Here, the detective is referring to the common belief among criminal justice professionals that investigations are most critical in their early moments. Police detectives in Baltimore told rape crisis advocates that their chances of making an arrest diminished after the first 24 hours had passed. Similar policing strategies are seen in popular television series like *The First 48*.
5. This case introduced ethical complexity for me as both a researcher and an advocate. Did I afford each alter the right to consent to or refuse my presence? Did I treat Dory as generally lacking the capacity to give affirmative consent and remove myself from the context? I opted to treat Dory as others did, affirming her capacity to consent. I then asked her how to introduce myself to her alters and whether they might object to my presence. She told me to remain and that she thought it was unlikely they would not want me to stay. In most cases, the other alters would ask me who I was and then nod and wave at me dismissively when I offered to leave, indicating that they cared very little about my presence at all.
6. DSM-IV is the *Diagnostic and Statistical Manual of Mental Disorders, Fourth Edition*, published in 1995 by the American Psychiatric Association in Washington, DC. The fifth edition, updated in 2013, has some changes to the diagnostic criteria, expanding them in several ways but using the same nomenclature.
7. For an excellent account of how dissociative identity disorder raises complex questions about consent, see Stone (1995).
8. I always asked nurses who were arriving to speak with me later as I didn't want to delay their response time if they were on their way to see a patient. This day, Abigail was just dropping off paperwork and seemed to want to debrief immediately.
9. Marital rape was brought before the court in *Lane v. State* (1991), and the appellate court upheld the judgment that a man could be found guilty of raping his wife with whom he was cohabiting, referring to legislative reforms in the 1980s

and stating that, "The legislative intent to remove any marital 'exemption' for the substantive offenses is absolutely clear and unmistakable."

NOTES TO THE CONCLUSION

1. This was a quality they attributed to my work, as I always told them that while I had an interest in these issues and would do my best to share my research findings, I could not guarantee that my work might affect real change. They also conceded that they wanted someone else to talk to and listen to them. While my only qualification was as an ethnographer and a rape crisis advocate (and not a therapist, on this point I was also very clear), I would do.
2. First, one cannot generalize the experience of four victims, no matter how different they are from one another, to those of all victims in general. Second, the reader might recall that I described my methodology in the opening chapter, and that this precluded interviewing any victims whose cases I had attended as rape crisis advocate beyond the forensic intervention. Thus, the four men and women I worked with following the forensic intervention were all victims whose examinations I had not observed. It is quite possible, then, that they had an exceptionally positive experience with their forensic nurse, and that this accounted for the increasingly positive sense of the interaction as the days passed. What's more, it is also quite possible that anyone who had a very negative experience with the forensic nurses or the sexual assault intervention would be wary to respond to a flyer they were given with their discharge materials. I raise these issues to draw some boundaries around what it is that I can presume to know or not to know, and with the commitment to the depth and detail that marks anthropological projects where statistical breadth cannot.
3. For example, see the "Vision of Ethical Practice," of the International Association of Forensic Nursing (www.iafn.org/displaycommon.cfm?an=1&subarticlenbr=56).
4. I have mentioned earlier in the book the 2005 study by Campbell, Patterson, and Lichty that does demonstrate that a forensic examination in general and a finding of genital redness specifically are predictive of a prosecutorial outcome in cases in Michigan. The other studies cited draw on cases in multiple states, and thus speak to national trends in forensic examination and prosecutorial outcome in the United States.
5. I hope it is clear by now that allegiance to the criminal justice system may not be the intent of the individual nurse, but that the institution is "greedy" and claims the nurses' allegiance by diverting all of their energy and expertise to the anticipation of the trial (Coser 1974). It does this through its protocols and technologies that are encumbered by the structure of anticipation, no matter how "victim-centered" a nurse may be.
6. The procedural proclivity to remove the social context, even an epidemiological one, from the cases to individualize each one is also characteristic of neoliberal governance.

BIBLIOGRAPHY

Agamben, Giorgio. 2000. *Means without End: Notes on Politics*. Minneapolis: University of Minnesota Press.

Agar, Michael and Heather S. Reisinger. 2002. "A Heroin Epidemic at the Intersection of Histories: the 1960s Epidemic among African-Americans in Baltimore." *Medical Anthropology* 21(2):115–56.

Alcoff, Linda and Laura Gray. 1993. "Survivor Discourse: Transgression or Recuperation?" *Signs* 18(2):260–90.

Allen, Beverly. 1996. *Rape Warfare: The Hidden Genocide in Bosnia-Herzegovina*. Minneapolis: University of Minnesota Press.

All-Pro Imaging. 2003. Medscope Overview. Electronic document, www.allproimaging.com/medscope.htm, accessed January 3, 2003.

Anderson, Benedict R. 1991. "Census, Map, Museum." *Imagined Communities: Reflections on the Origin and Spread of Nationalism*. Rev. ed. London: Verso, pp. 163–86.

Anderson, Sarah, Natalie McClain, and Ralph Riviello. 2006. "Genital Findings of Women after Consensual and Nonconsensual Intercourse." *Forensic Nursing* 2(2):59–65.

Andrias, Richard. 1992. "Rape Myths: A Persistent Problem in Defining and Prosecuting Rape." *Criminal Justice* 7(2):2–7, 51–53.

Angel-Ajani, Asale. 2004. "Expert Witness: Notes Toward Revisiting the Politics of Listening." *Anthropology and Humanism* 29(2):133–44.

Antognoli-Toland, Paula. 1985. "Comprehensive Program for Examination of Sexual Assault Victims by Nurses: A Hospital-based Project in Texas." *Journal of Emergency Nursing* 11(3):132–35.

Arnold, David. 1993. *Colonizing the Body: State Medicine and Epidemic Disease in Nineteenth Century India*. Berkeley: University of California Press.

Austin, J. L. 1962. *How to Do Things with Words*. Cambridge, MA: Harvard University Press.

Baber, Harriet E. 1987. "How Bad Is Rape?" *Hypatia* 2(2):125–38.

Bailey, F. G. 1983. *The Tactical Uses of Passion: An Essay on Power, Reason and Reality*. Ithaca: Cornell University Press.

Banks, Marcus and Howard Morphy. 1997. *Rethinking Visual Anthropology*. New Haven, CT: Yale University Press.

Barkin, Robert, Bennett Braun, and Richard Kluft. 1986. "The Dilemma of Drug Therapy for Multiple Personality Disorder." In *Treatment of Multiple Personality Disorder*, B. Braun, ed. Arlington: American Psychiatric Press, pp. 107–132.

Baszanger, Isabelle. 1998. *Inventing Pain Medicine: From the Laboratory to the Clinic*. New Brunswick, NJ: Rutgers University Press.

Baxi, Pratiksha. 2005. "Medicalisation of Consent and Falsity: The Figure of the Habitué in Indian Rape Law." In *The Violence of Normal Times: Essays on Women's Lived Realities*, Kalpana Kannabiran, ed. New Delhi: Women Unlimited in Association with Kali for Women, pp. 266–311.

Ben Ari, Eyal. 1996. "From Mothering to Othering: Organization, Culture and Nap Time in a Japanese Day-Care Center." *Ethos* 24(1):136–64.

Benjamin, Walter. 1979. "Critique of Violence." In *One-Way Street and Other Writings*. London: NLB, pp. 1–28.

Bennett, Jane. 2010. *Vibrant Matter: A Political Ecology of Things*. Durham: Duke University Press.

Bennett, Jane Foress. 1995. "Credibility, Plausibility and Autobiographical Oral Narrative: Some Suggestions from the Analysis of a Rape Survivor's Testimony." In *Culture, Power and Difference: Discourse Analysis in South Africa*, Ann Levett, ed. Highlands, NJ: Zed Books, pp. 96–108.

Bennett, Jill. 2002. "Art, Affect, and the 'Bad Death': Strategies for Communicating the Sense Memory of Loss." *Signs* 28(1):333–51.

Beres, Melanie, Barbara Crow, and Lise Gottell. 2009. "The Perils of Institutionalization in Neoliberal Times: Results of a National Survey of Canadian Sexual Assault and Rape Crisis Centres." *Canadian Journal of Sociology* 34(1):135–63.

Bergson, Henri. 1908. *Matière et mémoire, essai sur la relation du corps à l'esprit*. Paris: Alcan.

Berlant, Lauren. 2000. "Intimacy: A Special Issue." In *Intimacy*, L. Berlant, ed. Chicago: University of Chicago Press, pp. 1–8.

Betzig, Laura L. and Paul W. Turke. 1985. "Measuring Time Allocation: Observation and Intention." *Current Anthropology* 26(5):647–50.

Bevacqua, Maria. 2000. *Rape on the Public Agenda: Feminism and the Politics of Sexual Assault*. Lillington: Northeastern University Press.

Bhrigenti, Andrea. M. 2012. "New Media and Urban Motilities: A Territoriologic Point of View." *Urban Studies* 49(2):399–414.

Blanchot, Maurice. 1986. *The Writing of the Disaster*, Ann Smock, trans. Lincoln: University of Nebraska Press.

Bletzer, K. V. and M. Koss. 2004. "Narrative Constructions of Sexual Violence as Told by Female Rape Survivors in Three Populations of the Southwestern United States: Scripts of Coercion, Scripts of Consent." *Medical Anthropology* 23(2):113–56.

Bourgois, Philippe. 1998. "The Moral Economies of Homeless Heroin Addicts: Confronting Ethnography, HIV Risk, and Everyday Violence in San Francisco Shooting Encampments." *Substance Use and Misuse* 33(11):2323–51.

Bowers, Ariene A. and L. J. Veronen. 1993. "Sexual Assault and People with Disabilities." *Journal of Social Work and Human Sexuality* 8(2):135–59.

Brewer, Paul and Barbara Ley. 2010. "Media Use and Public Perceptions of DNA Evidence." *Science Communication* 32(1): 93–117.

Brison, Susan. 2002. *Aftermath: Violence and the Remaking of the Self.* Princeton: Princeton University Press.

Brownmiller, Susan. 1975. *Against Our Will: Men, Women and Rape.* New York: Simon & Schuster.

Buchwald, Emily, Pamela Fletcher, and Martha Roth. 1993. "Living in a Rape Culture." In *Transforming a Rape Culture*, E. Buchwald, P. Fletcher, and M. Roth, eds. Minneapolis: Milkweed Editions, pp. 7–10.

Buckley, Liam. 2000. "Self and Accessory in Gambian Studio Photography." *Visual Anthropology Review* 16(2):71–91.

Bumiller, Kristen. 2008. *In an Abusive State: How Neoliberalism Appropriated the Feminist Movement Against Sexual Violence.* Durham: Duke University Press.

Campbell, Kirsten. 2002. "Legal Memories: Sexual Assault, Memory, and International Humanitarian Law." *Signs* 28(1):149–78.

Campbell, Rebecca. 2001a. *Emotionally Involved: The Impact of Researching Rape.* New York: Routledge.

———. 2001b. "Preventing the 'Second Rape': Rape Survivors' Experiences with Community Service Providers." *Journal of Interpersonal Violence* 16(12):1239–259.

Campbell, Rebecca, Debra Patterson, and Lauren Lichty. 2005. "The Effectiveness of Sexual Assault Nurse Examiner (SANE) Programs: A Review of Psychological, Medical, Legal and Community Outcomes." *Trauma, Violence, and Abuse* 6(4):313–29.

Canguilhem, Georges. 1991. *The Normal and the Pathological.* New York: Zone Books.

Carr, Summerson. 2010. *Scripting Addiction: The Politics of Therapeutic Talk and American Sobriety.* Princeton: Princeton University Press.

Carsten, Janet. 2004. *After Kinship.* New York: Cambridge University Press.

Carter, Albert H. 1997. *First Cut: A Season in the Human Anatomy Lab.* New York: Picador.

Caruth, Cathy. 1996. *Unclaimed Experience: Trauma, Narrative, and History.* Baltimore: Johns Hopkins University Press.

Castoriadis, Cornelius. 1987. *The Imaginary Institution of Society.* Cambridge, MA: MIT Press.

Cavell, Stanley. 1979. *The Claim of Reason: Wittgenstein, Skepticism, Morality, and Tragedy.* Oxford: Clarendon Press.

———. 1995. *A Pitch of Philosophy: Autobiographical Exercises.* Cambridge: Harvard University Press.

Center for HIV Surveillance and Epidemiology. 2010. *Maryland HIV/AIDS Epidemiological Profile. Fourth Quarter 2010.* Infectious Disease and Environmental Health Administration, Maryland Department of Health and Mental Hygiene.

Chasteen, Amy L. 2001. "Constructing Rape: Feminism, Change, and Women's Everyday Understandings of Sexual Assault." *Sociological Spectrum* 21(2):101–39.

Chaudhary, Zahid. 2005. "Phantasmagoric Aesthetics: Colonial Violence and the Management of Perception." *Cultural Critique* 59:63–119.

Chen, Xiaohong Denise. 2002. "Human Olfactory Communication of Emotions." Institute of Mind and Biology, University of Chicago, Chicago, IL.

———.2004. "The Smell of Emotion: Olfactory Communication of Emotion in Humans." Society of Rice University Women, Austin, TX.

Child Welfare Information Gateway. 2013. *Foster Care Statistics 2011*. Washington, DC.

Collins, Patricia Hill. 2004. *Black Sexual Politics*. New York: Routledge.

Colomina, Beatriz. 2007. *Domesticity at War*. Cambridge, MA: MIT Press.

Conley, John and William O'Barr. 1997. *Just Words: Law, Language and Power*. Chicago: University of Chicago Press.

Coons, Philip, Elizabeth Bowman, Richard Kluft, and Victor Milstein. 1991. "The Cross-Cultural Occurrence of MPD: Additional Cases from a Recent Survey." *Dissociation: Progress in Dissociative Disorders* 4(3):124–28.

Coreil, Jeannine. 1991. "Maternal Time Allocation in Relation to Kind and Domain of Primary Health Care." *Medical Anthropology Quarterly* 5(3):221–35.

Corrigan, Rose. 2013a. "The New Trial by Ordeal: Rape Kits, Police Practices, and the Unintended Effects of Policy Innovation," *Law and Social Inquiry* 38(4):920–49.

———. 2013b. *Up Against a Wall: Rape Reform and the Failure of Success*. New York: New York University Press.

Corrigan, Rose, Lesley McMillan, Sameena Mulla, Gethin Rees, and Deborah White. 2013. "Compliance and Credibility: A Critique of Sexual Assault Forensic Examinations from International Perspectives." Unpublished article manuscript.

Coser, Lewis. 1974. *Greedy Institutions: Patterns of Undivided Commitment*. New York: Free Press.

Cosgrove, Lisa. 2000. "Crying Out Loud: Understanding Women's Emotional Distress as Both Lived Experience and Social Construction." *Feminism and Psychology* 10(2):247–67.

Crary, Jonathan. 1990. *Techniques of the Observer: On Vision and Modernity in the Nineteenth Century*. Cambridge, MA: MIT Press.

———. 2000. *Suspensions of Perception: Attention, Spectacle, and Modern Culture*. Cambridge, MA: MIT Press.

Crossmaker, Maureen. 1991. "Behind Locked Doors: Institutional Sex Abuse." *Sexuality and Disability* 9(3):201–19.

Crowley, Sharon. 1999. *Sexual Assault: The Medical-Legal Examination*. Stamford: Appleton and Lange.

Crozier, Ian and Gethin Rees. 2011. "Making a Space for Medical Expertise: Medical Knowledge of Sexual Assault and the Construction of Boundaries Between Forensic Medicine and the Law in Late-Nineteenth Century England." *Law, Culture and the Humanities* 8(2):285–304.

Daniels, D. E., A. A. René, and V. R. Daniels. 1994. "Race: An Explanation of Patient Compliance—Fact or Fiction?" *Journal of the National Medical Association* 86(1):20–25.

Das, Veena. 1995. "National Honor and Practical Kinship." In *Critical Events: An Anthropological Perspective on Contemporary India*. Delhi: Oxford India, pp. 55–83.

———. 1996a. "Language and Transactions in Pain." In *Social Suffering*, A. Kleinman, V. Das, and M. Lock, eds. Berkeley: University of California Press, pp. 67–92.

———. 1996b. "Sexual Violence, Discursive Formations and the State." *Economic and Political Weekly* 31(35/37):2411–13, 2415–18, 2420–23.

———. 2000. "The Act of Witnessing: Violence, Knowledge and Subjectivity." In *Violence and Subjectivity*, V. Das, A. Kleinman, M. Ramphele, and P. Reynolds, eds. Berkeley: University of California Press, pp. 205–25.

———. 2002. "Sexual Violation and the Making of the Gendered Subject." In *Discrimination and Toleration*, Kristin Hastrup and George Urlich, eds. London: Kluwer Law International, pp. 257–74.

———. 2006a. *Life and Words: Violence and the Descent into the Ordinary*. Berkeley: University of California Press.

———. 2006b. "Secularism and the Argument from Nature." In *Powers of the Secular Modern: Talal Asad and His Interlocutors*, D. Scott and C. Hirschkind, eds. Stanford: Stanford University Press, pp. 93–112.

———. 2008. "Violence, Gender and Subjectivity." *Annual Review of Anthropology* 37: 283–99.

Das, Veena, Arthur Kleinman, Margaret Lock, Mamphela Ramphele, and Pamela Reynolds. 2001. *Remaking a World: Violence, Social Suffering, and Recovery*. Berkeley: University of California Press.

Das, Veena and Deborah Poole. 2004. *Anthropology at the Margins of the State*. Santa Fe, NM: School of American Research Press.

Das, Veena, Jonathan Ellen, and Lori Leonard. 2008. "On the Modalities of the Domestic." *Home Cultures* 5(3):349–72.

Dattilio, Frank and Arthur Freeman. 2007. *Cognitive-Behavioral Strategies in Crisis Intervention, Third Edition*. London: Guilford Press.

Davis, Milton. 1968. "Physiologic, Psychological and Demographic Factors in Patient Compliance with Doctors' Orders." *Medical Care* 6(2):115–22.

Dawes, Robyn. 2001. *Everyday Irrationality*. Boulder, CO: Westview Press.

De Alwis, Malathi. 1997. "Production and the Embodiment of 'Respectability': Gendered Demeanors in Colonial Ceylon." In *Sri Lanka Collective Identities Revisited*, M. Roberts, ed. Colombo: Marga Institute, pp. 105–43.

Delaney, Carol. 2001. "Cutting the Ties That Bind: The Sacrifice of Abraham and Patriarchal Kinship." In *Relative Values: Reconfiguring Kinship Studies*, S. Franklin and S. McKinnon, eds. Durham and London: Duke University Press, pp. 445–67.

De Lauretis, Teresa. 1984. *Alice Doesn't: Feminism, Semiotics, Cinema*. Bloomington: Indiana University Press.

DelVecchio Good, Mary-Jo. 1995. *American Medicine: The Quest for Competence.* Berkeley: University of California Press.

Department of Health and Human Services. (DHHS). 2007. Foster Care FY2000–FY2005 Entries, Exits, and Numbers of Children in Care on the Last Day of Each Federal Fiscal Year. Washington, DC. National Clearinghouse on Child Abuse and Neglect Information.

Derrida, Jacques. 2002 (1990). "Force of Law: The 'Mystical Foundation of Authority.'" In *Acts of Religion,* J. Derrida and G. Anidjar, eds. New York: Routledge, pp. 228–98.

Desjarlais, Robert. 1996. "The Office of Reason: On Politics of Language and Agency in a Shelter for 'The Homeless Mentally Ill.'" *American Ethnologist* 23(4):880–900.

Des Rosiers, Nathalie, Bruce Feldthusen, and Oleana Hankivsky. 1998. "Legal Compensation for Sexual Violence: Therapeutic Consequences and Consequences for the Judicial System." *Psychology, Public, and Law* 4(1/2):433–51.

Di Leonardo, Micaela. 1992. "White Lies: Rape, Race, and the Black 'Underclass.'" *Village Voice*, September 22, 1992: 29–36.

Douglas, Mary. 1966. *Purity and Danger: An Analysis of Concepts of Pollution and Taboo*. New York: Routledge.

Dumit, Joseph. 2004. *Picturing Personhood: Brain Scans and Biomedical Identity*. Princeton: Princeton University Press.

Du Mont, Janice and Deborah Parnis. 1999. "Judging Women: The Pernicious Effects of Rape Mythology." *Canadian Woman Studies* 19(2):102–9.

———. 2000. "Sexual Assault and Legal Resolution: Querying the Medical Collection of Forensic Evidence." *Medicine and Law* 19(4):779–92.

———. 2001. "Constructing Bodily Evidence through Sexual Assault Kits." *Griffith Law Review* 10(1):63–76.

———. 2003. "Forensic Nursing in the Context of Sexual Assault: Comparing the Opinions and Practices of Nurse Examiners and Nurses." *Applied Nursing Research* 16(3):173–83.

Du Mont, Janice and Deborah White. 2007. *The Uses and Impact of Medico-Legal Evidence in Sexual Assault Cases: A Global Review.* World Health Organization.

Du Mont, Janice, Deborah White, and Margaret J. McGregor. 2009. "An Investigation of the Medical Forensic Examination from the Perspectives of Sexually Assaulted Women." *Social Science and Medicine* 68(4):774–80.

Dunkle, Kristin, Gina Wingood, Christina Camp, and Ralph DiClemente. 2010. "Economically Motivated Relationships and Transactional Sex Among Unmarried African American and White Women: Results from a U.S. National Telephone Survey." *Public Health Report* 125(4):90–100.

Edin, Kathryn. 2000. "What Do Low-Income Single Mothers Say About Marriage?" *Social Problems* 47(1):112–43.

Edmond, Gary, Simon Cole, Emma Cunliffe, and A. Roberts. 2012. "Admissibility Compared: The Reception of Incriminating Expert Opinion (i.e. Forensic Science)

Evidence in Four Adversarial Jurisdictions." *Forensic Ignorance.* Annual Meeting of the Law and Society Association, Honolulu, HI.

Ehrlich, Susan. 2001. *Representing Rape: Language and Sexual Consent.* New York: Routledge.

Emm, Deborah and Patrick C. McKenry. 1988. "Coping with Victimization: The Impact of Rape on Female Survivors, Male Significant Others, and Parents." *Contemporary Family Therapy* 10(4):272–79.

Estrich, Susan. 1988. *Real Rape: How the Legal System Victimizes Women Who Say No.* Cambridge: Harvard University Press.

Ewick, Patricia and Susan S. Silbey. 1998. *The Common Place of Law: Stories from Everyday Life.* Chicago: University of Chicago Press.

Fabian, Johannes. 1983 (2002). *Time and the Other: How Anthropology Makes Its Object.* New York: Columbia University Press.

Fahy, T. A. 1988. "The Diagnosis of Multiple Personality Disorder: A Critical Review." *British Journal of Psychiatry* 153:597–606.

Faigman, David. 1999. *Legal Alchemy: The Use and Misuse of Science in Law.* New York: W. H. Freeman.

Faubion, James and Jennifer Hamilton. 2007. "Sumptuary Kinship." *Anthropological Quarterly* 80(2):533–59.

Felman, Shoshana. 1992. "The Return of the Voice: Claude Lanzman's Shoah." In *Testimony: Crises of Witnessing in Literature, Psychoanalysis, and History*, S. Felman and D. Laub, eds. New York: Routledge, pp. 204–83.

Felman, Shoshana and Dori Laub. 1992. *Testimony: Crises of Witnessing in Literature, Psychoanalysis, and History.* New York: Routledge.

Fineman, Martha A. and Roxanne Mykitiuk. 1994. *The Public Nature of Private Violence: The Discovery of Domestic Abuse.* New York: Routledge.

Fisher, Bonnie, Francis Cullen, and Michael Turner. 2000. "The Sexual Victimization of College Women." Washington, DC: National Institute of Justice, NCJ 182369.

Fisher, Siobhan K. 1996. "Occupation of the Womb: Forced Impregnations as Genocide." *Duke Law Journal* 46(1):91–133.

Fisher, Sue. 1995. *Nursing Wounds: Nurse Practitioners, Doctors, Women Patients, and the Negotiation of Meaning.* New Brunswick, NJ: Rutgers University Press.

Flood, Dawn. 2005. "'They Didn't Treat Me Good': African American Rape Victims and Chicago Courtroom Strategies during the 1950s." *Journal of Women's History* 17(1):38–61.

Fortes, Meyer. 1945. *Dynamics of Clanship among the Tallensi.* London: Oxford University Press.

———. 1949. "Time and Social Structure: An Ashanti Case Study." *Social Structure: Studies Presented to A. R. Radcliffe-Brown*, M. Fortes, ed. Oxford: Clarendon Press, pp. 54–84.

Forth, Christopher and Ivan Crozier, eds. 2005. *Body Parts: Critical Explorations in Corporeality.* New York: Lexington Books.

Foucault, Michel. 1965 (1988). *Madness and Civilization: A History of Insanity in the Age of Reason*. New York: Vintage Books.

———. 1973. *The Birth of the Clinic: The Archaeology of Medical Perception*. New York: Vintage Books.

———. 1979. *Discipline and Punish: The Birth of the Prison*. New York: Vintage Books.

———. 1999. *Abnormal: Lectures at the Collège de France, 1974–1975*. New York: Picador.

Franklin, Sarah and Susan McKinnon. 2001. "Introduction." In *Relative Values: Reconfiguring Kinship Studies*, S. Franklin and S. McKinnon, eds. Durham: Duke University Press, pp. 1–28.

Gershon, Ilana. 2003. "Knowing Adoption and Adopting Knowledge," *American Ethnologist* 30(3):439–46.

Gillig, Paulette M. 2009. "Dissociative Identity Disorder: A Controversial Diagnosis." *Psychiatry* 6(3):24–29.

Ginsburg, Faye, Lila Abu-Lughod, and Brian Larkin. 2002. *Media Worlds: Anthropology on New Terrain*. Berkeley: University of California Press.

Ginsburg, Faye and Rayna Rapp. 1991. "The Politics of Reproduction." *Annual Review in Anthropology* 20:311–43.

———. 1995. *Conceiving the New World Order: The Global Politics of Reproduction*. Berkeley: University of California Press.

Girardin, Barbara, W., Diana Faugno, Patty Seneski, Laura Slaughter, and Margaret Whelan. 1997. *The Color Atlas of Sexual Assault*. St. Louis and Philadelphia: Mosby.

Gluckman, Max. 1968. "The Utility of the Equilibrium Model in the Study of Social Change." *American Anthropologist* 70(2):219–37.

Goffman, Erving. 1961. *Asylums*. Chicago: Aldine Publishing.

Goodfellow, Aaron. 2002. "Queer Family Portraiture and Lines of Skepticism." Paper presented in the Johns Hopkins University, Department of Anthropology Colloquium Series; Baltimore, MD.

———. 2006. "Critical Excess: Sex, Drugs, Intervention." In *Bordering Biomedicine*, Vera Kalitzkus and Peter L. Twohig, eds. Amsterdam and New York: Rodopi, pp. 159–76.

———. 2008. "Pharmaceutical Intimacy: Sex, Death, and Methamphetamine." *Home Cultures* 5(3):271–300.

Goodfellow, Aaron and Sameena Mulla. 2008. "Compelling Intimacies: Domesticity, Agency and Sexuality." *Home Cultures* 5(3):257–70.

Goody, Jack. 1962. *The Developmental Cycle in Domestic Groups*. Cambridge: Cambridge University Press.

Gose, Peter.1991. "House Rethatching in an Andean Annual Cycle: Practice, Meaning and Contradiction." *American Ethnologist* 18(1):39–66.

Gray, Bennison. 1971. "Repetition in Oral Literature." *Journal of American Folklore* 84(333):289–303.

Greene, Jeremy. 2004. "Therapeutic Infidelities: 'Non-Compliance' Enters the Medical Literature, 1955–1975." *Social History of Medicine* 17(3):327–43.

Gregory, Sam. 2006. "Transnational Storytelling: Human Rights, WITNESS, and Video Advocacy." *American Anthropologist* 108(1):195–204.

Griffin, Susan. 1979. *Rape: The Power of Consciousness*. San Francisco: Harper and Row.

Grosz, Elizabeth. 1994. *Volatile Bodies: Toward a Corporeal Feminism*. Bloomington: Indiana University Press.

Halpern, Orit. 2005. "Dreams for Our Perceptual Present: Temporality, Storage, and Interactivity in Cybernetics." *Configurations* 13(2):283–319.

Halpern, Sydney A. 2004. "Medical Authority and the Culture of Rights." *Journal of Health Politics Policy and Law* 29(4–5):835–52.

Hambleton, Elsie L. 2001. "'Playing the Rogue': Rape and Issues of Consent in Seventeenth-Century Massachusetts." In *Sex without Consent: Rape and Sexual Coercion in America*, Merrill Smith, ed. New York: New York University Press, pp. 27–43.

Hammer, Muriel and Amy Schaffer. 1975. "Interconnectedness and the Duration of Connections in Several Small Networks." *American Ethnologist* 2(2):297–308.

Haraway, Donna. 1988. "Situated Knowledges: The Science Question in Feminism and the Privilege of Partial Perspective." *Feminist Studies* 14(3):575–99.

Hardman, Charlotte. 2001. "Can There Be an Anthropology of Children?" *Childhood* 8(4):501–17.

Harper, Richard. 2000. "The Social Organization of the IMF's Mission Work: An Examination of International Auditing." In *Audit Cultures: Anthropological Studies in Accountability, Ethics, and the Academy*, M. Strathern, ed. London and New York: Routledge, pp. 21–54.

Harris, Lucy Reed. 1976. "Towards a Consent Standard in the Law of Rape." *University of Chicago Law Review* 43(3):613–45.

Harvard Law Review. 2004. "Acquaintance Rape and Degrees of Consent: 'No' Means 'No,' but What Does 'Yes' Mean?" 117(7):2341–64.

Hasday, Jill. 2000. "Contest and Consent: A Legal History of Marital Rape." *California Law Review* 88(5):1373–1505.

Hatley, James. 2000. *Suffering Witness: The Quandary of Responsibility after the Irreparable*. Albany: State University of New York Press.

Hawkes, K., J. F. O'Connell, and N. G. Blurton Jones. 1997. "Hadza Women's Time Allocation, Offspring Provisioning, and the Evolution of Long Postmenopausal Life Spans." *Current Anthropology* 38(4):551–77.

Hayden, Robert M. 2000. "Rape and Rape Avoidance in Ethno-National Conflicts: Sexual Violence in Liminalized States." *American Anthropologist* 102(1):27–41.

Hazan, Haim. 1984. "Continuity and Transformation Among the Aged: A Study in the Anthropology of Time." *Current Anthropology* 25(5):567–78.

Hazlewood, Robert and Anne Burgess. 2008. *Practical Aspects of Rape Investigation: A Multidisciplinary Approach, Fourth Edition*. Boca Raton, FL: CRC Press.

Health Resources and Services Administration. 2010. "Registered Nurse Population Findings from the 2008 National Sample Survey of Registered Nurses." Washington, DC: U.S. Department of Health and Human Services.

Hengehold, Laura. 2000. "Remapping the Event: Institutional Discourses and the Trauma of Rape." *Signs* 26(1):189–214.

Henslin, James M. and Mae A. Biggs. 1971. "Dramaturgical Desexualization: The Sociology of the Vaginal Examination." In *Studies in the Sociology of Sex*, J. M. Henslin, ed. New York: Appleton-Century Crofts, pp. 243–72.

Herz, Rachel and Geral Cupchik. 1995. "The Emotional Distinctiveness of Odor-Evoked Memories." *Chemical Senses* 20(5):517–28.

Herzfeld, Michael. 1993. "In Defiance of Destiny: The Management of Time and Gender at a Cretan Funeral." *American Ethnologist* 20(2):241–55.

Hirsch, Susan. 2007. "Writing Ethnography after Tragedy: Toward Therapeutic Transformations." *PoLAR: Political and Legal Anthropology Review* 30(1):151–79.

Hlavka, Heather R. 2010. "Child Sexual Abuse and Embodiment." *Sociological Studies of Children and Youth* 13:131–65.

Hochschild, Arlie. 2003 (1983). *The Managed Heart: Commercialization of Human Feeling*. Berkeley: University of California Press.

Hodes, Matthew. 1987. "Time in Sickness and Health." *Anthropology Today* 3(2):19–20.

Holmes, Dave, Amélie Perron, and Patrick O'Byrne. 2006. "Understanding Disgust in Nursing: Abjection, Self and the Other." *Research and Theory for Nursing Practice* 20(4):305–16.

Holmes, Ronald M. and Stephen T. Holmes. 2002. *Profiling Violent Crimes: An Investigative Tool, Third Edition*. London: Sage Publications.

Hoyson, Laura. 2009. "Rape Is Tough Enough without Having Someone Kick You from the Inside: The Case for Including Pregnancy as Substantial Bodily Injury." *Valparaiso University Law Review* 44(2009):565–610.

Hyde, Alan. 1997. *Bodies of Law*. Princeton: Princeton University Press.

International Association of Forensic Nursing. 2009. *Forensic Nursing: Scope and Standards of Practice*. Silver Spring, MD: American Nurses Association.

Jackson, John L. 2007. "Racial Paranoia and American Society." Seminar Series. Center for Africana Studies, Johns Hopkins University, Baltimore, MD. February 15.

James, Susan, Janice Johnson, Chitra Raghavan, Tessa Lemos, Michele Barakett, and Diana Woolis. 2003. "The Violent Matrix: A Study of Structural, Interpersonal, and Intrapersonal Violence among a Sample of Poor Women." *American Journal of Community Psychology* 31(102):129–41.

Jay, Martin. (1988) 1998. "Scopic Regimes of Modernity." In *Vision and Visuality*, Hal Foster, ed. New York: New Press, pp. 3–28.

———. 1993. *Downcast Eyes: The Denigration of Vision in Twentieth Century French Thought*. Berkeley: University of California Press.

Jetmore, Larry. 2006. "Investigating Rape Crimes, Part 2: Evidence Collection and Analysis." http://www.policeone.com/writers/columnists/LarryJetmore/articles/139768/

Johnson, Donald, Joseph Peterson, Ira Sommers, and Deborah Baskin. 2012. "Use of Forensic Science in Investigating Crimes of Sexual Violence: Contrasting Its Theoretical Potential with Empirical Results." *Violence Against Women* 18(2):193–222.

Jones, Yvonne. 1980. "Kinship Affiliation through Time: Black Homecomings and Family Reunions in a North Carolina County." *Ethnohistory* 27(1):49–66.

Jordanova, Ludmilla. 1989. *Sexual Visions: Images of Gender in Science and Medicine between the Eighteenth and Twentieth Centuries.* Madison: University of Wisconsin Press.

Just, Peter. 1991. "Going Through the Emotions: Passion, Violence, and 'Other-Control' Among the Dou Donggo." *Ethos* 19(3):288–312.

Kafka, Franz. 1919. *A Country Doctor.* Prague, CZ: Twisted Spoon Press.

Kapsalis, Terry. 1997. *Public Privates: Performing Gynecology from Both Ends of the Speculum.* Durham: Duke University Press.

Kerstetter, Wayne A. 1990. "Gateway to Justice: Police and Prosecutorial Response to Sexual Assaults against Women." *Journal of Criminal Law and Criminology* 81(2):267–313.

Kirk, Paul L. 1953. *Crime Investigation: Physical Evidence and the Police Laboratory.* New York: Interscience Publishers.

Kleinman, Arthur and Peter Benson. 2006. "Anthropology in the Clinic: The Problem of Cultural Competency and How to Fix It." *PLoS Medicine* 3(10):e294.

Kilpatrick, Dean, Benjamin Saunders, and Daniel Smith. 2003. Youth Victimization: Prevalence and Implications. U.S. Department of Justice, National Institute of Justice (NCJ 194972).

Konradi, Amanda. 1997. "Too Little, Too Late: Prosecutors' Pre-Court Preparation of Rape Survivors." *Law & Social Inquiry* 22(1):1–54.

———. 2007. *Taking the Stand: Rape Survivors and the Prosecution of Rapists.* Westport, CT: Praeger.

Korsmeyer, Carolyn and Barry Smith. 2004. "Visceral Values: Aurel Kolnai on Disgust." In Aurel Kolnai, *On Disgust*, C. Korsmeyer and B. Smith, eds. Chicago: Open Court Press, pp. 1–28.

Kristeva, Julia. 1982. *The Power of Horror: An Essay on Abjection.* New York: Columbia University Press.

Kuriyama, Shigehisa. 1999. *The Expressiveness of the Body and the Divergence of Greek and Chinese Medicine.* New York: Zone Books.

Lacan, Jacques. 2007. *Écrits: The First Complete Edition in English*, Bruce Fink, trans. New York: W. W. Norton.

Lakoff, Andrew. 1996. "Freezing Time: Margaret Mead's Diagnostic Photography." *Visual Anthropology Review* 12(1):1–18.

Lamb, Sarah. 1999. *New Versions of Victims: Feminists Struggle with the Concept.* New York and London: New York University Press.

Lamphere, Louise. 2005. "Providers and Staff Respond to Medicaid Managed Care: The Unintended Consequences of Reform in New Mexico." *Medical Anthropology Quarterly* 19(1):3–25.

Langton, Lynn. 2010. "Women in Law Enforcement, 1987–2008." Washington, DC: Bureau of Justice Statistics and U.S. Department of Justice (NCJ 230521).

Larcombe, Wendy. 2002. "The 'Ideal' Victim v. Successful Rape Complainants: Not What You Might Expect." *Feminist Legal Studies* 10(2):131–48.

Latour, Bruno. 2005. *Reassembling the Social: An Introduction to Actor-Network Theory*. Oxford: Oxford University Press.

Latour, Bruno and Steve Woolgar. 1986. *Laboratory Life: The Construction of Scientific Facts*. Princeton: Princeton University Press.

Law, John and John Hassard. 1999. *Actor Network Theory and After*. Oxford: Blackwell.

Lawrence, Susan C. 2007. "Access Anxiety: HIPAA and Historical Research." *Journal of the History of Medicine and Allied Sciences* 62(4):422–60.

Ledray, Linda E. 1999. "Sexual Assault: Clinical Issues: Date Rape Drug Alert." *Journal of Emergency Nursing* 17(1):1–2.

———. 2001. Evidence Collection and Care of the Sexual Assault Survivor, The SANE-SART Response. *Violence Against Women On-Line Resources*. Available on at: http://www.mincava.umn.edu/documents/commissioned/2forensicevidence/2forensicevidence.pdf

Lee, Matthew R. 2000. "Community Cohesion and Violent Predatory Victimization: A Theoretical Extension and Cross-National Test of Opportunity Theory." *Social Forces* 79(2):683–706.

Lee, S. Agnes and Michelle Farrell. 2006. "Is Cultural Competency a Backdoor to Racism?" *Anthropology News* 47(3):9–10.

LeFebvre, Henri. 1974. *The Production of Space*. Malden, MA: Blackwell.

———. 1992 (2004). *Rhythmanalysis: Space, Time and Everyday Life*. London: Continuum International Publishing.

Lefevre, Joyce. 2001. *Laboratory and Diagnostic Tests with Nursing Implications*. Englewood Cliffs, NJ: Prentice-Hall.

Levine, Nancy. 2008. "Alternative Kinship, Marriage, and Reproduction." *Annual Review of Anthropology* 37:75–89.

Levi-Strauss, Claude. 1949. *The Elementary Structures of Kinship*. London: Eyre & Spottiswoode.

Lock, Margaret. 1993. "Cultivating the Body: Anthropology and Epistemologies of Bodily Practice and Knowledge." *Annual Review of Anthropology* 22:133–55.

Lourau, René. 1970. *L'analyse institutionnelle*. Paris: Editions de Minuit.

Lowie, Robert. 1956. "Reminiscences of Anthropological Currents in America Half a Century Ago." *American Anthropologist* 58(6):995–1016.

Lugbill, C. 2007. "Summary of IAFN's International Initiatives and Next Steps for Moving Forward Internationally." White Paper for International Association of Forensic Nursing. Arnold, MD.

Luhmann, Niklas. 1995. *Social Systems*. Stanford: Stanford University Press.

Luhrmann, T. M. 2000. *Of Two Minds: The Growing Disorder in American Psychiatry*. New York: Knopf.

Luo, Tsun-Yin. 2000. "'Marrying My Rapist?!': The Cultural Trauma Among Chinese Rape Survivors." *Gender and Society* 14(4):581–97.
Lutz, Catherine and Jane Collins. 1991. "The Photograph as an Intersection of Gazes: The Example of National Geographic." *Visual Anthropology Review* 7(1):134–49.
Lynch, Virginia. 2006a. "Forensic Nursing Science." In *Forensic Nursing: A Handbook for Practice*, R. Hammer, B. Moynihan, and E. Pagliaro, eds. Boston and Toronto: Jones and Bartlett, pp. 1–40.
———. 2006b. *Forensic Nursing*. St. Louis: Elsevier.
Lynch, Michael, Simon Cole, Ruth McNally, and Kathleen Jordan. 2008. *Truth Machine: The Contentious History of DNA Fingerprinting*. Chicago: University of Chicago Press.
Mace, Jane. 1998. *Playing With Time: Mothers and the Meaning of Literacy*. Philadelphia: Routledge.
Mackinnon, Catharine. 1993. "Turning Rape into Pornography: Postmodern Genocide." *Ms* 4(1):24–30.
———. 1994. "Rape, Genocide and Women's Human Rights." *Harvard Women's Law Journal* 17:5–16.
Madigan, Lee and Nancy Gamble. 1991. *The Second Rape: Society's Continued Betrayal of the Victim*. New York: Lexington Books.
Madriz, Esther. 1997. *Nothing Bad Happens to Good Girls: Fear of Crime in Women's Lives*. Berkeley: University of California Press.
Makarius, Raoul. 1977. "Ancient Society and Morgan's Kinship Theory 100 Years After." *Current Anthropology* 18(4):709–29.
Malinowski, Bronislaw. 1939. "The Essentials of the Kula." *American Journal of Sociology* 44:938–47.
Manderson, Lenore. 1996. *Sickness and the State: Health and Illness in Colonial Malaya, 1870–1940*. Cambridge: Cambridge University Press
Mansell, Sheila and Dick Sobsy. 2001. *Counseling People With Developmental Disabilities Who Have Been Sexually Abused*. Kingston, NY: NADD Publishing.
Mardorossian, Carine M. 2002. "Towards a New Feminist Theory of Rape." *Signs* 743–75.
Martin, L. J. 2002. "Forensic Evidence Collection for Sexual Assault: A South African Perspective." *International Journal of Gynecology and Obstetrics* 78(1):S105–S110.
Martin, Patricia Y. 2005. *Rape Work: Victims, Gender and Emotions in Organization and Community Context*. New York and London: Routledge.
Martin, Patricia Y. and Marlene Powell. 1994. "Accounting for the Second Assault: Legal Organizations' Framing of Rape Victims." *Law & Social Inquiry* 14:853–90.
Martin, Susan E. 1999. "Police Force or Police Service? Gender and Emotional Labor." *Annals of the American Academy of Political and Social Science* 561:111–26.
Massumi, Brian. 1987. "Notes on the Translation and Acknowledgements." In *A Thousand Plateaus*, Gilles Deleuze and Felix Guattari, eds. Minneapolis: University of Minnesota Press, pp. xvi–xix.

Matoesian, Gregory. 1993. *Reproducing Rape Domination through Talk in the Courtroom*. Chicago: University of Chicago Press.

Matthews, Sandra and Laura Wexler. 2000. *Pregnant Pictures*. New York: Routledge.

Mattingly, Cheryl. 1994. "The Concept of Therapeutic 'Emplotment.'" *Social Science and Medicine* 38(6):811–22.

———. 1998. "In Search of the Good: Narrative Reasoning in Clinical Practice." *Medical Anthropology Quarterly* 12(3):273–97.

McCabe, Marita and Michelle Wauchope. 2005. "Behavioral Characteristics of Men Accused of Rape: Evidence for Different Types of Rapists." *Archives of Sexual Behavior* 34(2):241–53.

McGrath, Roberta. 2002. *Seeing Her Sex: Medical Archives and the Female Body*. Manchester: Manchester University Press.

McKegany, Neil and Marina Barnard. 1992. *AIDS, Drugs, and Sexual Risk: Lives in the Balance*. Buckingham: Open University Press.

McKeon, Michal. 2005. *The Secret History of Domesticity*. Baltimore: Johns Hopkins University Press.

McKeown, Thomas. 1976. *The Modern Rise of Population*. London: Edward Arnold.

McLaglan, Margaret. 2005. "Circuits of Suffering." *PoLAR: Political and Legal Anthropology Review* 28(2):223–39.

McLay, W.D.S. 1990. *Clinical Forensic Medicine*. London: Pinter.

McLean, Iain, Stephen Roberts, Cath White, and Sheila Paul. 2011. "Female Genital Injuries Resulting from Consensual and Non-Consensual Vaginal Intercourse." *Forensic Science International* 204(1–3):27–33.

McMehen, Emily. 2004. "Thrill Kill and the Beautiful Wound." In *Cultures of Violence: Papers from the Fifth Global Conference*, J. E. Lynch and G. Wheeler, eds. E-Books On-line Publication.

McMillan, Lesley. 2010. *Understanding Attrition in Rape Cases ESRC End of Award Report*. RES-061-23-0138-A. Swindon: ESRC.

McMillan, Lesley and Michelle Thomas. 2009. "Police Interviews of Rape Victims: Tensions and Contradictions." In *Rape: Challenging Contemporary Thinking*. M. Horvath and J. Brown, eds. Cullompton: Willan Publishing, pp. 255–80.

Meliker, Jaymie R. and Chantel D. Sloan. 2011. "Spatio-temporal Epidemiology: Principles and Opportunities." *Spatial and Spatio-temporal Epidemiology* 2(1):1–9.

Menon, Nivedita. 2000. "Embodying the Self: Feminism, Sexual Violence and the Law." *Subaltern Studies XI*. P. Chatterjee and P. Jeganathan, eds. Delhi: Permanent Black, pp. 67–105.

Merry, Sally Engle. 1990. *Getting Justice and Getting Even: Legal Consciousness Among Working-Class Americans*. Chicago: University of Chicago Press.

———. 2001a. "Rights, Religion, and Community: Approaches to Violence Against Women in the Context of Globalization." *Law and Society Review* 35(1):39–88.

———. 2001b. "Spatial Governmentality and the New Urban Social Order: Controlling Gender Violence through Law." *American Anthropologist* 103(1):16–30.

———. 2003. "Kapiʻolani at the Brink: Dilemmas of Historical Ethnography in Nineteenth-Century Hawaiʻi," *American Ethnologist* 30(1):44–61.

———. 2009. *Gender Violence: A Cultural Perspective*. Malden, MA: Wiley-Blackwell.

———. 2012. "What Is Legal Culture? An Anthropological Perspective." *Journal of Comparative Law* 5(2): 40-58.

Merry, Sally Engle and Jessica Shimin. 2011. "The Curious Resistance to Seeing Domestic Violence as a Human Rights Violation in the USA." In *Human Rights in the United States: Beyond Exceptionalism*, K. Libal and S. Hertel, eds. Cambridge: Cambridge University Press, pp. 113–31.

Merskey, H. 1992. "The Manufacture of Personalities: The Production of Multiple Personality Disorder." *British Journal of Psychiatry* 160:327–40.

Messick, Brinkley. 1989. "Just Writing: Paradox and Political Economy in Yemeni Legal Documents." *Cultural Anthropology* 4(1): 6–50.

Metz, Christian. 1985. "Photography and Fetish." *October* 34:81–90.

Meyers, Todd. 2013. *The Clinic and Elsewhere: Addiction, Adolescents and the Afterlife of Therapy*. Seattle: University of Washington Press.

Miller, Robert H. and Randall R. Bovbjerg. 2002. "Efforts to Improve Patient Safety in Large, Capitated Medical Groups: Description and Conceptual Model." *Journal of Health Politics, Policy and Law* 27(3):401–40.

Miller, William. 1998. *The Anatomy of Disgust*. Cambridge, MA: Harvard University Press.

Mitchell, Timothy. 2002. *Rule of Experts: Egypt, Techno-Politics, Modernity*. Berkeley: University of California Press.

Mitchell, W. J. T. 1995. *Picture Theory: Essays on Verbal and Visual Representation*. Chicago: University of Chicago Press.

Mittleman, R., H. Goldberg, and D. Waksman. 1983. "Preserving Evidence in the Emergency Department." *American Journal of Nursing* 83(12):1652–56.

Morgan, Lewis Henry. 1877 (1985). *Ancient Society*. Tucson: University of Arizona Press.

Mosko, Mark S. 1989. "The Developmental Cycle among Public Groups." *Man* 24(3):470–84.

Mulder, Monique Borgerhoff. 1995. "Bridewealth and Its Correlates: Quantifying Change Over Time." *Current Anthropology* 36(4):573–603.

Mulla, Sameena. 2001. "Rape, Resistance, and the Law: Reading Gender, Race and Violence in the Memphis Riots of 1866." Master's thesis. New School for Social Research, New York.

———. 2008. "There's No Place Like Home: The Body as the Scene of the Crime in Sexual Assault Intervention." *Home Cultures* 5(3):301–26.

———. 2011. "Facing Victims: Forensics, Visual Technologies, and Sexual Assault Intervention." *Medical Anthropology* 30(3):271–94.

———. 2014. "Sexual Violence, Law, and Qualities of Affiliation." In *Wording the World: Veena Das and Scenes of Inheritance*, R. Chatterji, ed. New York: Fordham University Press.

Munn, Nancy. 1992. "The Cultural Anthropology of Time: A Critical Essay." *Annual Review of Anthropology* 21:93–123.

Nader, Laura. 2002. *The Life of the Law: Anthropological Projects*. Berkeley: University of California Press.

National Research Council. 2009. *Strengthening Forensic Science: A Path Forward*. Washington, DC: Committee on Identifying the Needs of the Forensic Science Community.

National Service Guidelines for Developing Sexual Assault Referral Centres (SARCs). 2005. Joint Department of Health and National Institute for Mental Health in England (NIMHE), and Victims of Violence and Abuse Prevention Programme (VVAPP), in partnership with the Home Office.

Nations, Marilyn K. and Mara Lucia Amaral. 1991. "Flesh, Blood, Souls and Households: Cultural Validity in Mortality Inquiry." *Medical Anthropology Quarterly* 5(3):204–20.

Navaro-Yashin, Yael. 2007. "Make-believe Papers, Legal Forms and the Counterfeit: Affective Interactions between Documents and People in Britain and Cyprus." *Anthropological Theory* 7(1):79–98.

Nielsen, Bianca. 2005. "Home Invasion and Hollywood Cinema: David Fincher's Panic Room." In *The Selling of 9/11: How a National Tragedy Became a Commodity*, Dana Heller, ed. New York: Palgrave Macmillan.

Nikolow, Sybilla. 2001. "A. F. W. Crome's Measurements of the 'Strength of the State': Statistical Representations in Central Europe around 1800." *History of Political Economy*, Annual Supplement 33:23–56.

Ning, Ana M. 2005. "Games of Truth: Rethinking Conformity and Resistance in Narratives of Heroin Recovery." *Medical Anthropology* 24(4):349–82.

Nolan, James. 1998. *The Therapeutic State: Justifying at Century's End*. New York: New York University Press.

Nurco, David N., Norma Wegner, Howell Baum, and Abraham Makotsky. 1980. "A Case Study: Narcotic Addiction Over a Quarter of a Century in a Major American City, 1950–1977." Rockville, MD: National Institute on Drug Abuse.

O'Daniel, Alyson. 2008. "Pushing Poverty to the Periphery: HIV-Positive African American Women's Health Need, the Ryan White Care Act, and a Political Economy of Services Provision." *Transforming Anthropology* 16(2):112–27.

Office on Violence Against Women. 2004. A National Protocol for Sexual Assault Forensic Examinations. U.S. Department of Justice (NCJ 206554).

Olshaker, Jonathan, M. Christine Jackson, and William S. Smock. 2006. *Forensic Emergency Medicine: Mechanisms and Clinical Management, Second Edition*. Philadelphia: Lippincott, Williams and Wilkins.

Olujic, Maria B. 1998. "Embodiment of Terror: Gendered Violence in Peacetime and Wartime in Croatia and Bosnia-Herzegovina." *Medical Anthropology Quarterly* 12(1):31–50.

Parnis, Deborah and Janice Du Mont. 1999. "Rape Laws and Rape Processing: The Contradictory Nature of Corroboration." *Canadian Woman Studies* 19(1 & 2):74–78.

———. 2002. "Examining the Standardized Application of Rape Kits: An Exploratory Study of Post-Sexual Assault Professional Practices." *Health Care for Women International* 23(8):846–53.

———. 2006. "Symbolic Power and the Institutional Response to Rape: Uncovering the Cultural Dynamics of a Forensic Technology." *Canadian Review of Sociology and Anthropology* 43(1):73–93.

Pateman, Carole. 1980. "Women and Consent." *Political Theory* 8(2):149–68.

———. 1988. *The Sexual Contract*. Stanford: Stanford University Press.

Peletz, Michael G. 1995. "Kinship Studies in Late Twentieth-Century Anthropology." *Annual Review of Anthropology* 24(1):343–72.

———. 2001. "Ambivalence in Kinship since the 1940s." In *Relative Values: Reconfiguring Kinship Studies*, S. Franklin and S. McKinnon, eds. Durham and London: Duke University Press, pp. 413–44.

Peterson, Joseph, Ira Sommers, Deborah Baskin, and Donald Johnson. 2010. "The Role and Impact of Forensic Evidence in the Criminal Justice Process: Revised Final Report." National Institute of Justice, Document No. 231977

Peterson, M. S., W. Green, and C. Boyle. 2003. "SAFE, SANE, CARE and SART Nurse and Nurse Practitioner Examination Teams." In *Child Abuse and Neglect: Guidelines for Identification, Assessment and Case Management*, M. Peterson and M. Durfee, eds. Volcano, CA: Volcano Press, pp. 277–81.

Petryna, Adriana. 2002. *Life Exposed: Biological Citizens after Chernobyl*. Princeton: Princeton University Press.

Picart, Carolyn. 2003. "Rhetorically Reconfiguring Victimhood and Agency: The Violence against Women Act's Civil Rights Clause." *Rhetoric & Public Affairs* 6(1):97–125.

Pierce, Jennifer L. 1995. *Gender Trials: Emotional Lives in Contemporary Law Firms*. Berkeley: University of California Press.

Pinney, Christopher. 1997. *Camera Indica: A Social Life of Indian Photographs*. Chicago: University of Chicago Press.

Pinney, Christopher and Nicolas Peterson. 2003. *Photography's Other Histories*. Durham: Duke University Press.

Plichta, S. B., P. T. Clements, and C. Houseman. 2007. "Why SANEs Matter: Models of Care for Sexual Violence Victims in the Emergency Department." *Journal of Forensic Nursing* 3(1):15–27.

Poole, Deborah. 1997. *Vision, Race and Modernity: A Visual Economy of the Andean Image World*. Princeton: Princeton University Press.

———. 2004. "Between Threat and Guarantee: Justice and Community in the Margins of the Peruvian State." In *Anthropology at the Margins of the State*, V. Das and D. Poole, eds. Santa Fe, NM: School of American Research Press, pp. 35–66.

———. 2005. "An Excess of Description: Ethnography, Race, and Visual Technologies." *Annual Review of Anthropology* 34:159–79.

Poovey, Mary. 1998. *History of the Modern Fact: Problems of Knowledge in the Sciences of Wealth and Society*. Chicago: University of Chicago Press.

Porter, Dorothy. 1994. *The History of Public Health and the Modern State*. Amsterdam: Editions Rodopi.

———. 1999. *Health, Civilization and the State: A History of Public Health from Ancient to Modern Times*. London: Routledge.

Porter, Roy and Mikuláš Teich. 1994. *Sexual Knowledge, Sexual Science: The History of Attitudes to Sexuality*. Cambridge and New York: Cambridge University Press.

Porter, Theodore. 1995. *Trust in Numbers: The Pursuit of Objectivity in Science and Public Life*. Princeton: Princeton University Press.

Pounds, Ruth P. 1993. "AIDS in African-American Communities and the Public Health Response: An Overview." *Transforming Anthropology* 4(1):9–16.

Povinelli, Elizabeth. 2002. "Notes on Gridlock: Genealogy, Intimacy, Sexuality." *Public Culture* 14(1):15–38.

Prakash, Gyan. 1999. *Another Reason: Science and the Imagination of Modern India*. Princeton: Princeton University Press.

Procupez, Valeria. 2008. "Beyond Home: Forging the Domestic in Shared Housing." *Home Cultures* 5(3):327–48.

Putnam, Frank W. 1989. *Diagnosis and Treatment of Multiple Personality Disorder*. New York: Guilford Press.

Rabinow, Paul. 1996. *Making PCR: A Story of Biotechnology*. Chicago: University of Chicago Press.

Raffles, Hugh. 2002. "Intimate Knowledge." *International Social Science Journal* 54(173): 325–35.

Raine, Nancy Venable. 1998. *After Silence: Rape and My Journey Back*. New York: Three Rivers Press.

Rees, Gethin. 2010. "'It is not for me to say whether consent was given or not': Forensic Medical Examiners' Justifications for 'Neutral Reports' in Rape Cases." *Social and Legal Studies* 19(3):371–86.

———. 2011. "'Morphology is a witness which doesn't lie': Diagnosis by Similarity Relation and Analogical Inference in Forensic Medicine." *Social Science and Medicine* 73(6):866–72.

Regan, Linda, Jo Lovett, and Liz Kelly. 2004. "Forensic Nursing: An Option for Improving Responses to Reported Rape and Sexual Assault." UK Home Office Development and Practice Report 31.

Reitan, Eric. 2001. "Rape as an Essentially Contested Concept." *Hypatia* 16(2):43–66.

Remick, Lani Anne. 1993. "Read Her Lips: An Argument for a Verbal Consent Standard in Rape." *University of Pennsylvania Law Review* 141(3):1103–51.

Reverby, Susan. 1987. *Ordered to Care: The Dilemma of American Nursing, 1850–1945*. New York: Cambridge University Press.

Reynolds, Pamela. 2000. "The Ground of All Making: State Violence, the Family, and Political Activists." In *Violence and Subjectivity*, V. Das, A. Kleinman, M. Ramphele, and P. Reynolds, eds. New Delhi: Oxford University Press, pp. 141–70.

Riggs, Netti, Debra Houry, Gayle Long, Vincent Markovchick, and Kim M. Feldhaus. 2000. "Analysis of 1,076 Cases of Sexual Assault." *Annals of Emergency Medicine* 35(4):358–62.

Roberts, Dorothy. 1997. *Killing the Black Body: Race, Reproduction and the Meaning of Liberty*. New York: Pantheon.

Robins, Lee N. and George E. Murphy. 1967. "Drug Use in a Normal Population of Young Negro Men." *American Journal of Public Health* 57(9):1580–96.

Rodrigues, Isabel, Fabienne Grou, and Jacques Joly. 2001. "Effectiveness of Emergency Contraceptive Pills Between 72 and 120 Hours After Unprotected Sexual Intercourse." *American Journal of Obstetrics & Gynecology* 184(4):531–37.

Rose, Vicki M. 1977. "Rape as a Social Problem: A Byproduct of the Feminist Movement." *Social Problems* 25(1):75–89.

Rosen, George. 1974. *From Medical Police to Social Medicine: Essays on the History of Health Care*. New York: Science History Publications.

Rosen, Hannah. 1999. "'Not That Sort of Women': Race, Gender and Sexual Violence during the Memphis Riot of 1866." In *Sex, Love, Race: Crossing Boundaries in North American History*, M. Hodes, ed. New York and London: New York University Press, pp. 267–93.

Ross, Fiona. 2002. *Bearing Witness: Women and the Truth and Reconciliation Commission in South Africa*. London: Pluto Press.

Roth, Klaus. 1990. "Socialist Life-Cycle Rituals in Bulgaria." *Anthropology Today* 6(5):8–10.

Roth, Michael and Charles Salas. 2001. *Disturbing Remains: Memory, History and Crisis in the 20th Century*. Los Angeles: Getty Research Institute.

Russell, Diana E. H. 1982 (1990). *Rape in Marriage: Expanded and Revised Edition*. Bloomington: Indiana University Press.

Saferstein, Richard. 2006. "Evidence Collection and Preservation." In V. Lynch, *Forensic Nursing*. St. Louis: Elsevier, pp. 101–8.

Sahlins, Marshall. 1976. *Culture and Practical Reason*. Chicago: University of Chicago Press.

Sanday, Peggy Reeves. 1981. "The Socio-cultural Context of Rape: A Cross-Cultural Study." *Journal of Social Issues* 37(4):5–27.

———. 1990. *Fraternity Gang Rape: Sex, Brotherhood, and Privilege on Campus*. New York: New York University Press.

———. 1996. *A Woman Scorned: Acquaintance Rape on Trial*. Berkeley: University of California Press.

Sandelowski, Margarete. 2000. *Devices and Desires: Gender, Technology and American Nursing*. Chapel Hill: University of North Carolina Press.

Scaglion, Richard. 1986. "The Importance of Nighttime Observations in Time Allocation Studies." *American Ethnologist* 13(3):537–45.

Scarry, Elaine. 1985. *The Body in Pain: The Making and the Unmaking of the World*. New York: Oxford University Press.

Schneider, David. 1968. *American Kinship: A Cultural Account*. Englewood Cliffs, NJ: Prentice-Hall.

Schweitzer, N. J. and M. J. Saks. 2007. "The CSI Effect: Popular Fiction about Forensic Science Affects the Public's Expectations about Real Forensic Science." *Jurimetrics* 47(3):357.

Segal, Daniel A. 1988. "A Patient So Dead: American Medical Students and Their Cadavers." *Anthropological Quarterly* 61(1):17–25.

Serres, Michel with Bruno Latour. 1990. *Conversations on Science, Culture, and Time.* Ann Arbor: University of Michigan Press.

Shelton, Donald E., Young S. Kim, and Gregg Barak. 2006. "A Study of Juror Expectations and Demands Concerning Scientific Evidence: Does the 'CSI Effect' Exist?" *Vanderbilt Journal of Entertainment & Technology Law* 9(2):330.

Sinason, Valerie. 2002. *Attachment, Trauma and Multiplicity: Working with Dissociative Identity Disorder*. New York: Routledge.

Slaughter, L., C. R. Brown, Sharon Crowley, and R. Peck. 1997. "Patterns of Genital Injury in Female Sexual Assault Victims." *American Journal of Obstetrics and Gynecology* 176(3):609–16.

Smialek, J. 1983. "Forensic Medicine in the Emergency Department." *Emergency Medicine Clinics of North America* 1(3):1685.

Smith, Merril D. 2001. *Sex without Consent: Rape and Sexual Coercion in America*. New York: New York University Press.

Smith, M. E. 2005. "Female Sexual Assault: The Impact on the Male Significant Other." *Issues in Mental Health Nursing* 26(2):149–67.

Smock, Ann. 1986. "Translators Remarks." In Maurice Blanchot, *The Writing of the Disaster.* Lincoln: University of Nebraska Press, pp. vii–xiii.

Smock, W., G. Nichols, and P. Fuller. 1993. "Development and Implementation of the First Clinical Forensic Medicine Training Program." *Journal of Forensic Sciences* 38(4):835–39.

Sommers, Ira and Deborah Baskin. 2011. "The Influence of Forensic Evidence on the Case Outcome of Rape Incidents." *Justice System Journal* 32(3):315–34.

Sommers, Marilyn. 2007. "Defining Patterns of Genital Injury from Sexual Assault: A Review." *Trauma, Violence and Abuse* 8(3):270–80.

Spencer, Herbert. 1860. "The Social Organism." *Westminster Review* 17:51–68.

Spitulnik, Deborah. 1993. "Anthropology and Mass Media." *Annual Review of Anthropology* 22:292–315.

Spohn, Cassia and Julia Horney. 1991. " 'The Law's the Law, but Fair Is Fair': Rape Shield Laws and Officials' Assessments of Sexual History Evidence." *Criminology* 29(1):137–61.

———. 1992. *Rape Law Reform: A Grassroots Movement and Its Impact*. New York: Plenum Press.

Stinchcombe, Arthur L. 1997. "On the Virtues of the Old Institutionalism." *Annual Review of Sociology* 23:1–18.

Stokes, Martin. 1997. "Voices and Places: History, Repetition and the Musical Imagination." *Journal of the Royal Anthropological Institute* 3(4):673–91.

Stone, Allucquere Rosanne. 1995. "Identity in Oshkosh." In *Posthuman Bodies*, J. Halberstam and I. Livingston, eds. Bloomington: Indiana University Press, pp. 23–37.

Strathern, Marilyn. 1992. *After Nature: English Kinship in the Late Twentieth Century*. London: Cambridge University Press.

———.1995. "Displacing Knowledge: Technology and the Consequences for Kinship." In *Conceiving the New World Order: The Global Politics of Reproduction*, F. Ginsburg and R. Rapp, eds. Berkeley: University of California Press, pp. 346–64.

———. 2005. *Kinship, Law and the Unexpected: Relatives Are Always a Surprise*. New York: Cambridge University Press.

Strauss, Anselm, Shizuko Fagerhaugh, Barbara Suczek, and Carolyn Wiener. 1985. *Social Organization of Medical Work*. Chicago: University of Chicago Press.

Strong, Pauline Turner. 1986. "Fathoming the Primitive: Australian Aborigines in Four Explorers' Journals, 1697–1845." *Ethnohistory* 33(2):175–94.

Strong, Thomas. 2002. "Kinship between Judith Butler and Anthropology? A Review Essay." *Ethnos* 67(3):401–18.

Suggs, Adrienne, Richard Lichtenstein, Clare McCarthy, and M. Christine Jackson. 2001. "Child Abuse/Assault—General." In *Forensic Emergency Medicine*, J. Olshaker, M. Jackson, and W. Smock, eds. Philadelphia: Lippincott, Williams and Wilkins.

Süskind, Patrick. 1986. *Perfume: The Story of a Murderer*. New York: Knopf.

Tan, Sooi-Beng. 1989. "From Popular to 'Traditional' Theater: The Dynamics of Change in Bangsawan of Malaysia." *Ethnomusicology* 33(2):229–74.

Taslitz, Andrew. 1999. *Rape and the Culture of the Courtroom*. New York: New York University Press.

Taylor, Janelle. 2005. "Surfacing the Body Interior." *Annual Reviews in Anthropology* 34: 741–56.

Taylor, W. K. 2002. "Collecting Evidence for Sexual Assault: The Role of the Sexual Assault Nurse Examiner (SANE)." *International Journal of Gynecology and Obstetrics* 78 (Supplement 1):S91–S94.

Temkin, Jennifer. 1986. "Women, Rape and Law Reform." In *Rape*, S. Tomaselli and R. Porter, eds. Oxford: Basil Blackwell Press, pp. 16–40.

Terrell, F., K. L. Mosley, A. S. Terrell, and K. J. Nickerson. 2004. "The Relationship between Motivation to Volunteer, Gender, Cultural Mistrust, and Willingness to Donate Organs among Blacks." *Journal of the National Medical Association* 96(1):53–60.

Thomas, Nicholas. 1992. "Substantivization and Anthropological Discourse: The Transformation of Practices into Institutions in Neotraditional Pacific Societies." *History and Tradition in Melanesian Anthropology*, J. Carrier, ed. Berkeley: University of California Press, pp. 64–85.

Timmermans, Stefan and Marc Berg. 1997. "Standardization in Action: Achieving Local Universality through Medical Protocols." *Social Studies of Science* 27:273–305.

Tjaden, Patricia. 2009. "A Comment on White and Du Mont's 'Visualizing Sexual Assault: An Exploration of the Use of Optical Technologies in the Medico-legal Contact.'" *Social Science and Medicine* 68:9–11.

Tjaden, Patricia and Nancy Thoennes. 2000. *Full Report of the Prevalence, Incidence, and Consequences of Violence against Women*. Washington, DC: National Institute of Justice. Report (NCJ 183781).

———. 2006. *Extent, Nature and Consequences of Rape Victimization: Findings from the National Violence against Women Survey*. Washington, DC: National Institute of Justice. Report (NCJ 210346).

Todeschini, Maya. 2001. "The Bomb's Womb? Women and the A-Bomb." In *Remaking a World: Violence, Social Suffering and Recovery*, Veena Das et al., eds. Berkeley: University of California Press, pp. 102–56.

Tofte, Sarah. 2009. *Testing Justice: The Rape Kit Backlog in Los Angeles City and County*. New York: Human Rights Watch.

Trawick, Margaret. 1990. *Notes on Love in a Tamil Family*. Berkeley: University of California Press.

Trinch, Shonna. 2003. *Latinas' Narratives of Domestic Violence: Discrepant Versions of Violence*. Amsterdam: John Benjamins Publisher.

Turman, Kathryn. M. 2001. "Understanding DNA Evidence: A Guide for Victim Service Providers." Bulletin of the Office for Victims of Crime, U.S. Department of Justice, Office of Justice Programs.

Turner, Victor. 1957. *Schism and Continuity in an African Society: A Study of Ndembu Village Life*. Manchester: Manchester University Press.

Turton, David and Clive Ruggles. 1978. "Agreeing to Disagree: The Measurement of Duration in Southwestern Ethiopian Community." *Current Anthropology* 19(3):585–600.

Tyler, Tom R. 1990. "Justice, Self-Interest and the Legitimacy of Legal and Political Authority." In *Beyond Self-Interest*, J. Mansbridge, ed. Chicago: University of Chicago Press, pp. 171–79.

———. 2006. "Viewing CSI and the Threshold of Guilt: Managing Truth and Justice in Reality and Fiction." *Yale Law Journal* 115(5):1050–85.

Tylor, Edward Burnett. 1871. *Primitive Culture*. London: John Murray.

Umphrey, Martha M. 2007. "Law's Bonds: Eros and Identification in Billy Budd." *American Imago* 64(3):413–31.

U.S. Bureau of Justice Statistics. 2005. Criminal Victimization in the United States. 12/06. Washington, DC: National Justice Statistics, Publication 215244.

U.S. Department of Justice. 2004. A National Protocol for Sexual Assault Medical Examinations: Adults/Adolescents. Office on Violence against Women. Washington, DC.

Van Oosterhout, Dianne. 2000. "Tying the Time String Together: An End-of-Time Experience in Irian Jaya, Indonesia." *Ethnohistory* 47(1):67–99.

Vogeley, Ev, Mary Clyde Pierce, and Gina Bertocci. 2002. "Experience with Wood Lamp Illumination and Digital Photography in the Documentation of Bruises on Human Skin" *Archive of Pediatrics and Adolescent Medicine* 156(3):265–68.

Von Hertzen H., G. Piaggio, and J. Ding. 2002. "Low Dose Mifepristone and Two Regimens of Levonorgestrel for Emergency Contraception: A WHO Multicentre Randomized Trial." *Lancet* 360:1803–10.

Wagner, Sarah. 2008. *To Know Where He Lies: DNA Technology and the Search for Srebrenica's Missing*. Berkeley: University of California Press.

Waldram, James. 2012. *Hound Pound Narrative*. Berkeley: University of California Press.

Wallace, Aurora. 2009. "Mapping City Crime and the New Aesthetic of Danger." *Journal of Visual Culture* 8(1):5–24.

Warshaw, Robin. 1988. *I Never Called It Rape: The* Ms. *Report on Recognizing, Fighting, and Surviving Date and Acquaintance Rape*. New York: Harper and Row.

Weber, Max. 1946. "Science as Vocation." In *From Max Weber: Essays in Sociology*, H. H. Gerth and C. Wright Mills, trans. and eds. New York: Oxford University Press, pp. 129–56.

Weber, Samuel. 1999. "Family Scenes: Some Preliminary Remarks on Domesticity and Theatricality." *South Atlantic Quarterly* 98(3):355–66.

———. 2001. *Institution and Interpretation*. Stanford: Stanford University Press.

Weeks, Margaret, Merrill Singer, Maryland Grier, and Josephine Haughton, 1993. "AIDS Prevention and the African-American Injection Drug User." *Transforming Anthropology* 4(1):39–51.

Weist, Mark, Jennifer Pollitt-Hill, Linda Kinney, Yaphet Bryant, and Laura Anthony. 2009. *African American Experience of Sexual Assault in Maryland, 2003–2006*. Ann Arbor, MI: Inter-university Consortium for Political and Social Research.

White, Deborah and Janice Du Mont. 2009. "Visualizing Sexual Assault: An Exploration of the Use of Optical Technologies in the Medico-legal Context." *Social Science and Medicine* 68(1):1–8.

White, Priscilla N. and Judith C. Rollins. 1981. "Rape: A Family Crisis." *Family Relations* 30(1):103–9.

Williams, Raymond. 1977. *Marxism and Literature*. Oxford: Oxford University Press.

Wilson, E. F. and R. S. Fisher. 1969. "Death from Narcotics Use: Baltimore City, 1963 through 1968." *Maryland State Medical Journal* 18(10):49–52.

Winkler, Cathy. 1991. "Rape as Social Murder." *Anthropology Today* 7(3):12–14.

———.1994. "Rape Trauma: Contexts of Meaning." In *Embodiment and Experience: The Existential Ground of Culture and Self*, T. Csordas, ed. Cambridge: Cambridge University Press, pp. 248–68.

———. 2002. *One Night: Realities of Rape*. New York: Alta Mira Press.

Winkler, Cathy with Penelope J. Hancke. 1995. "Rape Attack: Ethnography of the Ethnographer." In *Fieldwork Under Fire: Contemporary Studies of Violence and Survival*, C. Nordstrom and A. Robben, eds. Berkeley: University of California Press, pp. 155–85.

Wittgenstein, Ludwig. 1953. *Philosophical Investigations*. Oxford: Blackwell.

———. 1961. *Tractatus Logico-Philosophicus*. New York: Routledge.

Wynn, L. L. and James Trussell. 2006. "The Social Life of Emergency Contraception in the United States: Disciplining Pharmaceutical Use, Disciplining Sexuality, and Constructing Zygotic Bodies." *Medical Anthropology Quarterly* 20(3):297–320.

Yablon, Charles. 1992. "Forms." In *Deconstruction and the Possibility of Justice*, D. Cornell, M. Rosenfeld, and D. Carlson, eds. New York: Routledge, pp. 258–64.

Zimmer, Lynn. 1987. "How Women Reshape the Prison Guard Role." *Gender and Society* 1(4):415–31.

INDEX

ABOUT THE AUTHOR

Sameena Mulla is Assistant Professor of Anthropology in the Department of Social and Cultural Sciences at Marquette University. Her research broadly considers the multiple dimensions of sexual violence within scholarly traditions that explore the cultural dimensions of human suffering.